Blogwars

Blogwars

David D. Perlmutter

OXFORD
UNIVERSITY PRESS
2008

OXFORD
UNIVERSITY PRESS

Oxford University Press, Inc., publishes works that further
Oxford University's objective of excellence
in research, scholarship, and education.

Oxford   New York
Auckland   Cape Town   Dar es Salaam   Hong Kong   Karachi
Kuala Lumpur   Madrid   Melbourne   Mexico City   Nairobi
New Delhi   Shanghai   Taipei   Toronto

With offices in
Argentina   Austria   Brazil   Chile   Czech Republic   France   Greece
Guatemala   Hungary   Italy   Japan   Poland   Portugal   Singapore
South Korea   Switzerland   Thailand   Turkey   Ukraine   Vietnam

Published by Oxford University Press, Inc.
198 Madison Avenue, New York, New York 10016

www.oup.com

Library of Congress Cataloging-in-Publication Data
Perlmutter, David D., [date]
Blogwars / by David D. Perlmutter.
p. cm.
ISBN 978-0-19-530557-9
1. Communication in politics—United States.
2. Communication—Political aspects—United States.
3. Blogs—United States. I. Title.
JA85.2.U6P45 2008
320.97301'4—dc22   2007016441

9 8 7 6 5 4 3 2 1

Printed in the United States of America
on acid-free paper

To bloggers, who boldly go where many of us could only dream of going before.

Acknowledgments

A comprehensive acknowledgment page for this book would be prohibitively long, since literally up to 400 people helped, including my students working on various projects through the last three years; colleagues who read and responded to various drafts of the manuscript; and the bloggers whom I interviewed or who filled out surveys for me. Suffice it to say that almost every blogger or individual named within the text of the book contributed to its completion. Special thanks, however, go to my wife, Christie; my agent, Sydelle Kramer; and my editors at Oxford, Timothy Bartlett, Dedi Felman, and finally Timothy Bent and Keith Faivre. Misti McDaniel and Nathan Rodriguez were invaluable graduate assistants. A number of bloggers, including Scott W. Johnson, Jerome Armstrong, John Donovan, Mark Blumenthal, Joan Carter, and especially Natasha Chart, were of greatest help. Institutionally, this book would not have been started without the help of the Manship School of Mass Communication at LSU and Dean John Hamilton and would not have been completed without the support of the William Allen White School of Journalism & Mass Communications at the University of Kansas and Dean Ann Brill.

Contents

Preface

When future historians chronicle the interactive, instant, always-on, open-source, globally accessible communications era, they will note that the initial years of the twenty-first century heralded many markers of radical change. *Time* magazine pictured a mirrored computer screen on its 2006 Person of the Year issue and thus affirmed the power of the self-expressive i-generation. In July 2007, *Wired* magazine teamed with Xerox to allow 5,000 subscribers to send in their own portraits for its cover. Ordinary people with cell phone cameras loaded up the first verbal and pictorial news from "ground zero" scenes of sensational news events like the South Asia tsunami, the London 7/7 bombings, and the Virginia Tech massacre. One U.S. television station fired its staff and opened up all on-air content to such "citizen journalists" while many others explored variations of the "I-reporter" or "you-report" format. Former vice president Al Gore began a network devoted to the same concept. More than 6 million gamers played *World of Warcraft* via colorful avatars each night. Perhaps they foreshadowed the future of education—at least online education—as well as entertainment because in the spring of 2007 a film class at my home, the University of Kansas, was virtually taught and attended with students and teachers encountering each other via avatars in the *Second Life* webworld.

Text messaging became the dominant communication technology of "tweenagers." Young fans of the "old" *Star Trek* television series created new episodes (with modern special effects) along with former actors and writers of the original. The remix/mash-up phenomenon proliferated on YouTube and personal Web sites, offering such hits as *Brokeback to the Future* (a gay-themed recut trailer of the Michael J. Fox movie) and *Chad Vader: Day Shift Manager* (the adventures of the Dark Lord as second in command of a small supermarket). Even creators of media products that used to be solipsistic enterprises like, say, writing a novel were putting drafts online asking for public critiques. Such developments—small and large, trivial and globe-shaking—reflected a time when we began to speak less of producers and receivers of media content and rather of "interactors," people who selfcast—that is, both create and consume information and entertainment online.[1]

Politics by Blog

Early bimillennial politics also radiated signs and portents of a communications revolution. An increasing number of younger Americans sought political information from nontraditional sources: stand-up comics, the *Daily Show,* the *Onion.* Politicians responded: Senator John McCain announced that he was running for president on the *David Letterman Show.* A creatively tonsured liberal activist attending a George Allen for Senate rally in Virginia videotaped the senator's use of an ethnic slur (against him) and created a new transitive verb, to "YouTube"; the "macaca moment" was cited as affecting the narrow race and thus shifted control of the U.S. Senate. Barack Obama supporters attempted to make his Facebook page the first to reach the "1 million friends" level. From France came news that supporters of candidates in the 2007 presidential election had set up virtual headquarters in the *Second Life* online fantasy game: Hillary Rodham Clinton, Obama, and John Edwards were doing the same. Candidates also embraced the newest and coolest tech: send a text message to the subject header "Hope" and the Obama campaign will respond; "Peace" will get you Dennis Kucinich. More darkly, the chief of intelligence of the U.S. military central command proclaimed that "the Internet was the number one recruiting tool for radical Islam." According to a March 2007 study by Burst Media, the Internet was rated by Americans as the best source from which to find out more information about the positions of the 2008 presidential candidates.[2] In all, according to Pew Foundation studies, a majority of Americans under thirty years of age and at least a third of all of us seek out campaign information and share it with others through online venues. And the great confluence of popular culture, new media, and politics was exemplified when the Hillary Clinton campaign posted on YouTube a parody of the ending of *The Sopranos*, featuring the ex– (and hoping to be next) first family. Of course, the ad closed with a reference to Hillary's Web site.

Most notorious among the newcomer technologies shaking up our culture, society, and politics was the weblog, or blog. A widely quoted assessment of blogging for corporations announced that the venue was "the new on-ramp for mainstream media."[3] One study of print and broadcast media workers found that they overwhelmingly tended to read political blogs.[4] Bloggers noted that when, in February 2005, California's Barbara Boxer gave a speech on the floor of the Senate, she held in her hands notes that were a printout from BradDeLong.com, the eponymous blog by a professor of economics at UC, Berkeley.[5] Conversely, mainstream photojournalism was shaken to its core by right-wing bloggers who pointed out errors, malfeasance, inconsistencies, miscaptions, and outright fakery in press "fauxtography" from the 2006 Israel–Lebanon war. Then there were the mainstream movie critics who, tired of being preempted by bloggers, began pushing film reviews earlier and earlier before the actual release date.

Blogs, too, showed success by old-fashioned metrics: audience and money. According to Nielsen/NetRatings, in July of 2005, DailyKos, the go-to blog for liberals and Democrats, received 4.8 million unique visitors.* In contrast, the population of Iowa, the first state to hold a presidential caucus every four years, was at that time about 2.9 million, and the population of New Hampshire, the first state to hold a presidential

---

*As noted later, such numbers are problematic; Kos himself wrote to tell me that they did not "feel right."

primary, was around 1.2 million. To illustrate the value of popularity, at one point, when it was receiving almost 700,000 hits a day, the blog Instapundit could charge Paramount Pictures $2,000 for an ad.[6] The election season of Bush versus Kerry was widely heralded as the "Internet's coming of age as a formidable force in American politics,"[7] and every major political campaign's communications strategy included blogs.[8] One study found that 9 percent of people online consulted blogs during the campaign.[9] Another report concluded that in the 2006 races,

> Some 15% of all American adults say the Internet was the place where they got most of their campaign news during the election, up from 7% in the mid-term election of 2002 . . . a notable class of online political activists [emerged]. Some 23% of those who used the Internet for political purposes . . . actually created or forwarded online original political commentary or politically-related videos.[10]

During the runup to the 2006 midterm elections, prominent bloggers become sought-after political consultants and raised millions for candidates of their choice. By the summer of 2007, big-name presidential hopefuls routinely racked up monthly page views on their Web sites and blogs in the millions.

Overall, it seemed like everyone running, from alderman to commander in chief, was blogging or trying to use blogs to raise money, rally supporters, and achieve every politician's dream of bypassing the mainstream press and communicating directly to the voters (for a lot less money than a television ad). Mitt Romney's Mitthead Blogroll boasted more than 6,700 pro-Mitt blogs while the candidate held "blogger-only" briefings from which the regular news media were excluded. Hillary Clinton hired a blogger in chief for her campaign for the presidency, and her husband, the former president, held a lunch with top liberal and progressive bloggers. Barack Obama, perhaps the most techno-savvy presidential candidate of our time, guest blogged and podcasted. The president of the United States himself decided to address the 2007 convention of milbloggers (military bloggers) via video link to rally support for his war in Iraq. Blogging also registered as the "early warning system" of the political world when, for several weeks in spring 2007, bloggers chatted about a possible run by retired Senator Fred Thompson (of *Law & Order* fame) for the presidency. One political blogger I know mentioned the rumors to a close political friend of Thompson, who dismissed the speculation; but then, to the surprise of insiders, there was the senator on a Fox talk show thinking aloud about running. The 2007 Yearly Kos convention of liberal and progressive bloggers featured the entire cast of 2008 Democratic presidential hopefuls and was dubbed by the press as the "second Democratic party convention." Nor is political blogging a top-down affair. My former students run blogs and vlogs (video logs) for campaigns; my political consultant friends note (and sometimes complain) that, as one put it, these under-twenty-five-year-old staffers "think I'm old-fashioned to use e-mail from a computer and watch TV on a television."

The future leaders of politics in America live in MySpace, see in YouTube, and write in blog.

But of all these events and occurrences, Hillary Clinton's invitation, "Let's talk," was in my opinion the most significant. The senator from New York, wife of a former president, and frontrunner for the Democratic nomination for the presidency in 2008 was often critiqued for being too measured, distant, and cautious. In evident response, she offered a countertype: Hillary as friendly, open, and even chatty: "I'm not just starting a campaign, though. I'm beginning a conversation with you, with America. . . . Let's talk about how to bring the right end to the war in Iraq, and to restore respect for America around the world." The Clinton campaign posted the announcement on the Web before the senator spoke to reporters, and surely it read like a blogpost rather than a presidential address. Hillary followed up with three live "Web chats" with supporters and in 2007 her campaign innovated many new Web and blog political strategies.

The verdict was in: Blogging—good and bad, enriching and frightening—was now part of the style, content, form, and function of politics and public affairs. In fact, 2008 was already called the political "Year of the Conversation"—with many wondering which candidates would exploit the promises and avoid the perils of interactivity. "Let's talk" was also a confirmation for me to write this new medium's story from the perspective of my own conversation with political blogging and bloggers.

Electronic Commilito: A Personal Revolution?

In perspective, each semester for the last dozen years, I have tried to introduce several hundred college students to modern media theory, research, effects, and professional practices by teaching the 101 Intro course in my field. One lesson I learned from my charges is that novel technologies grow old fast. It would puzzle university freshmen if I called e-mail and Web pages "*new* media." Satellite reception, Wi-Fi, laptops, cell phones, PDAs, digital photography, and the Internet are as familiar to eighteen-year-olds as pencils and paper; they know what it is to snope out a fact, wiki a term paper, and twitter a class session, even if their parents (or their teachers) don't.

A staple of my classroom instruction, however, which I did not foresee having to revise for the length of my career, was that mass media products are created by *industries*. Print press stories and editorials, icons of photojournalism, Hollywood movies, and HBO television series alike are produced by large, impersonal, megareturn-seeking corporations that crave "mass" audiences. Certainly, the intended consumers may be selected for their demographics and psychographics. A magazine's target population segment, for example, might be "career-oriented cosmopolitan Hispanic women under thirty." Political media consultants may design a television ad for "soccer moms." Still, if Disney, Merck, the Sierra Club, or the Republican National Committee seek niche audiences for some of their messages, we are nevertheless talking about *large* organizations trying to persuade via *mass* media *significant* numbers of people. In contrast, in the early days of the American republic, the founders considered a "press" to be a hand-cranked machine in Ben Franklin's workshop, with his staff consisting of one ink boy. I never imagined we would or could go back to the days of individual production of mass media products.

And then came blogs, bloggers, and blogging. In 1999, I first noticed something called a "we-blog" (pronounced *wee*-blog) and then a "blog" through the summer of 2003 and into February 2004, where, from the vantage point of Ames, Iowa, I gauged the impact of blogs on the campaign of Howard Dean for president. I appreciated that something innovative and exciting was changing political communication as I knew and taught it. People were (a) bypassing regular big media, (b) creating mass communication messages without formal training (like, say, attending my journalism school), (c) reaching, in some cases, large audiences, (d) inviting others to "wiki" or coauthor accretive knowledge, and (e) producing a range of effects on contemporary public opinion, political campaigns, public affairs argumentation, and even governmental policymaking.

In addition, to paraphrase *The Godfather*, political blogging was and is not just business; it's personal. Long ago, the Romans had a name for the ability of leaders to bond with ordinary soldiers by tending their wounds, sharing their chow, or congratulating them on their bravery: *commilito* (fellow soldiership). Even earlier, of course, for most of the history of our species, we were creatures of small groups and personal ties: Bigness, as in cities, crowds, or news networks, has not changed our affinity for one-on-one love, friendship, and affinity. Hence, the master truth of persuasion is that *successful mass communication is that which best approximates successful personal communication*. When you watch a political candidate in a thirty-second television ad or in a televised debate or speech and you feel moved, swayed, or impressed by her, you think, "I felt as if she were talking to me personally." Blogs allow officeholders (and seekers) and us a vehicle for even more intimacy.

Consider, for example, Aaron Pena, a Democratic State House Representative in Texas, who started a blog for his 2006 campaign. He described to one of my grad students why he blogged.

> Sometimes it's as personal as [sigh], philosophical feelings about death or my outings with my family. Sometimes it's biographical, sometimes it's humorous. It runs the gamut of human emotions. My son's . . . [pause] . . . the anniversary of his passing . . . I had a son who passed away, that day I typically make note of his passing and do not blog on that day out of respect for his memory. . . . It's almost like I'm speaking to my next door neighbor.[11]

Pena understands that his constituents want to be spoken to not as a political mass but as the friends next door.

Yet, for political candidates who blog, too much candor may hurt the candidate. "Americans want to know who their presidents are,"[12] notes retired *USA Today*'s political correspondent Richard Benedetto, but campaigns worry that we won't like what we find. Read what Deborah Wallace, a Democratic State Representative in Washington, wrote in her blog.

> This weekend the whole Wallace family came up to help cut the blackberry vines that have taken over the back yard. It was hard work to the point that I almost couldn't move after I sat down! . . . When I'm cutting the vines, it gives me time to think about all the important projects we've been working on in the legislature. I cut a vine and I think to myself how best to write a letter to coordinate our transportation project request in SW Washington. I ponder for several more cuts. I cut another vine and think about the priorities I have for the budget. And 100 cuts later (the vines, not my skin where the vines have tried to grab) I think about the approach to lower our medical costs through changes in state law. . . . And to all of you gardeners out there, any tips about how to get rid of all those cut blackberry vines?[13]

Here the officeholder consistently uses the pronoun "I," she invites reader response, and she offers personal details of her family and hobbies. But she also weaves in comments on government policy and legislative work, indirectly valorizing her own labors. We, as (possible) constituents, might perceive a sensitive, intelligent, hardworking woman who cares about issues of the day and who exhausts herself in our service.* When Wallace writes, "When I'm cutting the vines, it gives me time to think about all the important projects we've been working on in the legislature," she expresses the personal touch of the blog form and style, mixing her inner feelings with bigger political issues. But do we want that?

---

*I'm reminded of the classic case of the leader intimating to the group how he suffered for them: General George Washington, at his last address to his officers, pulled out his spectacles to read his speech and said, "Gentlemen, I have grown gray in your service, and now I am going blind."

Must Blog!

I will speak to this personal dimension in *Blogwars* because it is the essence of the attraction and repulsion of political blogging to millions and to me. In late 2005, I started my own blog (policybyblog.square-space) about political blogging, nonpartisan and sedate, and now I am the editor of the blog of the bipartisan Robert J. Dole Institute of Politics where (I hope) my commentary is neutral and restrained. Earlier in 2005, however, I had accepted invitations to guest blog (cloaked by a nom de guerre) at two hot, partisan political blogs. It was a case study in fervor and fever. For one particular week, I stopped work on the manuscript for this book and neglected my family and my personal hygiene. Whether it was news from Iraq, bombings in London, or fill-ing a supreme court vacancy, my thoughts ran: *I must keep up with all the news, I must say my piece, must . . . M . . . U . . . S . . . T . . . BLOG!* You don't have to be a political junkie to grasp that blogging is passion personified. According to one study, political blog readers spent more time consuming blogs than readers of other kinds of blogs (five blogs a day, up to ten hours a week),[14] and many hardcore weblog enthusiasts tell me that their own blogday is much, much longer.

I was also dazzled by the instant "message in a bottle" quality of blogs—that my thoughts could end up within milliseconds on a video display on some distant and exotic shore. To one of my posts, some-one in Pakistan responded with a comment in minutes; a few hours later, a Belgian chimed in. Everything I had written before—books, book chapters, research articles, newspaper and magazine essays, even film scripts—was so *sloooow*, static, and tame by comparison. Here, my musings were picked up, trackback quoted, and commented on by other bloggers, both positively and negatively. Blogging was fun, addic-tive, and liberating.

On the other hand, political blogging (a) required work and time, (b) prompted me to get wound up (read: almost crazed) about my political opinions, (c) aroused my resentment at criticism of those same, and (d) revealed some elitist feelings that I didn't know I pos-sessed. At times, I wanted to shout (or type in red and all caps) the fol-lowing at pests (i.e., "trolls") who attacked me in comments,

*PEASANT! I HAVE SPENT MY LIFE STUDYING THIS
TOPIC; WHAT RIGHT HAVE YOU, `$%&(#@, TO ARGUE
WITH ME?!!!*

So I took negative criticism of me (actually of my pseudonymous avatar) much too personally. "You have to have thick skin to survive as a
political blogger," advised DailyKos's mcjoan to a class of my students.
I learned my skin is too tender; I now only analyze politics and leave
partisan political blogging to my rhino-hided superiors. As I will talk
about later, such heat may be natural in the online world where the
lack of true face-to-face interactivity leads to more confrontation than
dialogue in the accepted sense.

No surprise that political bloggers I meet and talk to sound like
warriors going to battle.[15] They take politics more seriously than politicians, political reporters, pundits, and political professionals I know.
For example, Republican and Democratic political consultants, staffers, and politicians in Washington, D.C., generally have friends (or
even lovers and/or spouses) across the fence or the chamber. Many
view politics as a business or even a game. But only a handful of right
bloggers I know are pals with a left blogger. There are plenty of incentives and opportunities for a Republican congressional staffer and a
Democratic Party worker to have lunch in Washington, to play ten-
nis, or even to marry. A right blogger in Des Moines, Iowa, and a left
blogger in Manchester, New Hampshire, are confined largely to sniping
at each other, sometimes viciously, online; many I know living in the
same city won't talk to each other offline. The political bloglands offer
a marketplace of ideas if we care to buy from them, but the vendors in
the stalls don't shake hands and go have drinks after a day of heated
competition.*

Hence Blog*wars*. There are battles online over the offices of power,
the resolution of vital issues, and the ideas that dominate the minds of
the nation. The question of what effects blogs, bloggers, and blogging

---

*Dialogue can exist, however. When I have invited right and left bloggers to speak in my
classes or on panels, even the feistiest online opponents were cordial and constructive.
The venue counts! Bloggers are not attack dogs twenty-four hours a day.

will have on politics, public affairs, public opinion, and policymaking is, then, one that will affect all of us, whether we blog or not.

Reasons Not to Write a Book on Blogs

That said, there are caveats to writing a book about blogs, political or other kinds, in 2005–2007.

We are in the childhood of online, interactive communication and the infancy of the medium, genre of literature, and technology that is the blog or whatever it evolves into. The course of development and utility of any new invention is hard to predict. Thomas Edison expected that his sound recording and playing machine would find its market largely among businessmen dictating letters to their secretaries; he could not foresee Edward R. Murrow describing the bombing of London, The Beatles harmonizing "Love Me Do," or Osama bin Laden taping threats to destroy America. Although I don't believe that interactive media will disappear, their incarnations (like one called "blog") may change or morph into others, and we are foolish to try to predict what will come with certainty.

A book is linear; blogs are nonlinear. One blogger asked me, "Why write a book when you can blog?" Writing about the blog from outside a blog is analogous to Leonardo da Vinci's distinction between looking at a painting and reading a book: We read the words of a text one at a time and turn the pages, linearly, but a picture offers itself to us "all at once." It is hard to describe the world of blogs and politics step by step because all of their elements are so intimately related.

A book on blogs must serve multiple audiences. Although millions of intense bloggers know details of the experience intimately—by one estimate, a new blog is created every second[16]—many studies show that substantial portions of the population have no idea what blogging is. A book about blogs must address the cognoscenti without confusing readers unfamiliar with blogs with too much insider jargon.

The passion of bloggers (and not a few antibloggers in the professional press) means that any statement that appears pro- or anti-blogging will variously draw catcalls or cheers from one group or the other. When, in

2006, I wrote an article for *Editor & Publisher*, the trade magazine of the print news business, asking if some stratospheric estimates of the numbers of blogs were perhaps inflated, apparently a number of bloggers, including one famous former print news journalist, classified me as "anti-blog" and poured out some startlingly hot invectives about me. It was my first, but not last, lesson that bloggers care about blogging and will wonder if you are "for us" or "against us" just as they would in a war. But that I am a partisan for blogging does not preclude me from attempting to critique the practices and realistically assess the effects of political blogs.

Blogs are always unfinished, their work always to be continued, revised, and extended later. Describing political blogging in a book that took three years to research and write and another year to publish is like reporting a NASCAR race with stone tablets. Much information will be dated by the time you read this book. But that is the point: A blogger's work is never done, nor, I hope, is that of a student of blogs. You cannot coast or rest on your laurels; your readers will abandon you or, worse, ask why you are failing them. The implied points of ellipsis at the end of every essay or post in a blog are one of the crucial features of blogstyle and content that makes it a joint enterprise rather than a monologue.

Finally, the blogform is sufficiently intricate that we should be careful in making sweeping statements about it; the returns, in a political sense, are not in yet, and perhaps the election is never really over. A basic rule of discussing blogs is that everything one says about blogs is true and at the same time false. In other words, Charles Dickens's neat paradox of "the best of times" and "the worst of times" fits well in describing blogging. Take a simple query: How many blogs are there? Ratings and tracking services exist that are reporting increasingly precise counts of blogs—tens of millions by summer of 2007—but many cases remain unaddressed with any metrics, such as abandoned blogs, blogs created to attract unsuspecting customers, and blogs posted by commercial corporations as press releases for politicians or political causes. Furthermore, the word *blog* has become so hip that every Web page is calling itself a blog. MySpace (owned by Rupert Murdoch) has as many as 85 million users. Are they bloggers? When we say "blogger," do we mean someone who physically created a blogpage—that is, edits her own blog—or the people who participate in the blog with responses or their own posts, or just people who read blogs? Finally, there are bloggers and there are *uber*bloggers, the elite with large audiences, heavily linked by other bloggers, and whose pronouncements tend to attract mainstream media attention. One could make a case for there being a few dozen political bloggers, a few million, or perhaps hundreds of millions.

Blogging is full of such counterweights and paradoxes. Blogger Dan Riehl (riehlworldview) tells his readers that his favorite line is from Walt Whitman: "I am large. I contain multitudes. I contradict myself." He adds, "I believe that's true of all of us." A correct summation of both human beings and blogs.

Blogwars, thus, is my first extended post in what I hope will be a long thread of speculative conversation about a fast-moving phenomenon whose direction, development, and destinations are unknown and probably unknowable. But I claim that one fact is certain: Blogs have changed and will change our politics and our world.

Road Map for Blogwars

Accordingly, I will try, in a linear fashion, to map out the world of *Blogwars* in the following manner.

In chapter 1, I offer an overview of the different kinds of political blogs, a sketch of what we know about the qualities and quantities of their audiences and participants. I also discuss the major investigatory themes of political blogging. First, blogs are special political media not because they are new but because they enable an old political impulse, to reach large numbers of people with personal messages and to gather others who are like-interested and like-minded about political causes. Second, I review research and observations about bloggers and those who participate as readers or responders and ask to what extent they represent "the people" as in an electoral mass or some specialized constituency or even power elite "influentials." Finally, I look at the seeming paradox of blogs being marked both by aggression and partisanship and also by bridge building and offering a marketplace of ideas.

Chapter 2 offers a prehistory of blogs. I make the case that blog-like entities and aspirations are very old and recur with new personalized, additive technologies, from the ancient Greeks writing letters through Franklin Roosevelt's radio fireside chats. But most of the chapter is devoted to the development of bloglike forms of content on the Internet and its forebears. I especially address the development of online politics and ask whether blogs are the ultimate incarnation of such political ideas and practices. I note that we have debated for the last two decades the extent, efficacy, and downsides of cyberdemocracy as we evolved into an age of so-called new media and politics.

In chapter 3, I look at the year of the "blogthrough," the 2004 election and its buildup, when blogs seemed to explode into the national political consciousness and then into the 2006 midterm elections. In particular, I examine the presidential run of Howard Dean, who typified the advantages and drawbacks of using blogs as a vehicle of political persuasion and organization. I also review the Dan Rather "Memogate" affair and blog involvement in the 2004 election exit poll controversies. My primary argument is that blogs have become part of the media system not by accident but because of the particular qualities of blogging that allowed them to exploit opportunities that events afforded them. By 2006, then, blogs became insiders while at the same time retaining their outsider mystique.

In chapter 4, I posit that bloggers are part of the political system's citizen-press component, people who don't make policy or run campaigns but who write or talk about them. These include blogger as reporter of political information, collector and collator, reviser and extender, and investigative journalist. Bloggers progressively are being read as experts, analysts, and watchdogs on political events, issues, ideas, and persons.

In chapter 5, I study the culmination of blogging's arrival in modern American politics, the rise of the blogger as political professional, acting as a working political consultant or, ultimately, as a politician. I show that blogging is becoming part of running for office, of governing, with bloggers taking roles such as speechwriters, advertising creators, and even king- and queenmakers. At the same time, I cite the real perils of blogging for the politician, from the gaffe-prone nature of blogstyle to the sheer time it takes to blog or to be blog friendly. In a final section, I ask, "Should a presidential candidate blog?" with Hillary Clinton as a case study in pro and con ambivalence.

Finally, in an afterpost, I offer some lessons and predictions about blogs and politics. The main three are that (a) bloglike forms will become part of almost every campaign, (b) blogs, or whatever blogging becomes, will stimulate political participation and in turn make us more responsible citizens, and (c) a decade from now, students of politics and the press will look back at the "blogged years" and say 2006 to 2008 was the time blogs "got down to business" in politics and commerce.

Blogwars

1

Beyond the Blog "Revolution"

In 1996, a colleague and I conducted one of the first studies of presidential campaign Web sites.[1] Our main finding was that they were mostly online "tackboards," posting information rather than developing content that exploited the hyperlinking and interactive qualities of the Internet. But as an afterthought, I began looking at "personal political Web sites" created not by the campaign apparatus—political consultants, managers, advisers, or parties—but by individuals who supported the candidate or some cause. Many were raucous and crude, but they offered a new form of public affairs media, a private news bulletin sent from one individual to, potentially, the whole world. *Personalized mass political communication* was finally possible. Here were ordinary folks—dry cleaners, cops, high school juniors—grabbing a bullhorn and insisting, "Listen to me, I have something to say!" about presidential politics, terrorism, the Supreme Court, and so on. If you had Web access, you could read and interact with them for your own enrichment or bemusement.

In contrast, for thousands of years of human history, the elites (or their paid scribes, artists, and heralds) were the *only* ones disseminating messages via *mass* communication. The top stratum has always had the ability to broadcast and upload, ever since civilization raised its first

castle or obelisk. Sometimes, they did so by means of written communication, an activity often limited to the few. Consider, for example,
Isocrates (no relation to Socrates), a Greek philosopher who lived to
ninety-eight years of age in an era just before Alexander the Great's
conquest of Southwest Asia. Isocrates' "about me" page reads much like
that of a stereotype of today's blogger: He was fascinated by politics
but did not want to be a politician; he enjoyed pontificating about his
opinions on politics and education but had no desire to attend town
meetings; he craved popular support but eschewed meeting the public.
As a modern translator put it,

> He endeavored to direct the affairs of Athens and Greece without
> ever holding an office and to mould public opinion without ever
> addressing a public assembly, by issuing from his study, political
> pamphlets or essays in oratorical form, in which [he] then set
> forth the proper conduct of the Greeks in the light of broad
> ideas.[2]

And most interesting, he put to use a new technology called "the alphabet" to publicize his ideas. In one long letter (c. 374 B.C.), he wrote to the
new young king of Cyprus offering advice on how to rule a country:

> You will be a wise leader of the people if you do not allow the
> multitude either to do or to suffer outrage, but see to it that the
> best among them shall have the honors while the rest shall suffer
> no impairment of their rights; for they are the first and most
> important element of good government.[3]

Isocrates elsewhere affirms that he is a rhetorical combatant as it was
his duty to be "waging war against the false pretenders to wisdom."[4]

His great project was to convince the Greeks to band together, to stop
squabbling, and to defeat the great enemy from the east, the Persians. So
he would also write letters to Philip of Macedon (Alexander's father)
summoning him to lead the Greeks into Asia. A later Greek literary
critic, Demetrius of Phaleron, wrote that such letters were less intimate
asides than public documents intended to gain popular currency (a mix-
ture of diary and policy statement, as in blogposts). To go even further,
Isocrates may have been the first author to, like a blogpost, both invite

and include responsive commentary. As my colleague Charles Marsh pointed out to me, in his last great essay, "Panathenaicus," Isocrates actually writes about completing a draft of the work, worrying about how fair it was, and consequently, calling in an opponent to critique it. He then paraphrases the opponent's response and comments.[5] In the same essay, Isocrates complains of enduring criticism, which is a major problem for political bloggers as well: "I am continually being misrepresented by obscure and worthless sophists and being judged by the general public, not by what I really am, but by what they hear from others."[6]

So do blogs spur political participation (attending campaign events, working for the candidate, voting) or just channel political interest into blogposts and comments in an Isocratean fashion? Many bloggers give advice to or rant about the powerful on public affairs issues, campaign strategy, and all sorts of political topics. For blogposts, the headline often reads literally: "What Kerry Must Do" or "What Bush Must Do" and so on. For example, on August 1, 2005, readers of RedState.org, a Republican political blog, were offered insight by Jay Cost, creator of The Horserace Blog, on "Nine Tips for Bush on [Filling] the Supreme Court Vacancy" of Sandra Day O'Connor. Among Cost's counsels: "He should find somebody with a short paper trail: This will also put Bush's political opponents off-balance. Again, they will oppose Bush regardless of whom he appoints. But, if he appoints somebody who has not published very much, they will have a more difficult time constructing arguments reasonable to the mind of moderate Senate Democrats, who are Bush's real audience here."[7]

What were Cost's credentials for being a presidential adviser? He was "a graduate student at the University of Chicago . . . currently working toward his Ph.D. in political science." Thus is blogging: People who in a previous era would have had no political capital (although in Cost's case he would have developed more years later after much publication) can write memos to the powerful that instantly become public documents. And of course, RedState is an open blog, a community of conservatives. Readers replied to Cost with advice of their own for the president, hardly the smoke-filled room of yesteryear's politics. Others wrote posts in response on their own blogs. But was anybody listening? Isocrates must have asked himself the same question.

Suppose, however, that in ancient times you needed to *mass* communicate, influence not just one king but most of his subjects? One solution for societies without printing was *massive* communication. In about 1300 B.C.E., the Pharaoh Ramses II and his army fought a battle against a Hittite force at Kadesh, in what is now Syria. The battle was a draw; in fact, the Egyptians ended up retreating. But Ramses' memorial temple shows on its 100-foot walls pictures and hieroglyphics of the great ruler as victorious. As originally painted, Ramses is bronze skinned, broad shouldered, long armed, resolute of face, wearing the twin crowns of Upper and Lower Egypt, and many times larger than the Hittites and his own men—a superman in the anthropological as well as comic book sense.*

In the written records accompanying the images, Ramses boasts that he personally routed "every warrior of the Hittite enemy, together with the many foreign countries which were with them."[8] In contrast, the Pharaoh blames his own men for early problems in the battle: "You have done a cowardly deed, altogether. Not one man among you had stood up to assist me when I was fighting . . . not one among you shall talk about his service, after returning to the land of Egypt."[9]

I wonder whether some spearman veteran of Kadesh, walking by the tableaus, did not squint up, shake his head, and growl to his wife, "The lying bastard; it was his bad leadership that screwed up everything, we were no cowards." Of course, we do not know; foot soldiers in Pharaoh's army did not record their campaign memoirs. They may not have even been able to read hieroglyphics, although they would not have failed to observe their own portrayal in the picture writing as the tiny supporting cast for the monarch's vainglory.

Today, however, their contemporary counterparts blog. Take a post from CaptB, a Marine blogger in Iraq (now promoted in stateside duty to Major Pain). It follows a picture of the good officer on his modern steed of war (see Figure 1.1). I quote the passage in full to render a

---

* Shelley's "Ozymandias," patterned on the Pharaoh, commanded, "Look upon my works, ye mighty, and despair."

Figure 1.1. CaptB, a Marine blogger in Iraq.

flavor of the authenticity and intenseness that the milblogger at the front, in a war without fronts, can offer us at home trying make sense of it all:

SMOKE EM IF YA GOTEM! Another fine day here in Iraq. Thanksgiving has come and gone and we are that much closer to getting outa here. The holiday was nice although it was the same as every other day here as we maintained vigilance and on guard for attacks and concluded operations. The chow was hot . . . It resembled turkey, really it did . . . kinda . . . oh well I digest. It was hot chow and I am thankful for that. As I remember back in Afghani living months on MRE's, yes it was hot chow and Im damn glad to have it. On our Thanksgiving some of my guys were wrapping up a convoy as they would on the typical day here when they were ambushed and hit with an IED. Probably an 81mm mortar size. Because there were many civilians in the area they weren't able to fire into the crowed where the known triggerman was hiding within. No Marines were injured due to their training, gear and armor hummers. Its was the fourth IED for us. Not a lot compared to others but about four too many, trust me one was plenty and I have the T-shirt Im good to go. Now we race down what we call the White Knuckle Express? It's a road to our destination similar to others with names like ambush alley, dead mans curve and the gauntlet. I really hate this road and respect it a lot because of how dangerous it is. The second time we were scheduled to travel this route I rewrote some items in a last letter? to my family the night before . . . just in case the worse happened because this is where it would happen. I did this because the first time really got my attention if you know what I mean. We maneuver down the bare street (never a good sign) and have to jump the curb to go around an M1 Tank that is

7

protecting our flank. M1's are great to have around as they bring a lot of fire power to the fight. Watch the bag on the right with wires? says truck one, as we continue our movement through the dirty trash covered streets. What doesn't look like an IED at this point??? Everything you see looks like it could hide an artillery shell underneath it. A pack of 5 dogs begins to chase truck 2 in the street as the other trucks continue their paths. We aren't moving or stopping for anything. In this area its survival of the meanest as these same dogs are probably some that have been seen feeding on dead enemy, a real pleasant sight. I could explain every detail to you about it but you wouldn't feel the sneaky eyes peeking around corners with cell phones calling trigger men ahead waiting to try to blow you up or you wouldn't feel the weight on your chest as you swerve to miss the crater holes and the radio chatter is calling out the probable IEDs spotted. Its very surreal because while this is going on small kids are waving hello at you on the sidewalks. I guess that's better than them mashing their thumbs down imitating the act of detonating an IED like they sometimes do. This place is crazy. As we drive Ive now counted at least twenty IED crater holes in the road and have lost count there are so many. However, this fear keeps you razor sharp and alert with adrenalin pumping in your veins to where it takes an hour or so to chill the hell out. Smoke em if ya gotem! Just as we enter the friendly lines a large IED goes off behind us. It was triggered too late to hit us and no one was injured, well that was number five says one of the Marine, 6 if you count the one we discovered and detonated ourselves. As we pull in to our destination, prayer begins and the familiar Arabic chant is broadcasted throughout the area. You remind your Marines of where not to position themselves because of past sniper shots claiming warriors. The Marines are fired up and have lightening reflexes ready for anything. It's a good thing because I think if Bambi? the deer ran across them now the little thing would be vapor. We conduct our mission on scene and adjust to do the run again. Its another fine day here in Iraq. Semper Fi, time for a cigar!

How far such communication has come from the days of Ramses! An anonymous commenter aptly noted to CaptB, "Felt like I was there with you Capt, through your riveting account. How did you ever learn to write like that? It is an amazing gift! We can never thank you and your Marines enough for the outstanding service and sacrifice you are providing America every day. You are all in our hearts and prayers." Ordinary soldiers (and sailors, airmen, and Marines) can now tell their stories, in their own words, even with their own pictures, from ground zero. By doing so they are changing the world of media and politics— maybe even of war.

Or are they? A summer 2006 issue of *Congressional Quarterly Researcher* asked whether the "blog explosion" was a "passing fad or a lasting revolution?"[10] Since the summer of 2003, when Howard Dean's campaign for president seemed to be catching fire via a blog-driven rocket, many politicians, political workers (including media consultants, officeholders' staffers, and campaign managers), people who study and report on politics, and a few ordinary citizens (including many who blog) have been questioning the staying power of blogging. Certainly, America is the land of oversold technologies and collapsed marketing manias in popular culture and political society. But in this book, I want to shift the question by first asking whether our only two choices for the future of political blogs are a complete takeover of the political system or their collapse and disappearance.

Furthermore, if blogs are a revolution of sorts in certain areas of politics but not in others, what do we mean by the term? When America staged its first revolution, many in Europe—perhaps to mollify aristocratic egos astonished that overseas ruffians could overturn the hierarchy of the anointed sovereign—dismissed it as simply the transfer of power from one ruling class to another. (Some Marxists still argue this proposition today.) In retort, the pamphleteer-propagandist (who could be classified as proto-blogger) Thomas Paine proclaimed that the American Revolution was not just a political upheaval but a metaphysical leap: "Our style and manner of thinking have undergone a revolution more extraordinary, than the political revolution of the country. We see with other eyes; we hear with other ears; and think with other thoughts, than those we formerly used."[11] Are blogs changing the way we think about politics, not just the way we practice it?

My short answer is "no and yes." Blogs are not a revolution due to the fact that (a) what they say, their actual content, is not radically new; (b) they represent an ancient impulse in anatomically modern humans, the yearning for public political expression; and (c) they are not forcing all the old means and techniques of politics, policymaking, and campaigns and elections to grind to a halt, to retool, or to be abandoned. Television, for example, remains king, and if you want to be elected president, you'd better devote hundreds of millions of dollars to that tube, and not just YouTube, whatever you do with blogs. As an example, in February 2007, Tom Vilsack of Iowa (a much better blogger than Hillary Clinton of New York) dropped out of the presidential race because, he said, he did not have the money to compete. He meant the cash to buy television time.

But—another paradox of blogging—they are revolutionary in the following sense: *Hyperlinking structure creates the kind of nonlinear, endless jumping about and instant feedback that previous technologies, from cave paintings to television, simply could not.* Blogs allow ordinary people to mass communicate, an act impossible in any previous age of humankind. In fact, in line with Paine's "other thoughts," they present the crest of social eruptions of *IDS-castings*: the convergence of Internet-digital-satellite technology that allows all of us to be broadcasters, not just receivers, and to self-cast the "id" of our inner feelings. Furthermore, we can share the feelings of others, from potential lovers in the next county to politicians in Washington to people with whom we are at war a continent away. And above all, others can join in; blogs are, to use the term from political theory, *voluntary associations* of individuals who could previously have associated so intimately only in the union hall, at the town meeting, or among the mob on the street.

Whatever happens to blogs, whatever the term evolves into, I don't think IDS (Internet-digital-satellite-selfcasting) will fade away. The some 80 percent of American teens who are putting up personal Web pages, instant messaging their friends, podcasting, or creating their own clans with online worlds like that of City of Heroes are not going to return to watching three network channels on TV and reading one (print) newspaper every afternoon. Blogs will not go the way of last year's teen pop star.

So, as far as a complete revolution—where the old idols and kings are tossed away into what the revolutionary Trotsky called "the dustbin of history"—no, blogs are not that extreme, but they are a significant development in politics and public (and what was formerly known as private) life as well.

The Political Blog: Varieties of the Species

A phenomenon has gone mainstream when journalists no longer feel the need to define it as cute or weird. As of this writing in summer 2007, there are few "what is a blog" kinds of stories. How far we have come so fast! The first definition in mainstream media[12] of the word *blog* appeared in the British publication *New Statesman* on October 11,

1999, describing "a web page, something like a public commonplace book, which is added to each day. . . . If there is any log they resemble, it is the captain's log on a voyage of discovery."[13] The first newspaper reference to blogs came from Canada's *Ottawa Citizen* on January 7, 2000, in a story about pop star Sarah McLachlan. Blogs got their undignified television introduction on the *CNNdotCom* program of July 8, 2000, when a correspondent introduced the "nerdword" as follows: "Today's training in technobabble, 'blog.' No, it's not the way you feel in the morning after drinking too much tequila the night before. And no, it's not one of the creatures found in Dr. Seuss's zoo. . . . "[14] In sum, the main elements of the political blog as we know it today—a personal commentary on nonpersonal events, issues, ideas; a site for interaction; a spawning ground for activism; a vessel of wrath—were hazy to observers (and participants) at the dawn of the blog. Neither literally nor metaphorically did anyone exclaim, "Eureka, what a breakthrough for human communication!"

But some people are saying that now. In fact, the whole trend of blogging seems to attract (a) jargony neologisms such as "blook" (a paper book written by a blogger) and "blogola" (money spent to bribe a blogger to support one's party or candidate or consumer product) and (b) hyperbolic statements about blogging itself.

Following are a few of the latter in paraphrase form:

Soon, everybody on the planet, from yak herders in Mongolia to the pope of the Roman Catholic Church to jihadists in Indonesia, will be blogging!

Traditional mass media such as television, radio, and print are dead or dying and will be replaced by bloggers, blogs, and blogging!

Forget thirty-second political commercials, direct mail fundraising, and door-to-door GOTV (get out the vote); blogs are the new campaigns and elections stomping ground, bloggers are the new political constituency, and blogging is the new political medium!

I doubt that blogs will rule the world, that every peasant, pontiff, and president will blog, or that people will abandon their televisions and give up reading books to blog. But blogs are indeed changing media, including politics, campaigns and elections, and public affairs and, commensurably, have turned the traditional dynamics of the media producer–media consumer relationship on its head.

Types of Blogs

There are several ways to draw a portrait of the world of blogs. Scope or outlook is one. Many blogs (or bloglike venues) are inward looking, largely concerned with the personal problems or issues of the editor/author. Among the hundreds of thousands of personal sites at Web hosts MySpace.com and LiveJournal.com are writers who describe their life as a sex slave, the antics of their cats, their stalking of celebrities, and in one case, a student's cheating on one of my midterm exams. Others are veritable *Time* magazines of the Internet, focusing on public affairs issues of great scope, from Iowa politics to Shi'ite Islam to global climate change. Many blogs mix the intimate with the macroeconomic and read simultaneously like letters from a friend, diary entries, political pamphlets, Associated Press news reports, and newspaper editorials. Former *TV Guide* writer Jeff Jarvis (of JeffJarvis.com), for example, might discourse on topics as varied as the Iraq war, the problems he had with Dell computers, his canoeing vacation, and whether bloggers should be called "pajama media" or "open-source media." A not atypical blogpost on a political blog might run something like: "Got to stop ranting on the Iraq Troop Surge for now, the kids want to go play in the park."

That said, there are many attempts to map out the bloglands into constituent parts. A summer 2006 survey by the commercial Blogads network categorized blogging into four metagroups or blog communities: politics, gossip and celebrity news, motherhood and family issues, and music.[15] Wizbang's 2006 Weblog Awards offered the following topical categories, with awards granted based on some 500,000 reader votes:

- Best Blog
- Best New Blog
- Best Individual Blog

- Best Humor Blog
- Best Comic Strip
- Best Online Community
- Best Liberal Blog
- Best Conservative Blog
- Best Centrist Blog
- Best Media Blog
- Best Technology Blog
- Best Sports Blog
- Best Military Blog
- Best Law Blog
- Best Business Blog
- Best LGBT (Lesbian/Gay/Bisexual/Transgender) Blog
- Best Parenting Blog
- Best Educational Blog
- Best Science Blog
- Best Medical/Health Issues Blog
- Best Photo Blog
- Best Culture Blog
- Best Diarist
- Best Gossip Blog
- Best Music Blog
- Best Podcast
- Best Video Blog

Voters also judged blogs by region or nationality, such as Best Canadian Blog or Best Middle Eastern or African Blog. And there were distinctions based on "ecosystem"—that is, how popular a blog was in rankings—from Best of the Top 250 Blogs to Best of the Rest of the Blogs (8,751+).*

---

* As an aside, the bloglands are full of contests to decide which blogs are more important than others. Some are in jest: Right bloggers started a Conservative Blogress Diva competition. Wizbang's Awards are one of the most participated in. Several of my favorite bloggers urged me to vote once a day in their favor. I also learned of a loose plot by some right bloggers to promote for "leftblog of the year" the most left-kooky-extremist blog they could find so that they could then say, "Look at what kind of fruitcake the liberal bloggers elected!"

Obviously, many categories morph into each other: You can have a group, gay, liberal, Canadian, and/or photo blog. Some blogs are concerned with the home, family, and everyday life; others express fanaticism about certain television shows or rock-'n'-roll bands; still others are techie, citing, assessing, or carping about new types of iPods or even blogging itself.

Here are some examples:

- After Hurricane Katrina hit, my colleague Professor Jean Trumbo in faraway Reno, Nevada, was so overcome with the horror of the images that she took up blogging on riversad.blogspot.com, telling me, "Blogging was my catharsis. This medium became a way for me to SCREAM without standing in the middle of the street. And to cry without hiding in the basement."
- Wil Wheaton, formerly Wesley Crusher of the "new" (now old) *Star Trek*, blogs under his own name.
- Godblog.com, purportedly written by the Maker himself, offers "higher" guidance on personal, holy, and worldly affairs.
- My friend, the (allegedly) retired *Washington Post* Pulitzer Prize–winning political columnist Ed Yoder, has converted to blogging at www.yoderblog.com.
- Ask the English Teacher is the blog of Crawford Kilian, a retired college English professor, who answers questions on the use of hyphens and "the mysterious subjunctive."
- Prayersfortracy.com, created by one of my students, follows the developments of her sister who suffered brain trauma after an accident. The blog is maintained "to keep our large family and friends everywhere updated on what was going on."
- One woman uses Diary of an Army Wife to describe to her readers "my roller coaster ride through a deployment" of her husband.
- Vladimir Poetin, a young Dutch student and journalist, blogs From Holland to Kurdistan, independently reporting from the Kurdish region of Iraq (vladimirkurdistan.blogspot.com/).
- Dr. Pepper/Seven-Up brands publicized the Raging Cow milk-based drink by having an angry young cow post impressions from its cross-country trip of "udder madness."

Blogs are most often published by individuals, but there are many group blogs as well that proffer veritable staffs or militias of people blogging together. Charles Johnson's blog Little Green Footballs boasts its "lgf army" of bloggers. Kos has his "alumni," including Kos fellows such as mcjoan, who work as paid staff commenters. A number of conservative women bloggers have formed The Cotillion where, as they put it, "Everyone is entitled to our opinion."

In blogs as in street politics, there is initiative and power in friendship and numbers. And in some cases, the lines between the virtual and the actual do cross: Regional left and right bloggers hold soirees and pub nights in Washington, D.C.; [Daily]Kosites (or sometimes "Kossacks") organize a Yearly Kos convention. SusanG, a blogger in the Kos community, proclaimed about the 2006 Las Vegas gathering: "We are here. We are at the gates. We will no longer remain passive and meek in order to court favor. We, the people, are coming to power slowly and indefatigably, here in Vegas and here on the blog. We have arrived. And we'll never go back to silence again."[16] MSNBC's Tom Curry noted the sea change that the event represented:

> In the old days—not long ago, in 1998—reporters came to Las Vegas for the AFL-CIO convention to see union chieftain John Sweeney and allies such as House Minority Leader Dick Gephardt. Now reporters come to interview Markos Moulitsas Zúniga, the proprietor of DailyKos web site and Matt Stoller of Mydd.com.
>
> The presidential hopefuls, past and present, came too, —Wes Clark mingled with Kos attendees at the opening night reception; New Mexico Gov. Bill Richardson addressed a panel discussion on energy policy Friday; and Iowa Gov. Tom Vilsack flew in for an education panel Saturday.[17]

Mother Jones magazine (the icon of the "old" left press) described Yearly Kos on its own blog as "the progressive blogosphere's coming out party; more [for] the fact that such Democratic luminaries as Harry Reid and Nancy Pelosi feel it necessary to make the pilgrimage here to touch the feet of Kos, this event's presiding deity."[18] The courting of the Kosites by the powerful was testimony to the reality that blogging is no longer a fringe phenomenon in politics. That the *arrivistes* had arrived was confirmed at the 2007 gathering, when all the major Democratic candidates for the presidency spoke and the *Washington Post* and others dubbed it the "Democrats' Other National Convention." The road to the White House for Democrats now seemed to include three must-stops: Iowa, New Hampshire, and Yearly Kos (which in 2008 will be retitled, grandly but fittingly, the "Netroots Nation").

Interplay: Posting and Linking

The flagship of blogging, the essential physical element of the blog, is the short- to medium-length essay, the post.* Although posts look like pasted essays, their structural complexity is considerable compared to, say, what a Victorian gentleman might have put down in the *Edinburgh Review* of 1850 or Samuel Johnson's *Rambler* rants or Addison's essays in *The Spectator* of the eighteenth century. What makes posts blog worthy, what distinguishes their real political import, are, first, "hot" links—that is, embedded URLs or occasionally e-mail addresses. Such hyperlinks are crucial to the interactivity of a blog and a key to its success as a medium.[19]

The second element integral to making posts attractive is the ability for people to participate. Comments can accrete into discussions, especially in longer threads where one person makes a point, someone responds, a third person chimes in, the original writer extends her remarks, and so on. DailyKos and RedStateDiaries are powerhouses of the left and right, respectively, because they are not monologues but rather communities where many people have found a home for political

*The art of timing a post is a subtle one. Ambra Nykol, a guest editorial columnist for the *Seattle Post-Intelligencer*, who blogs via nykola.com, explained in an interview, "I generally write and post at night—sometimes into the wee hours of the morning. This way, readers come to my site first thing in the morning and see fresh content." David Yeagley of Badeagle.com told me that some of his readers complained that he was putting up new posts too often and that "by the time they get to it, by the time they're ready to comment the comment will be visible only a few hours and then I've changed to a new blog subject." Professional bloggers who are on somebody's payroll, like Wonkette (of Gawker media) or the bloggers on corporate PR sites, are required by contract to blogpost a certain number of times a day.

expression. Blogs can thereby ask their communities to work together on projects too large for any one reporter or one blogger. For example, when in March 2007 the Department of Justice released thousands of documents relating to the firing of a number of federal prosecutors, talkingpointsmemo's Josh Marshall called upon his readers to help sift and search them. His associate Paul Kiel announced on the tpm.muckraker site: "Josh and I were just discussing how in the world we are ever going to make our way through 3,000 pages when it hit us: we don't have to. Our readers can help." They could, they can, and they did because those interactors include both passionate laypeople and experts who want to pitch in.

Blogs are also porous portals not meant to be one-stop journeys. Even the most solipsistic blogs tend to link to friends or buddies or fellow conspirators. Sometimes, the links are made to random members of a prescribed group: a Web ring, where connecting through the link will take you to a random member of the ring. Most bloggers encourage linkage, building community by indicating via references, citations, hat tips, and blogrolls, signifying that "these people are with me" and "you should look at them, too." As my interviews with bloggers revealed, whether they accept comments or not, no one blogs alone— at least not intentionally. Numbers bolster the case for citation as the glue of the blog communities: According to a winter 2007 survey by the Vizu Answers Group and Ad Age, almost two thirds of people who read blogs locate a new blog because of a link on another blog.[20]

To take one example of such go-back and go-between, Ezra Klein, on his eponymous blog, posted a brief item on October 7, 2005, that critiqued a report on voting trends and argued, in part, "Mere Democratic/liberal turnout, if it doesn't also mobilize across the rest of the political spectrum, will not win us any elections." There were thirty-eight comments in response.[21] That is a key point about blogs: They allow, either within the space of post and comment pages or between blogs, a *full* discussion of issues of the day. Although mass media are chopping themselves up into smaller and smaller bits of clutter and hyperkinetic activity, bloggers can stop, think, read, talk, ponder, and rethink at length.

In the past, most of us have been allowed to talk politics only among ourselves or via very edited and constricted channels, like perhaps writing a letter to the editor. I recall many years ago when a high school friend appeared on a local news broadcast to offer a "citizen's response to an editorial"; apart from robbing a bank or winning a spelling bee, that was pretty much the only way he could have gotten any airtime. At present-day ezraklein, though, several dozen bright, thinking, knowledgeable folks debated the strategies of Democratic Party electoral politics unrestrained, to each other, although they may have been separated by a continent. As Klein himself put it, "*Great* f**king thread guys—lots of good stuff." That's crucial to *good* interactive blogging—threading the argument.

But a key concern about such hyperlinked and group interactivity for political bloggers is how to get *other people* to link to you and talk to you. Here's one personal example: In January 2006, I wrote a blogpost in my analysis blog on "Hillary Clinton's Blog Dilemma: Are the Grassroots Burning?" I speculated on whether Hillary Clinton had a blog strategy for the 2008 presidential race. She was being attacked hardest and supported least among left bloggers (like Kos), and I wondered whether this was an early indicator, a fire on the prairie horizon, of imminent rebellion against her on the left wing of the Democratic Party. The blog software at the time could tell me how many people per hour were viewing my site. I knew I had several hundred readers per day, a tiny audience. But then an uberblogger, Mickey Kaus of slate. com, commented on my comment, and his comments were responded to and picked up by others. By the end of the week, I had nearly 10,000 readers, about equal to the number of students I have taught in my entire career. A fellow blogger proclaimed, "You've made it, bub." Another cautioned, "But can you hold the audiences?" Well, I tried. I posted more on the same subject; I started dialogues with people who replied to my posts; I created publicity by notifying other bloggers and the posters what I was writing about. In turn, some other prominent bloggers, like Arianna Huffington, contacted me. Perhaps I was on my way to the B-list of semiprominent bloggers?

Alas, or rather fortunately for my academic career, my family, and my sanity, my blogging collapsed because I simply was unwilling to spend the four to five hours a day necessary to maintain fresh, interesting content. So I watched, or rather didn't watch, as my audience trailed off into the single digits. (I don't check my meter anymore.) I still blog but only when I feel like it, which by the tally of real bloggers is far too little. One noted to me: "It's tricky. You have to keep up with something each day or explain why you aren't. People expect you there." I was not willing to develop the "paper" each day, and so I could not sustain an audience. And that's another point: Bloggers have to work for their community; ignore it and it dies, like some Japanese-programmed computer pet, or rather disperses to other more faithful and dedicated bloggers.

Blogs as Personal Mass Communication and Voluntary Associations

In an age when public distrust of institutional sources of information—such as newspapers or the Department of Transportation—is the norm, blogging is a new opportunity for reinvigorating politics and political communication. In researching this book, getting to know blogs and bloggers of the left, right, and center via their blogs and through interviews, I was struck by how much that personal touch matters to bloggers and to their growing readership. This "I am there with you" quality is self-evident with someone like CaptB, who recounts his hell ride into Fallujah. But the personal factor also applies when a blogger offers an opinion on a significant issue of the day. For example, attorney La Shawn Barber (La Shawn Barber's Corner, lashawnbarber. com) describes herself as "a believer in and follower of Jesus Christ . . . a former liberal and current renegade supporter of conservative ideals [and] an Independent conservative, not a member of the Republican or Democratic parties." Her blog is well cited by many leading conservative blogs. I do not agree with her on a number of issues—indeed, she attacked me in one post!—but I like, respect, and regularly read her. On September 24, 2004, she offered the following post on "The Immorality of Race Preferences."

> I was asked to explain why I believe race preferences are immoral.
>
> Immorality is the state of being immoral. An immoral thing is that which is contrary to accepted principles of right and wrong. Morality is conformity to ideals of right human conduct. For a primer on right human conduct, I direct you to God's word, the Bible.

Natural rights, as well as those found in the Constitution, belong to *individuals*, not groups. If an individual is discriminated against because of his race, *he* should be compensated, not his entire racial group. There is no such thing as Group Rights. An individual has a right to seek redress from injury from a particular institution, not an entire race.

Skin color preferences bestow undeserved advantage on some and undeserved burdens on others. Such an idea is anathema to democracy and freedom. Why should people be compensated for a wrong they did not suffer? Why should some be penalized for a wrong they did not commit?

A person's sex or skin color doesn't entitle him to special favors or treatment. Skin color or sex doesn't entitle anyone to receive less or more consideration. Giving one group preferred status over another group is unjust, especially when done by our own government. It is against the law and in violation of the **U.S. Constitution**, regardless of intentions.

The idea that we can "fix" history by preferring the race once discriminated against over the race once doing the discriminating is flat out wrong, not to mention counterintuitive.

In his brief for the **Brown v. Board of Education**, the case that declared government-sanctioned race discrimination illegal, **Thurgood Marshall** wrote, "Distinctions by race are so evil, so arbitrary and invidious that a state, bound to defend the equal protection of the laws must not invoke them in any public sphere."

I'll concede this: I believe social engineers' hearts were in the right place, but they had no idea what their skin color schemes would look like thirty years out. Thanks to them, we're still entangled in race debates and race politics. These things will not pass until individual rights regain their proper place in this country.

Any questions?

A thoughtful post, regardless of one's personal opinion. More crucial, there were seventy responses, some of greater length than the original essay. They were readers, other bloggers agreeing, disagreeing, arguing, making claims and counterclaims, and adding points: a small town hall forum of Norman Rockwell flavor but in cyberspace. The discussion thread was taken up (trackbacked) on other blogs. In short, Barber's post *began* an interchange of ideas that continued for weeks, and anyone could join it.

Blogs also allow interaction between individuals that could in turn accrete their common knowledge, focus their activism, recruit others, and march, virtually, toward a goal. Such "smart mobs," or self-organizing networks, are discussed by many researchers concerned with the sociology of cyberspace.[22] In terms of politics, this is noteworthy because democracy is held to be based on and in favor of "individual" rights. However, democracies in fact tend to operate through the agencies of voluntary associations—that is, so-called interest groups such as unions, the Sierra Club, the oil industry, Mothers Against Drunk Driving, and now, groups of bloggers self-aggregating to champion a cause, reveal a scandal, or pillory a politician. Voluntary associations have always been foundations of the democratic experiment. Alexis de Tocqueville, that great student of the American political system, argued that a democratic "government . . . places each citizen, even the most humble, in a condition of [enabling him to act] with as much independence, and of making of his independence as much use as is available to the most exalted citizen."[23] But Tocqueville was not referring to independence from other independents; the American Constitution that he admired affirms the right to form groups to "lobby" government. (Gun rights, for example, are implicitly linked to joining a "militia.") Or, as the great twentieth-century Kansas newspaper editor William Allen White pointed out, every citizen has "two votes," one at the ballot box and another through affiliations with a party, a union, or any other organization with political interests.

Obviously, some communication communities within cyberspace are truly interactive: You play a monster multiplayer game such as City of Heroes, and you and your band of avatars cocreate the resulting outcomes, including, say, the burning of a city block. New media technology allows not only an individualistic revolution in media but also an interactive one; everyone can add to, or wiki, the message—that is, treat information as "open sourced." We used to think of mass media as a "closed-source" broadcast: Somebody distributes a television program, for instance, and lots of people choose to see it or not. But open source implies communities of meaning that recode data or code their own, not just decode it. Think of those *Star Trek* fans who are now CGIing (with special effects that would have astonished Gene Roddenberry) new episodes of the original series (with old cast members and writers!). Or the sticky mobs, people who happen to have taken images of the same event—for example, the London 7/7 bombings—upload them, and find them all grouped in the same Web space. Or the legion of photoshoppers, people who digitally edit vacation photos or news icons into alternative reality fantasies. Wikipedia, the online encyclopedia, allows anyone to contribute entries and change them (but is adding restrictions lately). In politics as well, interested voters seem to want and seek out interactivity with each other and with candidates.[24] As of the 2004 election, the Web sites of the presidential contenders had evolved and were much more hyperlinked and interactive than those of the class of 1996 that I examined.[25]

So if you are trying to assess a political blog, ask yourself a simple question: Is there evidence of people volunteering to be part of its association? To paraphrase an old saying about successful politicians, behind every great blogger is a supportive group of women and men.

Are Bloggers "The People"?

Many famous blog sages have made some statement to the effect that blogs are indeed a popular movement. In 2002, at a conference on Internet communication held at Harvard, Professor Jay Rosen of New York University sounded the bugle for a new age identifying "a new kind of public, where every reader can be a writer and people do not so much consume the news as they 'use' it in active search for what's going on, sometimes in collaboration with each other, or in support of the pros."[26] I agree. To express one's opinion about the Pharaoh (or the president), one need not carve a 100-foot obelisk or even get an op-ed in the *New York Times*; one can instead blog, and thousands, maybe millions, will observe. So, yes, we could assert that blogs are the "unedited voice of the people" as did Dave Winer, editor of *Scripting News*, a weblog started in 1997 that he claims "bootstrapped the blogging revolution." Likewise, Rebecca Blood, author of one of the main texts about blogging, correctly observed, "The weblog's greatest strength—its uncensored, unmediated, uncontrolled voice—is also its greatest weakness."[27] Dan Gillmor, in the title of his landmark book, affirmed that it is *We the Media* now, not "they" (the political, economic, and press elites).

But there are limitations to such a vision of blog-facilitated direct democracy. Winer and Blood had the *mainstream* press and the government in mind when they described blogs as "unedited" and "uncontrolled." Although bloggers certainly possess more autonomy about what to publish and what to ignore than even the most powerful journalists, blog content is in fact edited in one way or another. Policies, procedures, and protocols vary, but bloggers edit themselves; they may consult others on a post before putting it up, and they certainly may edit comments by their readers for considerations such as length and profane language. David Yeagley (Badeagle.com) declared, "I cull out the potty mouths; after a while they get it and move or clean up their language." Opinions can also get one cut from the pack. Some blogs block the comments of caustic partisans of the opposing side. Furthermore, as advertising revenues increase, blogs will bear the same commercial pressures that big media have always borne. Certainly, bloggers who are subsidized by political parties or corporations are susceptible to editorial control. They can become boring flags (PR blogs) or deceitful sock puppets.

Another problem with "the whole world blogging" mantra and the *vox populi* projection of blogs is that bloggers are not necessarily a representative slice of the population. An analogous adage in social science is that a majority of psychological experiments are done on college students because they are the most readily available population for researchers of human behavior to study. But as anyone who teaches college classes can attest, "sophomores are not people" in that the average eighteen- or nineteen-year-old is not really the best exemplar of society as a whole. Likewise, with blogs, a medium can be popular and populist without being *of* the people—that is, of *all* the people.

Elitism and Blogs: Lonesome Rhodes's Revenge?

In the youth of blogging, observers and participants commonly deemed it the "people's medium." But that bloggers are people—often ordinary people who don't seem to have the résumés of traditional media elites, tenures as journalists, academics, civil servants, and so on—is not considered a positive quality to many of those same traditional media elites. Bill Keller, editor of the *New York Times*, in one of a series of professional dismissals of bloggers, summed up their contribution to the information society with the following: "Bloggers recycle and chew on the news. That's not bad. But it's not enough."[28] Well, remember Perlmutter's rule on blogging: You can find blogs to support or contradict any generalization about blogs, bloggers, and blogging. It is true that, according to one study and lots of blog reading by me and my students, about half of blogposts make reference to news items that have appeared in newspapers, television, and so on.[29] But as detailed later, many bloggers are now media and political elites themselves. In December 2005, the *Times* started creating blogs for some of its reporters. News organizations regularly send out calls to on-the-scene bloggers (with cell phones) when breaking news occurs, as was the case after the London bombings, what researcher Steven Livingston calls the "Nokia effect."[30] Almost every news organization is blogging up or exploring ways to use citizen journalists.

But did Keller mean something else by his use of the word *chew?* The implications are found in a potent icon of individual populist autocracy gone mad, a lead character in the film *A Face in the Crowd.*

There were no blogs in 1956 when director Elia Kazan crafted his meditation on the perils of unfiltered democracy via the powerful new medium of the day, television. In his first (and best) movie performance, Andy Griffith plays Lonesome Rhodes, an Arkansas jailbird who, by his quick wit, raconteur style, and ruthless nature, rises to the top of the talk show radio and television industry. He ultimately abuses his power, crushes people who stand in his way, and even attempts to hogtie the course of the nation. In one famous sequence, he adopts the political fortunes of a well-known conservative senator with presidential ambitions. The latter is a dignified, thoughtful, old-fashioned politician, modeled perhaps on the late Robert "Mr. Conservative" Taft of Ohio (who died a few years earlier). Lonesome tries to morph the senator into a cracker-barrel populist, creating a television show in which he mingles with some good old boys at a country general store, chewing (actually "chawing") "tobacca," and offering dumbed-down political homilies. In the movie, the scene is meant to be both low comedy and high satire. The key points were that (a) the politician was demeaning himself with each chaw and (b) the relatively novel venue of television—which in 1956 was younger than blogs are now—offered many opportunities for demagoguery. Radio did the same in the era of Walter Winchell and again conspicuously in the 1980s with the wave of right-wing talk radio hosts like Rush Limbaugh.

That such populism and its demagogues are to be feared is an old theme, given its latest iteration in anti-blog prejudice. Thomas Carlyle, the English historian and a subscriber to the Great Man theory of history, reportedly said, "Democracy will prevail when men believe the vote of Judas as good as that of Jesus Christ." All the noted philosophers of democratic Athens, including Plato, Socrates, and Aristotle, eschewed democracy as their ideal form of government. Interestingly, Isocrates was one of the few to at least think democracy was no worse than monarchy. And until a few hundred years ago, democracy was a rare and scorned practice. By the sixth century A.D. in Byzantium, for example, the word *democrateria* meant an urban riot. When the idea of democracy was revived in revolutionary America, most of the Founding Fathers saw not democratic Athens as a role model but rather elitist republican Rome. Even Thomas Jefferson, that most "democratic" of our political leaders, despised the mobs of the big cities.

And in truth, the idea of ordinary folk broadcasting themselves and their opinions on everything is easy to satirize. The great conservative thinker and essayist Samuel Johnson once dismissed the discernment of the "rabble" (i.e., the nonelites of his day), declaring that "the vulgar are the children of the State, and must be taught like children."[31] In particular, he lampooned the affectation of the small man aspiring to effect great policy in his portrait of one Edward Elwall, a religious quack who wrote on Christian doctrine and boasted of being acquitted of heresy charges and thus defeating "the greatest potentates on Earth" when he in fact had made a fool of himself and, as Johnson put it, "failed in his scheme of making himself a man of great consequence."[32] The modern critic Cyril Connolly wrote that one could blame the playwright Robert Addison in the mid-eighteenth century for starting the fad of the small essay, or rather, "He enforced the essay on us, so that small boys who can hardly write are at this moment busy putting down their views on Travel, the Great Man, Courage, Gardening, Capital Punishment, and winding up with a quotation from Bacon."[33] More recently, in a famous panel of *Calvin & Hobbes*, Bill Watterson has his iconic "small boy" protagonist proclaim:

> I feel I have an obligation to keep a journal of my thoughts. . . . Being a genius, my ideas are naturally more important and interesting than other people's. So I figure the world would benefit from a record of my mental activities.[34]

Surely many of today's traditional elites, from university professors to Washington newspaper columnists (even if they blog!), view indy bloggers as at best an army of Elwalls or Calvins, at worst one of Lonesome Rhodes. Many indy bloggers conversely may perceive that media elites are Calvins with puffed credentials.

So, yes, to paraphrase Carlyle, democracy forces us to accept that idiots and fools (i.e., people who disagree with us) should be allowed to vote . . . or to blog.

Kings and Queens of the Bloglands

Are blogs anti-elitist at all? There is no question that a lot of people blog. In the United States, blogging has undergone explosive increases, from a few dozen in the late 1990s to many, many of millions today. Still, and keep this in mind when examining the numbers that follow, only about a fifth of blogs and blog traffic is political. According to several studies by the Pew Internet and American Life Project, blog readership increased 58 percent in 2004, marking blogs at "20% of the newspaper audience and 40% of the talk radio audience." At that time, at least 11 million Americans read blogs daily, and this number increases all the time.[35] A *Wall Street Journal*/Harris poll in April 2005 similarly reported that "two-fifths (44 percent) of Americans have read an online political blog, and more than a quarter read them once a month or more."[36] One study found that blog-perusing Americans in 2005 would spend a combined 551,000 years reading blogs while at work, or 3.5 hours each of their workweek.[37] Technorati's David Sifry reported in his "State of the Blogosphere" on October 17, 2005, that his company was tracking 9.6 million weblogs and that the number of weblogs had been doubling every five months for the last three years.

But blogs have a hierarchy of prominence, popularity, and power; there are kings and queens in the bloglands—that is, the A-list.[38] These are people who by brains, skill, luck, and moxie[39] receive a high billing by every metric, from numbers of other blogs that link to them to numbers of visitors to the site to numbers of folks who interact with the site. Several useful studies of this issue have pointed out that when people develop a new blog, one of their first acts is to create a blogroll of blogs they consult. And no surprise, the rich get richer because that list tends to include the most popular blogs, which thus add to their scores in numbers linked to.[40] Studies by Clay Shirky and others support the picture of the bloglands displaying a power law curve, which looks something like half of the familiar bell-shaped curve.[41] There is a narrow, tall spike (the top blogs) and then a *very* long "tail" formed by the many other blogs. My students and I have done similar work on how often particular blogs are mentioned in newspapers, magazines, television, and radio. Here as well, there are the tops (A-list), some middles (B-list), and many "one cite wonders." As detailed later, with such royal status comes political power: Kos and others are for all purposes political consultants. (Zúniga's writing partner Jerome Armstrong of MyDD.com is a working consultant.) So a critic of blogging might now say that the problem with blogging is not that it is populism run amok but rather the reverse: It is too elitist.

The royal status of some bloggers, however, is tempered by several factors. First, blogs are often produced by individuals but comprise what Drezner and Farrell call a "web of influence,"[42] meaning they are often operationalized by cross-links between bloggers and blogposts. There are several ways such voluntary associations are physically created by the kings and queens of the bloglands for their own good as well as democratically for the good of the many less popular bloggers. The most obvious is a citation, something to the effect of "Go to this Internet address and look at what this blog is saying." Sometimes, such references are very explicit. On July 14, 2004, Michelle Malkin (michellemalkin.com) told her readers in a short post titled "Proper Blog Etiquette" that "It has come to my attention that Nathan, a very cool blogger at Brain Fertilizer, is irked that I mentioned him in a previous post, but failed to provide a link to his fabulous blog. My bad. Please help me make amends and visit him at Brain Fertilizer. (And no, I'm not doing this for everyone!)." Finally, as discussed further in the final chapter, bloggers should not be judged by quantitative metrics alone. Many are performing important (and influential) functions while happily remaining numerical small-fry. Milblogger John Donovan (www.thedonovan.com) explained to me, "I follow the Small Business Administration's advice for small-town businesses that find themselves suddenly confronting Wal-Mart: 'Don't fight Wal-Mart at what they do best. Figure out what they don't do, and provide that service or commodity.'"

So blogs are not dangerous populism, whatever that is, nor are they hereditary autocracies; they are, simply, democratic (small *d*). You peruse, you pick, you choose. There is room in the marketplace of ideas for stalls of all sizes.

Activists and Tech Optimists, Not Peasants

I stated earlier that by the 2008 election cycle, I *hope* we live in the age after the myth, hype, oversell, and hyperbole of the blog. I hear fewer people insisting that blogs will all die out and few others asserting that blogs will be kings of all media. Such temperance is a healthy sign for blogs and for politics. Nevertheless, what if you are a politician looking for votes and for money, not just the support of a few big party bosses (the superbloggers)? In terms of the electorate, are bloggers the people—that is, the *voters*? And if they are voters, what kind and what groups? In the language of advertising and marketing (whether for minivans, toothbrushes, or congressmen and women), what target niche are bloggers? In the last section of the final chapter of the book, I will ask to what extent blogs replicate existing political venues such as, say, talk radio or direct mail advertising. But here I want to make the case that although the mass of political bloggers are not quite the people but also not quite aristocrats, there are certain qualities that make them important players in American politics.

Now, when we look at actual surveys of bloggers—both creators and interactors within the bloglands—we find that bloggers may be high in number but tend to come from the higher education and upper income portions of the population, which is as true in Kyrgyzstan or Nigeria as it is in the United States. In the United States, bloggers are overwhelmingly white, and the majority are male. One study of 2006 "Internet seekers" of political information found them to be much more likely to have an "annual household income $75K or more" and be "post-grads."[43] Another international survey found that in all nations, save Poland and Japan, blog readers were more often males than females.[44] Similarly, a report on Americans' use of technology issued by Forrester Research in summer 2005 found the country almost evenly divided between "tech optimists" (those who eagerly seek out technology to facilitate their lives and solve perceived problems) and "tech pessimists" (those who are skeptical about new technologies and find them less relevant to their daily lives). Tech optimists tend to be younger, have higher income, are much more likely to use the Internet, and spend almost double the hours of tech pessimists online. Strikingly, 78 percent of tech optimists reported reading blogs regularly, but only 6 percent of tech pessimists reported regular blog use.[45]

Such a lopsided demographic (and psychographic) has many implications. Our reading of "popular" politics in other countries can get skewed if we only listen to bloggers. This was the case in the Iranian election of 2005 where "Tehran-centered" political bloggers spoke for the middle class but not the mass of poorer voters.[46] On the domestic front is a quandary most male, white, middle-class bloggers don't tend to think about. Keith Jenkins, an African American editor at *The Washington Post* who also blogs, stated, "It has taken 'mainstream media' a very long time to get to [the] point of inclusion. . . . My fear is that the overwhelmingly white and male American blogosphere . . . will return us to a day where the dialogue about issues was a predominantly white-only one."[47] His point is an intriguing one: The A-list blogs include few ethnic or racial minorities, among them Michelle Malkin (Asian), Kos (Hispanic), and the late Steve Gilliard (African American). One of my graduate students, working on a project on black-written blogs, told me initially that she could not do the work because there weren't enough applicable blogs to inspect.

But if the bloglands are a democracy where people vote with their eyes, links, and clicks, does it matter who actually blogs?

Here we need to get philosophical as well as historical. Jenkins was talking about dialogue for good, history-driven reasons. While I was writing this book, civil rights pioneer Rosa Parks died. It was she who, by her refusal to give up her bus seat to a white man in Montgomery, Alabama, on December 1, 1955, helped initiate the modern Civil Rights movement. We should remember that Ms. Parks did not achieve vindication and the right to sit at any open seat on a bus through democratic means or by the will of the people. No one on the bus of any race that day argued for her cause: There was no wisdom of a crowd that day! If there had been a referendum in Montgomery the next week, the majority of participants (most of the whites and perhaps not a few blacks wishing to avoid "racial troubles") would have voted against the integration of buses. (The other black passengers did move to the back of the bus when the bus driver told them to; Parks alone remained seated.) Practically all the achievements of the Civil Rights movement were installed by courts over the objections of the majority of local citizens.

But of course, it is not a case of blacks or other minorities being segregated actively and purposefully from blogging. As Tiffany B. Brown of the blogs blackfeminism.org and tiffanybbrown.com explained in an interview, "If you haven't participated in the blogosphere, you don't understand its worth. You have to think blogging is important." If so, blogging will better live up to its ascription of universal popularity.

Even if blogs are not *vox populi*, it does not follow that, as blog critics love to taunt, bloggers are the tinfoil hatters of American political life. To the contrary, bloggers may not *be* the people, but there is growing evidence that they have an extraordinary and extraproportional effect *on* the people and on politics, campaigns and elections, public affairs, policymaking, press agendas and coverage, and public opinion. In political history, vocal minorities have, we should recall, changed the world and affected the fate of millions far out of relation to their size as a group. In revolutions, sheer numbers do not guarantee success or failure. A few thousand Bolsheviks toppled the Russian government in 1917, whereas millions of workers and protestors could not move the Chinese power structure in 1989. In the case of the former Soviet republic of Kyrgyzstan in 2005, just a few hundred demonstrators took over the government building and sent the president packing, partially instigated by local bloggers![48]

In democracies, too, a cadre of politically effective people can make a mighty impact. Obviously, political leaders can change our world by building wide support or by making fateful decisions. But almost a century of studies in the marketing of ideas suggests that the kind of people who blog could very well be players in politics, either as part of campaigns or in opposition to them. Communications researchers, starting in the 1950s, described a "two-step flow" of persuasion. The goal of persuasion campaigns, from "I like Ike" to "Drink a glass of orange juice with breakfast," was not to convince everyone directly. Rather, it was to persuade local opinion leaders within a community, who would then persuade those who respected their opinion or followed their leadership on political matters.

The modern term for such folks is *influentials*, people who probably have some influence, positive or negative, on the decision making of larger groups: pastors, politicians, journalists, even professors.[49] They were described by Ed Keller and John Berry as "canaries in the mineshaft for looming political ideas. . . . If word of mouth is like a radio signal broadcast over the country, influentials are the strategically placed transmitters that amplify the signal, multiplying the number of people who hear it."[50]

According to one study, "Americans who are politically active via the Internet are almost seven times more likely than the average American to serve as opinion leaders among friends, relatives and colleagues."[51] The Institute for Politics, Democracy and the Internet, in a study published in February 2004, profiled what it called "Online Political Citizens (OPCs)": These turned out to be disproportionately male, higher income, and more highly educated than the average American.[52] One later study of bloggers reported that 70 percent fit the enticing category of influential.[53] A 2005 profile found that "Weblog users tend to be young, highly educated men with high incomes [with] moderate to high levels of trust in government, high self-efficacy, and high interest in political and general news."[54] The Blogads network reported that more than 70 percent of political bloggers had contributed to a political campaign within the past six months, and more than 77 percent had a college degree.[55] In 2007, an international survey found that influencers read blogs at a much higher rate than the general population. In Japan, for example, 91 percent of the public opinion persuaders read blogs; the figure for the United States, a much more heterogeneous nation, was 34 percent.[56]

Bloggers are particularly attractive as being categorized as influentials because they seemingly have a built-in constituency. Political scientist Austin Ranney noted, "The people who regularly vote in presidential primaries are more interested in politics in general. Also, they are people with better formed and more elaborate political philosophies."[57] That describes the people who blog. As one political blogger put it, "I have 3,000 people who listen to what I say and, judging from posted comments, many of them pretty much agree with me." But does concurrence or even popularity bestow power? The last three chapters of this book are concerned with this question. But there is one certainty: Although political bloggers are many things, one quality they all possess is the *potential* for political power.

War by Blog: Blogs as Dividers or Uniters in Politics

The "face in the crowd" critique of vulgar populism is most visible when mainstream journalists and others make outright attacks on blogging and bloggers as "children" undeserving of their status. Visualize a horde of Lonesome Rhodes (or Calvins) with a vengeance, but online. MSNBC commentator and Democratic Party worker Bill Press, in a fit of anger and candor, attacked bloggers who tried to play journalist "with no credentials, no sources, no rules, no editors and no accountability."[58] During the "Memogate" affair, in which he was accused by bloggers of presenting forged memos about President Bush's National Guard service, Dan Rather was visibly irritated at blogsniping and, as one observer put it, treated his enemies like a "bunch of geeks in pajamas typing away in the dead of night."[59] Retired longtime CBS correspondent Eric Engberg offered an unkind analogy: "I worked on a school paper when I was a kid and I owned a CB radio when I lived in Texas. And what I saw in the Blogosphere on [Election Day] was more reminiscent of that school paper or a 'Breaker, breaker 19' gabfest on CB than anything approaching journalism."[60] Essayist Victoria A. Brownworth, while praising the postings of the likes of blogger and respected journalist Andrew Sullivan, complained that "any dot-commer can blog—a serious journalist with years of experience like, say, myself, or the teenager down the block spewing political rants during breaks from Grand Theft Auto. The problem in the blogosphere is that the kid and I will be received with equal credibility."[61]

Correspondingly, on July 3, 2005, Gary Trudeau, the Doonesbury cartoonist, featured in one strip a radio talk show interview with fictional blogger SlamZ88. The host asks, "Isn't blogging basically for angry, semi-employed losers who are too untalented or too lazy to get real jobs in journalism?" Later in the interview, the blogger is tricked into admitting that he eats cat food, a sure sign of crackpot status.* From another ideological corner, television pundit Bill O'Reilly referred to liberal bloggers as "simpletons who [are] cowards and they don't have any influence."[62] Columnist Steve Lovelady called bloggers "the salivating morons who make up the lynch mob" for their role in toppling CNN news head Eason Jordan.[63]

Many reporters and editors to whom I have spoken in the course of writing this book feel about blogs as baseball pros do when they endure catcalls and advice shouted at them by obnoxious fans in the bleachers. Every reporter or photographer has a potential online jeering section. As an older photojournalist told me, "Thirty years ago if somebody didn't like a picture I had in the paper, I got some letters passed on by my editor a few weeks later; now I get a hundred bloggers calling for my blood before I even see the paper." Indeed, if, as I subsequently outline, 2004 was the "Year of the Blog," the blowback to the upstart medium began then and continues to this day. First, Howard Dean lost his primary run, although it is hard to saddle blogs with that failure. Blogs were also blamed for leaking raw exit poll results on Election Day and setting up expectations of a Kerry landslide victory that never came. Mainstream media created many of their own blogs and so seemed to undercut the purity of blogs as the voice of the independent media and the nonmainstream elites. There were even minor blog scandals: bloggers outed for faking data; bloggers for the John Thune for Senate campaign in South Dakota revealed to be subsidized by the Republican Party; a blogger with a questionable background given a (limited) White House press pass. CNN also earned ridicule (of itself and of blogs) by creating an "Inside the Blogs" segment that consisted of people reading blogs on air, an exercise in synergy that drew laughs

---

*A year later, however, Trudeau was setting up his own community Web site for milbloggers (military bloggers).

even from bloggers. And then there was *The Daily Show*'s skewering of one of the intellectual fathers of blogging, New York University's Jay Rosen, in which the program's "correspondent" made fun of the entire idea of amateurs hosting a news and commentary Web site.* As late as summer 2007 bloggers were cast with the same stereotype as Dungeons & Dragons devotees. Stephen Colbert reported: "A serious disaster was threatening the country. I'm talking, of course, about the YearlyKos blogger convention in Chicago. For those of you who don't know what a blogger is, it is someone who has a laptop, an axe to grind, and their virginity."

Blogwar by Balkanization: Arguments For

Once upon a time, a new medium came along that was vilified by traditional media elites as being raucous, uncontrolled, full of unprofessional voices, and unschooled in the basic norms and values of news. The novelty was called radio. The practitioners of the print press in the 1920s and 1930s saw the arriviste as a threat not only to their livelihoods but also to the future of the republic itself. The *New York Times* warned, "If the American people . . . were to depend upon scraps of information picked up from air reporting, the problems of a workable democracy would be multiplied incalculably."[64] *Editor & Publisher*, the trade magazine of journalism, asserted that it was "inconceivable that a medium which is incapable of functioning in the public interest will be allowed to interfere with the established system of news reporting in a democracy."[65] Fast forward, and the print journalists of the White House Correspondents Association voted in 1961 not to allow television reporters to join because they were not considered real journalists. Go back further and you find Plato (in *Phaedrus*) attacking the lack of interactivity of writing and finding it far inferior to the mainstream communication venue of the day, speech, as a medium for political exchange and education. So in perspective, new media tend to generate fulminations among the elites of the old, and professional status is

* The segment was, of course, hyperlinked and enjoyed by many bloggers.

often a key point of contention. In each case, including radio, the rude innovator eventually became part of the mainstream; so will blogs.

But there has been a more serious critique of blogs and bloglike expression of political will by scholars. Remember Isocrates' self-description of his duty to be "waging war against the false pretenders to wisdom"?[66] Do such wars, like the blogwars, hurt those who fight in them, society, America, and democracy itself?

For quite some time, all forms of Internet interaction (and now especially blogs) have caused political scientists and commentators to speculate whether they spur community building, the voluntary associations that are often praised as bedrocks of democracy, or to take the darker alternative view, virtually break us up, Balkanize us, and heighten conflicts and tensions among Americans. The former thesis was famously articulated in Robert Putnam's *Bowling Alone,* in which he warned of "cyberapartheid" because "cyberspace represents a Hobbesian state of nature" where each individual is fundamentally self-interested.[67] Another scholar, Cass Sunstein, described a cocooning of the mind in cyberspace: "In a system in which each person can 'customize' his own communications universe, there is a risk that people will make choices that generate too little information, at least to the extent that individual choices are not made with reference to their social benefits."[68]

Indeed, partisan knowledge bases are also an increasing part of the Web, although, as in the case of other alternative media, their justification is based on alleged bias of mainstream media or, ironically, other alternative media. For example, several conservative groups protesting what they believe was "political correctness . . . anti-American, anti-Christian and anti-Western" bias on Wikipedia started Conservapedia, "an online resource and meeting place where we favor Christianity and America."

A school of thought among students of the Internet agrees that online involvement is a force to split the nation, not unite it.[69] A study of how congressional staffers viewed the effectiveness of blog communication found that they thought blogs were least effective for "communicating with political opponents."[70] Other research found that bloggers tend to link their partisanship; that is, conservative bloggers are much more likely to provide hyperlinks to right blogs, and liberal bloggers are much more likely to provide hyperlinks to left blogs.[71] A great divide of linkage between right bloglands and left seems incontrovertible, as was demonstrated in another study of forty prominent political bloggers.[72] (Both these latter studies found right bloggers slightly more likely to cross-link than their counterparts.)

As an illustration, consider the now famous map of the political blog universe by researchers Lada Adamic and Natalie Glance (available online but unreprintable here). The image shows the links between about 1,000 blogs, with blue dots representing liberal blogs and red dots representing conservative blogs shortly before the 2004 presidential election.[73] When a conservative blog links to its kin, the line is shown in red; blue to blue signifies a left to left connection; orange or purple are for cross-ideological links. Even more than on a red state–blue state map of the country, the Balkans recrudesce. As the study reported,

> Cross citing accounted for only 15% of the links, with liberals citing conservatives 247 times, and conservatives citing liberals 312 times. The interesting result is that even though the conservatives had 16% fewer posts, they posted 40% more links to one another, linking at a rate of 0.20 links per post, compared to just 0.12 for liberal blogs.

The great blog political divide indeed *looks* like two warring nations, divided and uncommunicative save for a no-man's land between them.

The Balkans metaphor also comes to mind when you realize that when you step into the public sphere, you must be ready for the catcalls and potshots: nasty e-mails in response to blog content, insulting or libelous comments, and falsehoods. It is also likely that combativeness is exacerbated by taking your arguments online. Much interesting research in communications psychology over the last few decades has found that "Internet dialogue" may be a contradiction in terms. Take one study published in July 2007 in the journal *Human Communication Research* by Donald G. Ellis and Ifat Moaz of "Online Argument Between Israeli Jews and Palestinians." I am oversimplifying their results, but basically, it seemed that, even when brought virtually together in the service of a dialogue toward peace, the participants in computer-mediated communication tended to just trade charges and challenges. In other words, they stated (or yelled) their positions and counterpositions at each other. Yes, the "dialogue" did allow them to hear the other side, but nobody moved past that to . . . well, what most of us think of as real dialogue.

You could argue as well that blogging brings out the worst in some people and attracts some of the worst people. In the winter of 2007, JillF, a blogger (feministe.us) and NYU student, found herself receiving hundreds of comments on "how I'm hideous and a fat ugly pig" on a college discussion board when someone allegedly posted a picture of her. One of her supporters stated, "I'm so sorry this happened to you. You have been and continue to be fiercely brave by just being you and sharing that with us." Indeed, but how many of us can remain "fiercely brave" while enduring the jabs of venomous slings and arrows? It's a situation that the technology of interactivity can make worse, as one person calling for greater online politeness discovered:

> Mena Trott, a co-founder of the blogging software company Six
> Apart, proposed elevating civility on the Internet in a speech
> she gave at a French blog conference. At the event, organizers
> had placed a large screen on the stage showing instant electronic
> responses to the speeches from audience members and those who
> were listening in online.
>
> As Ms. Trott spoke about improving online conduct, a heckler
> filled the screen with personal insults. Ms. Trott recalled "losing
> it" during the speech.
>
> Ms. Trott has scaled back her public writing and now writes
> a blog for a limited audience of friends and family. "You can't
> force people to be civil, but you can force yourself into a situation
> where anonymous trolls are not in your life as much," she said.[74]

The bloglands are strewn with the corpses of abandoned blogs whose owners likewise ultimately declined to post in the crosshairs of jerks.[75] The lesson for my students, especially my female ones, is not happy: one person's free speech can shut down that of another.

Another peril of polblogging is identity theft. Trillin, blogger of mnleftyliberal.com, announced that he was shutting down because, "It seems the GOP has set its sights on me. Not only is there a blog pretending to be me, but also I have become aware of no less than three attempts to get my identity in the last two weeks. As I have stated before, due to my job I cannot allow my identity to be known, as I would get fired."[76] A tpmcafe (blogger) warned, "There is a site that is ripping off Josh [Marshall] and his TPM site. They are using the URL: http://www.talkingpointmemo.com/. In case you miss it they removed the 's' from 'points.'" Blackfive, a top milblogger, complained, "Somebody is running around the blogosphere claiming to be me, leaving comments about me having a change of heart and disappointment with the Bush Administration."[77] Fauxblogging is definitely going mainstream as well: In August of 2007 Forbes.com adopted the very funny "Secret Diary of Steve Jobs" (http://fakesteve.blogspot.com/) as a regular feature.

Blogging, thus, can be bad for your reputation, your mental health, and even your wallet. Some bloggers have been forbidden to blog by their employers or worse. (The name of one woman's blog—*dooce*—has since become a term describing the act of terminating someone's employment for what they wrote in a blog.[78]) There are many other reports of bloggers being fired or reprimanded or their blogging curtailed or banned because they allegedly have revealed insider corporate information or have criticized their employers or managers. And political blogging can get red-hot nasty as well. For instance, Rockville, Maryland, high school teacher Michael Calderon had feuded with Justin Raimondo of Antiwar.com. In one article, Calderon described a possible post-apocalyptic future in which "Raimondo, et al. act out their sedition in a just-nuked America [and so] expect their bodies to be found shot full of holes."[79] Raimondo defined these words as "A Death Threat" by "Some maniac [who] wants to give me a permanent vacation"[80] and posted the contact information for the principal at Calderon's school.

Quite simply, as the evidence affirms, bloggers tend to be both more passionate about their politics and more partisan than the average voter. Only those who really cared about what they were doing would work so hard or endure such trouble, almost always for little monetary reward. And surely, there is a spiral of posting and passion: You write something, feel you need to defend it, and thus dig in more strongly on the position. One may legitimately describe political debates that rage in the bloglands as battles, whether over the Bush presidency, the Iraq war, Islam and terrorism, Supreme Court nominations, or many, many other ideas and issues. A hundred clashes fought by recognizable sides constitute to me, someone who writes about the military and the media a great deal, a war—of sorts.

Blogwar by Balkanization: Arguments Against

Community is where you find it: The "dividing us" argument often fails to take into account that a centripetal force can also be centrifugal. In the final chapter, I will argue that, in line with a century of speculation and research in social psychology, partisanship can be a unifier for many, whereby in facing off against enemies people become comrades of the trenches and may use online resources to find each other, coalesce, and mobilize for group action.

Among the contradictions and complexities that are blogs, then, there are counterarguments to the Balkanization thesis. The first is simple: There is no evidence that we live in a more partisan era today than at any previous time. Yes, veterans of the Senate decry that it is much harder to build consensus in, say, foreign policy than it was in the Cold War 1960s. But as for the country itself, are we more divided than in 1980 or 1972 or 1968 or 1952 or 1936 or 1860 for that matter? There were no blogs when the South seceded, no YouTube during the McCarthy era, and no Facebook during the Chicago riots of '68.

In fact, if we rewind the clock to the beginning of the republic, we find that the early American press—the one of which the founders were thinking when they bestowed on it unique freedoms—was not fair and balanced. The printers and publishers of the time would have chuckled at the notion of objectivity; the content of their pamphlets and broadsides and protonewspapers was downright angry and even violent. Benjamin Franklin (who "blogged"—that is, wrote journal entries on events and mores of the day under the pseudonym Silence Dogood) and others made their pennies not by providing a neutral platform for an advertising revenue stream but by attracting partisan readers. As late as the 1830s, Tocqueville noted that "the first newspaper over which I cast my eyes, upon my arrival in America," accused President Andrew Jackson of being

> a heartless despot, solely occupied with the preservation of his own authority. Ambition is his crime, and it will be his punishment, too: intrigue is his native element, and intrigue will confound his tricks, and deprive him of his power. He governs by means of corruption, and his immoral practices will redound to his shame and confusion.

If such vitriol reads like an anti-Bush (or anti-Clinton) blog, it is because it was written in the same spirit. The role of the newspaper in the first two generations of the new republic was to champion causes or parties. Tocqueville also observed with forensic astonishment that

> In America there is scarcely a hamlet that has not its newspaper. It may readily be imagined that neither discipline nor unity of action can be established among so many combatants, and each one consequently fights under his own standard. All the political journals of the United States are, indeed, arrayed on the side of the administration or against it; but they attack and defend it in a thousand different ways.

In 1830 as much as in 2007, one person's combatant sages were another's "salivating morons," but blogs now comprise the "thousand different ways."

Furthermore, as journalist William Powers argued, the "fractious, disunited, politically partisan media of the nineteenth century" did not retard the development of democracy, and in fact, they probably "heightened public awareness of politics and taught the denizens of a new democracy how to be citizens."[81] You can have violent political rhetoric that results in a healthy body politic; that was true for newspapers in 1804, and it is true for blogs in 2007. Tocqueville himself noted that "I admit that I do not feel toward freedom of the press that complete and instantaneous love which one accords to things by their nature supremely good. I love it more from considering the evils it prevents than on account of the good it does." The truth is, however, that by any objective measure, our postblog, post–talk radio era is *less* politically violent than the early republic, which we often idealize.[82] American political blogs, a decade or so into their being, have yet to lead to any physical *political* violence.

Perhaps, too, blog linking is not as one-sided as it may seem. Right and left bloggers are, after all, engaging each other. The technology of the blog form allows or even forces people to at least hear/see what the other person is saying. Hyperlinks take up the postings or writings that are attacked on one blog. News consumers can certainly try to insulate themselves from contrary opinions, but I think it is harder to do so with blogs. One Pew study found people who seek political information online more likely to be exposed to contrarian political data about, for example, the candidates they supported for office than people who did not use the Internet.[83] Other research reported that there are indeed "cross-ideological discussions among conservative and liberal bloggers" of various kinds occurring all the time.[84] My own students found the record spotty: Some blogs did cite like-minded people much more than the opposition, but others did not.

As a practical matter, if you try to limit the data to which your readers have access, you come off as both narrow-minded and churlish. As Suzanne Stefanac puts it in her guide to blogging, "Outbound links knit you into the blogosphere [so] be generous in linking to sources for your writings and imagery. . . . The more links you provide to valuable outside sources, the more often your visitors are likely to return."[85] A good right or left blogger does not try to pretend the other side does not exist; on the contrary, he or she endeavors to provide as information-rich a portal for readers as possible. Even more politically practical is the notion that, in a democracy, bipartisan coalitions focused on "what unites us" are more likely to succeed in passing legislation than partisan exploitation of "what divides us." So groups like MomsRising, though founded by online activists from the left, try via blogs and other interactive technologies to mobilize people of many political stripes around core issues of mutual agreement. Notably, none of the candidates for president in 2008 are pushing a "pro-division" platform.

Also, to Balkanize implies that the partisan sides are "deep"; that is, they are based on lifelong or thousand-year traditions of propinquity, ethnicity, or religion, thus making it unlikely that one person on one side will ever cross the line to the other. An orthodox Christian Bosnian Serb, for instance, is unlikely to defect to the Muslims. Furthermore, the Balkans conjures images of warlords or religious patriarchs who demand full obedience from their subjects and issue unchallengeable marching orders. I know of no one who seriously describes bloggers like that. For example, blogger Billmon (a liberal and a Kos alumnus) noted, "The idea that Kos could use his influence, such as it is, to intimidate Left Blogistan into a quivering reign of fear is simply laughable." Mcjoan, a full-time employee of DailyKos, explained to me: "Sure, Markos knows me and my opinions, but I've never had any sense that I have some party line to follow. He likes good writers and good thinkers, and that trumps ideological purity." Erik Erickson, the founder of RedState, similarly assured, "Nobody tells us what to say and what to do."

Case Study: Durbin's Dilemma—Bloggers Don't Take Orders

To illustrate that bloggers are not myrmidons or flacks, consider the blog blowback on Illinois Democratic Senator Dick Durbin. In the summer of 2005, he spoke on the floor of the Senate about the treatment of prisoners at Guantánamo Bay, Cuba. He reported seeing an e-mail from an FBI agent and stated,

> If I read this to you and did not tell you that it was an FBI agent describing what Americans had done to prisoners in their control, you would most certainly believe this must have been done by Nazis, Soviets in their gulags, or some mad regime—Pol Pot or others—that had no concern for human beings. Sadly, that is not the case. This was the action of Americans in the treatment of their prisoners.[86]

Durbin was attacked for his remarks by many, including military retirees, but soon a perfect storm of partisanship arose among bloggers. Conservative and pro-Iraq war bloggers heaped abuse on the senator. Paul Mirengoff of powerlineblog wrote, "It's not likely that [Durbin] intentionally set out to injure his country. Until I hear a better explanation, I'll put it down to a kind of sickness or derangement brought on by hatred—of President Bush, the military, etc.—coupled with a very weak immune system (i.e. intellect)."[87] Hugh Hewitt, another consequential right blogger, commented, "Durbin is a pathetic and repulsive political hack who should exit immediately after a lengthy and detailed apology. BTW: If you don't 'get' this, you are really far removed from the country's center. It isn't a Democrat-Republican, left-right thing. It is an American-anti-American thing. Period."[88] Illinois resident Ellis Wyatt found new fodder for his self-explanatorily named blog, Dump Dick Durbin, where he described his senator as a "lying, partisan hack."

Many left bloggers defended Durbin. Orcinus[blog]'s Dave Neiwert was prompted to post later that day: "conservatives are deliberately misrepresenting what Durbin said, and twisting his words into a campaign to paint liberals as treasonous vermin worthy of extermination."[89] Steve Gilliard of the popular NewsBlog fired off: "Americans have never been as morally clean as we pretend, our history lionizes criminals and murderers. But Gitmo is wrong. We know it is wrong, our enemies hope we continue it as it is the biggest thing they have to recruit others. When we release people from there, their stories serve as an excellent reason to fight the U.S."[90] DailyKos described the Durbin criticism as a "moronic Right-Wing smear attack" in which "the pea brains on the Right . . . claim Durbin is calling our troops Nazis."[91]

Durbin was not unaware of the dueling blogswarms in antipathy for and in sympathy with him. In fact, he held a consulting conference call with left bloggers about his strategy for responding to attacks and also used blogs as a forum for his own defense. The meeting was blogcast, a first for a politician-blogger rendezvous. Blogger Annatopia of MyDD.com offered a post of the proceedings,[92] which she described was in response to the Republican "shit storm."

But then suddenly (to bloggers, who were not informed beforehand), Durbin changed tack. He apologized for his previous remarks, again on the floor of the Senate. From a traditional political point of view, it was calculated damage control: say you are sorry, that you were misinterpreted, and get past the issue. Nevertheless, right bloggers did not forgive Durbin. Captain Ed of Captainsquarters stated, "His is yet another halfway dodge in putting the onus onto those whom you offended instead of taking responsibility for your own actions and comments. Color me unimpressed."[93] The affair eventually blew over as other events and issues captivated bloggers and the press. However, of more importance, and a crucial sign of bloggers not being simply a loyal constituency, many left bloggers—who, taking an analogy from *The Godfather*, had "gone to the mattresses" for Durbin—felt betrayed. Steve Gilliard told me, "Durbin reached out to us, we went to battle for him, but then he ran away without any explanation." His subsequent post was bluntly subtitled: "Gutlessness in the face of a challenge is dishonorable," and he argued the following:

> Look, I'm a practical person. I understand that politics requires compromise. I'm often far more tolerant of deal making than some of my peers. I've done politics and I get the point. You sometimes have to back down or make a deal you wouldn't otherwise want to.
>
> But Dick Durbin can go fuck himself.
>
> Senator,
>
> Don't ask for backchannel help to save your ass and then not even have the decency to send an e-mail out warning us your boss, Dick Daley, wanted you to back down. I know you did a conference call to explain your miserable ass, but I missed and well I am glad I did, because I am pissed. Why? Because if you thought what you said was wrong, you should have backed down without the plea for help.
>
> I don't like being played for an idiot. You had a lot of people step up for what you said and then, like a punk, you mumble out some apology. "Oh, I'm sorry I told the truth and that interrupted your fantasy" is what you should have said.
>
> It is that kind of continued guntlessness in the face of rank GOP corruption which enrages many Democrats. We are tired of leaders who will not fight, especially when 15 or so of your colleagues can take a pro-lynching stand and have nothing to pay for. Hey, it was just dead black people, so what if 15 Senators didn't have the decency to say lynching was wrong. I bet you'll all have a good chuckle over some Navy Bean Soup in the Senate Dining Room. The GOP can take the most outrageous stands, be totally protected by the media, and you people refuse to actially call them on their antics.
>
> We both know the defense of torture at Guantanamo is reprehensible, the report you read from came from an FBI agent. Yet because you lost your nerve, you became the issue and not the report. We know most service members are not torturers. But there are those that are and who shame this country and we need to acknowledge that.
>
> People were ready to stand up for you, it's a shame you wouldn't stand up for yourself.
>
> Next time you need help, go ask Dick Daley for it. If he and his administration aren't in jail, that is.

The lesson of the Durbin incident is that if many bloggers seem like attack dogs, they are not subject to control and training by any master. Conservative blogger Patrick Hynes, a blogging adviser to John McCain, explained, "It's a learning curve for politicians and their staffs; they think they can just send us a press release and we'll print it or parrot it. I have to tell them blogging does not work that way—good blogging that people trust, that is." Because most political bloggers are not paid political professionals and have no experience in politics, they tend to be passionate idealists about politics. Durbin *could* have used bloggers as a focus group, getting an honest reaction from them about his position. But when he decided to reverse course, he should have returned to the same bloggers and made his case to them as well. Instead, he treated them as lackeys, confusing their initial partisanship for blind loyalty to him.

Beyond the Balkans: Integrity and Bridge Building

Bloggers often display integrity before party loyalty. Take Bob Owens, aka confederateyankee (http://confederateyankee.mu.nu/). He is by any definition a hardcore right-wing blogger and proud of it. His posts almost always feature critiques of the left, liberal politicians, positions, and media (even bloggers). But he also cares about getting the facts right. I know this because when Vice President Richard Cheney shot his hunting partner, I got a note from Bob. He asked me about the ethics of going with a story that featured his enumeration of inconsistencies in Cheney's narrative, especially on details of the gun and the shotgun pellets. He was asking some good questions and making some observations unreported in mainstream media—not "chewing" but offering original investigative content. I told him that I thought if he believed his facts were correct, to go with the story. He did, to the illumination of all his readers of any political stripe.

Nor is it true that all bloggers take sides. As I hope to document, many bloggers set out to attack (although to champion a cause is not in itself being divisive), but many others want to simply inform and even build connections with those who might disagree with them—that is, to become, as Chinese blogger Xiao Qiang put it, "bridgebloggers."[94] One such example is Rick on Media Blog (http://allyourtv.com/rickonmedia but now http://www.allyourtv.com/mediablog/). Editor Rick Ellis, like most bloggers, seeks out media stories and comments on them. But he does so not to score points or to push a political agenda but to try to encourage his readers to freeze frame and to analyze news, not just to absorb it, a task that is difficult enough in the classroom but nearly impossible in the living room or the movie theater. For example, during the Dan Rather "Memogate" affair, Rick, instead of howling for the blood of Dan Rather, George Bush, or other bloggers or crying cover-up or conspiracy, announced, "I'm looking for people who would be willing to [do] a project I'm calling 'Dan For A Day.' I want to put as much of the original reporting and research as we can accumulate into a wiki format, and track everything."[95] In short, Rick is the opposite of the Calvin-like "boy genius"; he is stating that we don't know it all and proposing that we investigate and look things up ourselves from multiple sources, not just those that we regularly, selectively expose ourselves to because they support our prejudices. He is encouraging bloggers, thus, to become public (and self) political educators, not just knee-jerk opinion spewers.*

The eventual good, however, does not make the process pleasant to those who lack hard hides and strong stomachs. As I discuss in the final chapter of the book, this is the big hypothetical of blogging *by* politicians. So far, attempts to set up blogs where both right- and left-wing bloggers post as one community have tended to fail; the marketplace of ideas seems to require elbowroom between stalls. As Patrick Ruffini, e-campaign director at the Republican National Committee, explained to one of my students,

> I think everybody has to be able to recognize that this is really a no holds bar[red] medium. So you're going to be aggressively questioned on things you say [and if] you're not willing to engage in a debate then [you should not blog].[96]

---

* And to be sure, most political bloggers I have talked to think that you do not need to be neutral to be educational. You can learn political information, as is discussed in chapter 4, from partisans as much as bipartisans.

In sum, political war pervades the political bloglands, but it is not one that has shed any real blood (yet!). As I shall argue subsequently, it is a socially useful war of ideas that, despite its more distasteful projections, is improving rather than detracting from democracy in America.

2

From Cybercommunity to Blogland

Why do people blog? One study suggested the following reasons:[1]

- information seeking
- convenience
- personal fulfillment
- political surveillance
- social surveillance
- expression and affiliation

According to my own surveys (from 2004 to 2006) of some 900 of my undergraduate and graduate students who told me they visited a political blog at least once a week, they did so (not in rank order)

- for entertainment
- to find information on "what's new" in the political world
- to find commentary on existing political issues
- to engage in conversations about political topics
- to hear people who agree with them on political topics
- because they don't trust traditional media

I asked the same students why they preferred one political blogger to another. Their answers (not in rank order) were

- political blogger was entertaining
- political blogger was trustworthy
- political blogger added new material regularly (posted every day)
- political blogger held opinions similar to mine
- political blogger was informative about "new" items and issues in political world
- political blogger was informative in commenting about existing items and issues in political world

Such opinions and outcomes are not surprising if we define blogs as a form of interactive, personalized mass communication. In fact, in the responses to "why you blog" and "why you read blogs," we see echoes of the fundamentals of the success of the Internet itself. Blogs are a communication style and a venue as well as a technology. Although there are historical antecedents to blogging before the 1990s, the basic origins of blogging anything, including politics, are found within the short history of politics on the Internet and its precursors. To understand what blogging is, we need to step back and review how it evolved.

The Internet: Politics as Unusual

Early on, the potential to use new media technology for campaigns and elections was noted by researchers[2] because, as one put it, in that venue "candidates can do things that are nearly impossible or prohibitively expensive in other media."[3] The probable first use of e-mail by a campaign (Jerry Brown for governor of California) occurred in 1982. The 1992 Clinton campaign for president was the first political campaign to post the text of a candidate's speech online.[4] The first Web site put up for a major candidate was for Senator Ted Kennedy in 1992. By 1994–1995, political parties, candidates, and groups were exploiting the Internet more quickly than any previous new communications technology.[5] The expansion prompted many optimistic predictions of online campaigning displacing traditional campaign activities or creating new ways of politicking that promised to make all others obsolete.[6]

Such possibilities seemed to be confirmed in 1996 as "the year politics discovered the computer as a communications tool."[7] The elections of that year and 1998 showed campaigns increasingly adopting Web sites as a norm.[8] The Web site of Republican presidential primary contender Senator Phil Gramm recorded eight times more voter contacts on a cost per hit basis than his direct mail. One survey found as many as 20 percent of potential voters using online resources for gathering political information or for some other political activity.[9] Journalists as well increasingly assessed campaign Web sites as useful for getting campaign material such as press releases "faster in the home page than on PR Newswire or the fax machine."[10] As researcher John Tedesco summed up, "The expanse of the Internet offers candidates, citizens, and political groups unlimited space to articulate completely policy positions, biographical information, speech texts, press releases, and a variety of other important political information."[11] From the politician's perspective, the Net was an opportunity that bypassed the filtering, commentary, and "limited space" of big media.

On the other hand, ease of access to comprehensive information about a candidate and campaign had its downside. For one, the Web data fueled "'fire alarm' accountability" to "activists, political professionals, the media, electoral challengers, and others—who pose the threat of awakening the public's attention to an action."[12] Posting all of a candidate's documents on the Web, including his or her voting record, also constitutes a gold mine for oppositional research. Court records, archives, and other sources of compromising data on an enemy that used to be buried in boxes in libraries or government offices are now online and searchable. You can delete or reword faulty or embarrassing items from your own Web page but they live forever somewhere, ready to be examined by the press, your opposition, or anyone else.

Second, the online material of the '96 campaign tended to be unimaginative in content and drab in style. Only about one in four voters who consulted political Web sites found the information they procured to be "very useful."[13] Most senatorial Web sites did no more than post a few printed pages.[14] Likewise, in my study of 1996 presidential campaign sites, we found most to be repeats of content prevalent in newspapers, campaign literature, posters, handouts, and direct mail literature.[15] We called the sites "electronic tackboards" because they contained what, in our view, was a great deal of "pasted" information, with the Web used more as mass fax machine (the proverbial "blast fax") than as a tool for political interaction, inspiration, motivation, or group accretion. The only real innovation was in the failed candidacy of former U.S. Senator Lamar Alexander (R-Tennessee), who first conducted an online *discussion* with people who visited his Web site.

These initial difficulties suggested a future direction for the Internet and politics. It is a norm for new media technologies that audiences insist on an ever increasing amount of entertainment value as well as information richness and density. Early motion picture viewers, for example, were satisfied with one-minute films showing a train arriving at a station or, more titillating, *The Kiss*, but within a few years, they called for cowboys and Indians, chases, romances, gun battles, and other more sensational fare. Likewise, in 1996, campaign material simply posted on the Web might have been of use to journalists and of marginal interest to information-seeking members of the public. But to retain attention in a world saturated with colorful, action-packed, competitive media, campaign Web sites, and indeed any political Web site, would have to provide (a) information designed to be as interesting as possible, (b) information that could be personalized to the uses and needs of the individual Web viewer, and eventually, (c) a technology that allowed interactivity with political information and that further eroded the top-down, sender–receiver model.[16]

In 1998, the scope of online campaigning increased and widened. Utah Republican Congressman Chris Cannon, defending his conservative House record, posted on his Web site "446 differences" between himself and his opponent, a density of information not possible with most campaign media save (more expensive) mail-outs.[17] Cannon won reelection. Also, by 1998, federal elections saw almost two thirds of candidates for open House and Senate races sponsoring Web sites.[18] By 2000, 88 percent of Senate candidates featured their own Web page. Another signal event was the August 11, 1998, release of Independent Counsel Kenneth Starr's "Clinton" report to the House: Several million copies were downloaded the first day.[19]

In terms of the Web helping a candidate win a campaign, the successful run for Minnesota governor by Jesse Ventura in 1998 was the first headline. "The Body's" initial campaign was considered a joke by the political establishment. (I recall receiving e-mails from friends in my former hometown of Minneapolis amused at how an ex-wrestler and cheesy movie star was trying to win the highest office in the state.) But Ventura possessed several advantages. He was running as an independent at a time of great dissatisfaction with the evenly split Republican and Democratic candidates. He was noticeably more colorful than his opponents. His campaign was also open to innovative stunts: One humorous ad, modeled on Rodin's *The Thinker,* featured Ventura in the nude. Also via the Web, he launched a wave of guerrilla marketing. His campaign targeted groups normally disaffected by regular politics but tech-savvy, like college students. The campaign would send out an e-mail noting that the candidate would be speaking in Duluth on a given day; individuals would then spread the word on their own, creating small e-mailing groupings of friends. Ventura also used the Internet to raise cash—one twelfth of all the money for his campaign—and coordinated voters to get out on Election Day.[20] In all, the campaign highlighted two interconnected facets of the Web and politics: how campaigns can use the Web to organize people and how people can use the Web to organize themselves.

Cybercommunities as Voluntary Associations

Intentional aggregation is the key to the success of online politics. By the late '90s, the Web had become a place where "virtual" or "cyber" communities or "'villes" or "villages" (as per Marshall McLuhan's "global village") were major phenomena much studied by researchers. Early computer users "logged" onto user groups, LISTSERVs, and bulletin board services (BBSs). By 1995, when CompuServe, America Online (AOL), and Prodigy all began building giant customer bases, the number of online groups (e.g., of people jointly interested in Alfred Hitchcock movies, sex bondage, pet geckos, or California Democratic Party politics) was in the hundreds of thousands.[21] Tagged with "alt" or "soc" file extensions, these online groups made it possible for like-minded people to trade information and commentary on their favorite subjects. Social activists also formed free nets, seeking to mobilize forums toward various causes.[22] Cities like Berkeley, California, for example, set up e-mail access for the homeless "community." By the late 1990s, many major political theorists and technology futurists heralded the age of the "e-democracy," which, as one put it, would "enable a Jeffersonian revolution."[23]

To what extent such groups were really communities compared to the Rockwellian American small town, an infantry platoon, Teamsters at their union hall, or a high school cheerleading squad is still a subject of debate. On the one hand, there is the stereotype of the loner geek in his parents' basement whose only "social" interaction is playing Gorthnard, Lord of Darkness in the Everquest universe or having sex virtually via The Sims. On the other hand, many people obviously use the Web to increase physical contact via online dating and now Facebook, Friendster, Linkedin, MySpace, and the LiveJournal "buds."

The Web can link you up with the person a few blocks away who also opposes a new Wal-Mart in town, but it can virtually group you as well with a fellow gun rights activist (or antigun activist) a continental divide away. It also allows *naptime activists*, people who have limited time (like, say, homemakers who have an online window while their kids are asleep) and availability to involve themselves in traditional street or town hall activism, to do something with lesser physical effort and a flexible schedule. Usenet groups, for example, addressed real social needs among their constituents as much as did traditional face-to-face political accretions of people. One study found that people who use candidate Web sites tend to become less cynical about politics than they were before they clicked through.[24] Another investigation reported that being able to get more information via hyperlinks and Web interaction spurred people to seek knowledge out.[25] Blogs, as we shall see, are group magnets and information inciters: They draw people of similar interests; they may even prompt political participation. You can open a stall in the marketplace of big community blogs like DailyKos by registering for a week and then starting your own subblog within the main blog. More common, bloggers coalesce around threads of comments or guest blog on other people's blogs. One of the Howard Dean campaign's main claims—which I will challenge in part later—was that it was a Dean *nation* of like-minded bloggers. All politician group blogs have followed this style: Wesley Clark, for example, blogged at his Clark Community Nation.

The question of the nature of groups in cyberspace, and especially now on blogs, is political at a deeper level. As argued earlier, democracy comprises more than the collective rights of individuals. Individuals, historically, have joined together to gain and maintain rights. In ancient Athens, for example, people upheld their democratic rights by voluntary associations that included many persons who in fact did not have formal democratic rights.[26] In the great Greco-Roman world, we find evidence that all sorts of people, from prostitutes to military veterans, banded together in their own interests.[27] The Latin name for one such grouping, "the guild," survives in the word *college*. In the Middle Ages, associations of artisan guilds were commonplace among feudal and monarchical regimes.[28] Even today, most working political consultants will confirm, "we have to ask ourselves whether, in fact, we really do vote 'as individuals.'"[29]

So an optimistic view of cybercommunities in the 1990s and bloggers and their interactors would claim that they created the voluntary associations that have been part of democracy.

Downsides of Cyberdemocracy

Marc Andreessen once stated, "Every time a new net user arrives, the whole net gets more valuable to everyone on it." The rosy picture of virtual commilito, decentralized knowledge creation, and self-associative sharing does not convey the many problems such groups encountered and that blogs face today. When you create an open network or open discussion, anyone can enter, setting up the possibility of flame wars, psychotic rants, partisan attacks, and just plain folly, as in whoppers reported as fact on Web pages. I was briefly a member of several Web-platformed political discussion groups in the mid-1990s but dropped out because instead of Plato's *Dialogues,* what I got in my inbox was potty-mouthed diatribes. No surprise that one early study found that the anonymity of Web interactions, as well as the absence of a face-to-face exchange, encouraged e-mail correspondents to be more hostile than they would probably have been in real life.[30] (And, as I reviewed in the previous chapter, much current research supports the idea that online political dialogues are much lower in complexity and mutual exploration than face-to-face interactions.) Over the years of getting e-hate-mail responding to some of my newspaper op-eds, I have also noted the tendency of people putting the worst invectives and language into an electronic message that, I believe, they would not have expressed similarly in a phone call, in person, or even on paper. In my ill-fated political blogging tenures, too, I experienced considerable frustration: a zealot who attacked me viciously until I "trolled" him; an e-mail box stuffed with spam offering cheap Viagra and bank accounts in the Congo; making the enemies list of several bloggers who to this day won't talk to me. A number of my students who started political blogs orphaned them not because they ran out of things to say but because they no longer wished to put up with the abuse. One young lady asked me: "Is the price of expressing myself on Iraq [that I get] e-mails describing how I should be raped and burned?" While I sympathized with her plight, I replied, yes, unless you blog anonymously, don't accept comments, and don't have an e-mail address for the blog. Such voluntary associations of hurt I and many other people can do without, but they are a norm of frontline political blogging.

The downsides of cyberdemocracy raise even more ominous questions. In 1995, one could make an optimistic sweeping statement like Andreessen's about the online world, but now it is hard to sustain. Are we pleased when *antidemocratic* groups form voluntary associations on the Web? Hate organizations and hate-filled individuals, once separated and splintered, can form virtual cells of mutually supportive quackery, planning, and mobilization.[31] If Usenets and blogs are a boon for chinchilla owners, Harry Potter fans, and people opposed to new dam building, cyberconnectivity is equally helpful to Nazis, Stalinists, and Jihadists who want to MeetUp and get Linkedin. In the last case, I recall in the 1980s media ethics dilemmas such as: "What if terrorists threaten to kill hostages unless you broadcast their message on television?" How dated such debates seem today. Terrorists no longer demand that newspapers or networks publish their manifestos because they have the Web with which to announce or display anything they want, such as the brutal beheading of *Wall Street Journal* reporter Daniel Pearl. In Iraq, there have been several cases of the U.S. military finding that before a gun battle with insurgents is fully over, the jihadi Webmasters have uploaded their spin of the event online. Hate groups used to be hard-pressed to get any airtime; now they have a global forum twenty-four hours a day on Web sites and blogs. With little effort, their Web presence can look slick, professional, and enticing to young recruits a world away. David Weinberger, author of *Small Pieces Loosely Joined,* an incisive book about the Net, commented, "In the future, everyone will be famous to 15 people on the Web."[32] Such celebrity, however fleeting or enduring, can arise from evil or insanity as much as from virtue.

The Age of New Media and Politics

By the year 2000, the political Web had truly arrived and played a prominent role in many activities, including fund-raising. In John McCain's venture, technology allowed thousands of individuals to create Internet phone banks to financially support the candidate in their homes. John Kerry raised more than $80 million via Web sites in 2004.[33]

Blogs, however, were not yet on the academic or professional political map. Books dealing with the Internet and political campaigns published in 2001–2003 failed to even mention weblogs. Among students of cyberdemocracy, the normalization hypothesis ruled. As stated in Michael Margolis and David Resnick's book *Politics as Usual,* the Web provided analogs of what political campaigns already were doing, but electronically: Web as fund-raiser, Web as broadcaster, Web as get-out-the-vote organizer, and so on. These were familiar activities to political workers who then just needed to learn the new ways to use the Internet and the Web to activate them. True interactivity among voters and with candidates, however, was not fully developed by the first election of the millennium, and those interested in online political information wanted, as researcher Kaye Trammell put it, "interactivity at a higher rate than normal Web pages [with a] greater frequency of hyperlinks and feedback features."[34]

Blogs would provide that interactivity.

Still, even in the late '90s, there were hints of something new on the horizon. As a headliner example, one post on a proto-blog almost toppled a presidency. Sometime in the spring of 1994 (the exact date is in dispute), a man with the improbable but real name of Matt Drudge broadcast an e-mail seeking subscribers for his Web site that featured a "cross section of things that the editor Matt Drudge is focusing in on. . . . Already read by key players, this tip sheet will be sure to peak [*sic*] your interest."

The report featured then, and still does, a list of headlines (e.g., "China to Deploy Nukes Near Taiwan," "Rob Lowe Caught on Sex Tape") with minimal commentary (e.g., "Amazing pics!" or "Sick!"). The Web site hyperlinks its headline to a more detailed story on conventional press sites, often those of major U.S. newspapers. Drudge also provides hyperlinked lists of news publications, columnists, and other sites that he "frequently consult[s]." Drudge's innovation was that surveying the entire Web encouraged "sources" to reveal to him gossip about behind-the-scenes events in politics and the press. He was even able to occasionally scoop mainstream media and the slower news cycle that required editors to decide what stories to publish or air. In 1996, for instance, he was first to break the story that Republican U.S. Senator Bob Dole had chosen Jack Kemp as his vice-presidential candidate.

But Drudge's most famous post—the one that set the stage for the blogworld, overturned the convention that news came from above (i.e., traditional media), and established the possibility that an independent voice could drive the press and political agenda—came on a day in mid-January 1998.

Here I must give some personal background. At that time, I taught political communication in the politically obsessed state of Louisiana. Late one afternoon, a student of mine who was active in the local Democratic Party dropped by my office. He looked shaken. I recall his words to this day: "Clinton will be gone in a week—did you read Drudge?" I had not; Drudge Report was a Web site I only occasionally scanned, more for amusement than for edification or news gathering. Together, we pulled up www.drudgereport.com, and I read with astonishment the following: "Web Posted: 01/17/98 21:32:02 PST—NEWSWEEK KILLS STORY ON WHITE HOUSE INTERN X X X X X BLOCKBUSTER REPORT: 23-YEAR OLD, FORMER WHITE HOUSE INTERN, SEX RELATIONSHIP WITH PRESIDENT . . . blind chaos in media circles . . . The White House was busy checking the DRUDGE REPORT for details." The post was amazing on several levels beyond the central story of adultery at 1600 Pennsylvania Avenue. In terms of the conventions of journalism, here was an outsider, literally somebody webbing from his apartment, breaking a story that the mainstream media had killed (or had not yet published, anyway). Furthermore, in his moxie, this fellow was claiming a "world exclusive" and then stating that the famous journalist for the big-name publication "was not available for comment late Saturday." It was the world turned upside down—"blind chaos in media circles," indeed—and the great snowball of the alternative media challenging the mainstream media began.

Of course, *Newsweek* had not actually buried the story with the intention of never publishing it. The magazine was sitting on the story, deciding what to do, and attempting to get more information. That was proper journalism. If Drudge had not existed or had been a cub reporter for a local paper, Clinton–Lewinsky would still ultimately have seen the light of day, just not at that moment. Before the era of "breaking news" on the Internet, politicians and the press had news cycles, a period before the paper was printed or the evening broadcast was shown, when they could mull over what to do with a piece of unconfirmed information. For example, film news from the front in Vietnam took up to thirty-six hours to make it on air in New York; editors and politicians had time to think about what it meant, what to do about it, how to react.[35] Internet news, the rise of outsiders, the warlike culture of modern politics, and a huge demand for up-to-the-second news to fill Web sites and twenty-four-hour news operations of big media have combined to kill the news cycle as we knew it. Since Drudge's post, big media worry about being scooped not only by their competitors in the large glass-and-steel buildings down the street but by the millions of voices online. That is the legacy of the Clinton affair story: an anxiety about whether to withhold before verifying, dread of outing by independents both reliable and fantastic, of what is out there in the world.

To this day, Drudge is Drudge: one man, no interaction, no community. The combination of independent media, hyperlinked posting, and voluntary association that bypassed and critiqued regular media, however, was developing at the same time, and we would soon all know its name: blog.*

* Being cited by Drudge (as of this writing in the summer of 2007) significantly boosts traffic to a blog.

3

The Ascent of Blogs

If we describe a blog as (a) written in the style of a personal essay, journal entry, diary, or memoir, (b) interactive, (c) containing posts of varying length in reverse chronological order, (d) embedded with hyperlinks within text, (e) providing permalinks and allowing trackbacks, and (f) listing other blogs (blogrolling), then a true blog took almost a decade to develop after the christening of the Net. (The conversion from the government ARPANET to the independent and commercial Internet occurred in 1989.) In 1992, Tim Berners-Lee, one of the inventors of hypertext, posted a list of all new Web sites that attracted his attention. A year later, Marc Andreessen released his new Mosaic browser (later renamed Netscape) that introduced a generation of users to "surfing" the Web. Included in Mosaic was Andreessen's "What's New" page, where he noted happenings in the world of the Internet and computers, complete with hotlinks to other sites and documents. In 1994, a student at Pennsylvania's Swarthmore College, Justin Hall, started up a "filter log" on his home page that announced: "Howdy, this is twenty-first century computing . . . (Is it worth our patience?) I'm publishing this, and I guess you're readin' this, in part to figure that out." Such sites were, in the words of one of the pioneers and sages of blogging, Rebecca Blood, "link-driven," seeking and reporting what was on the Web and not just looking inward like personal diaries.[1] Indeed, Hall directed his readers to "check out" some "cool shit."

Blogs were officially born in December 1997, when Jorn Barger coined the term *weblog* on his site RobotWisdom.com. To him, the term was flexible, meaning a log *on* the Web, a log of observations, ideas, thoughts, links, notes, news that he was posting, but also a log *of* the Web, capsule descriptions of items he found along with hyperlinks to them. Barger had been an active Usenet participant.[2] On RobotWisdom, his posts were disjointed—for example, "40 AAA batteries for $7 shipped (Buy.com-DealNews)" and "Purported mp3 of December tsunami-quake (Columbia via Eureka) [wav?] I can't hear anything." Barger did not provide space for comments or any level of interaction. In January 1999, Jesse James Garrett (Infosift) uploaded the names and URLs of the then twenty-three known weblogs. In the spring of 1999, Peter Merholz, host of peterme.com and an Internet analyst, announced, "For What It's Worth I've decided to pronounce the word 'weblog' as wee'-blog. Or 'blog' for short." He recalled that he "enjoyed [the word's] crudeness . . . its dissonance. I like that it's roughly onomatopoeic of vomiting. These sites (mine included!) tend to be a kind of information upchucking."[3] His readers and correspondents adopted the term.

The commercial stamp was imprinted when in July 1999 the Pitas company began distributing software tools to build personal Web sites, "The fresh, healthy, delicious home of free, easy to update, weblogs, newslogs, all that junk." A month later, Pyra Labs released the program Blogger (later bought by Google) to the public, which made blogs user friendly, generally accessible, and particularly personal, as bloggers could name the sites themselves. Bloggers started reaching out, finding other bloggers to attack or to ally with or just to reference or seek help from. It was cumulative knowledge building about technology, from how to type HTML to what to blog about. In other words, what made blogs successful was not just personalization but affiliated voluntary associations and the ease of creating material and posting it. Today, one can "moblog" or "Twitter" from a cell phone or networked PDA. Many additional programs, like Typepad, MovableType, and Wordpress, simplified the blogging experience even further and helped the phenomenon become ubiquitous.

Mainstream media and most students of politics blogs were still under the radar. But many big events—the 2000 Florida ballot battles and especially 9/11—spurred more and more people to want to mass communicate; many found blogs the best and most accessible vehicle and venue with which to do so.

The old media started to pay attention when the first "blog-through" created a political firestorm. In 2002, Senate Majority Leader Trent Lott, while attending a 100th birthday party for South Carolina Senator Strom Thurmond, applauded the one-time Dixiecrat and segregationist's run for the presidency in 1948. Many members of the mainstream media attended the event, and although there was a negative reaction by the crowd, no substantive reports appeared in the papers or on television news. Only one major news outlet reported Lott's comments—on a Web site (The Note, which is a quasi blog for ABC's political reporters), not on the air. Slowly, however, the remarks came up for discussion on blogs like Atrios and TalkingPointsMemo. com. The latter blog's editor, Joshua Marshall, declared three days into the furor, "I don't want to overplay the political significance of this. And I'm certainly not going to say the guy is toast. But I think Trent Lott's in real trouble. The conventional wisdom on the news today was that Lott had pretty much put this story to bed with his 'apology.' I didn't think that was true. Now it seems clear that it's not true."[4]

As the percolation in the blogworld increased, some mainstream commentators and reporters took notice, and a scandal was born. *Time* magazine admitted, "The papers did not make note of [Lott's] comments until days after he had made them. But the stillness was broken by the hum of Internet 'bloggers' who were posting their outrage and compiling rap sheets of Lott's earlier comments."[5] Lott ended up resigning his leadership position under party pressure. Columnist John Podhoretz called the incident "The Internet's First Scalp."[6] However, while blogs gained stature as agenda setters, notably they remained relatively lightly cited by mainstream media.

Others would feel the tomahawk blade, although sometimes the wounds would be self-inflicted. But the "plucky independents topple the media giant" narrative, handed down as a much-cited example of the power of blogs, has a few holes. *Eventually,* the Lott story would have picked up champions in big media. There have been scandals in Washington that smoldered for some time but then erupted when, in the tradition of journalism, somebody broke the story. Quite a few regular reporters were developing the issue, including some from National Public Radio, which ran a mention of Lott's remarks the evening they were given, and PBS's *Washington Week in Review* with Gwen Ifill the next night. Thomas Edsall of the *Washington Post,* in particular, ran a piece on the weekend which garnered substantial attention. In fact, Jeffrey A. Dvorkin, ombudsman for NPR, claims that Edsall's piece was the real "tipping point" for the story.[7] By the early part of the week after Lott's Thursday night speech, the issue was everywhere in big media. Perhaps it felt like blogs were driving the story because blogs move so much faster and so much more nimbly— as other public personalities were later to learn. The old news cycle of "let's wait till Monday to see how this develops" is an eon in blog time, a fact that reporters and politicians must now keep in mind. Since those same reporters and their editors disproportionately read political blogs, one can say that a "blog effect" is perceptible.

So blogs played a role in the administrative fall of Lott, but it is not clear whether the result would ultimately have been the same, eventually, if blogs had not existed. What is true is that the sheer number of blogs makes any consensus to hold a leaked or rumored story back from publication online, on air, or on paper improbable and impracticable. It does happen that a story circulates in Washington—and in the pre-Watergate days, this was common, such as with the infidelity of a president—and nobody reports it for various reasons, including the quaint belief that politicians should have a private life. However, if a story gets out there, it is shouted from the mountaintops of the bloglands, and reporters who read blogs will find it impossible to refrain from their own coverage. Many warlike analogies seemed to fit: blogs as early warning radar, blogs as tribal drums, blogs as fire starters.

Another story confirmed that blogs were now part of the political landscape. In the early summer of 2003, Washington experienced its first blog sex scandal (sort of) when blogger Washingtonienne, a self-described young female congressional staffer, posted several descriptions of the sex-and-party culture of young staffers. She included such personal revelations as, "Most of my living expenses are thankfully subsidized by a few generous older gentlemen. I'm sure I am not the only one who makes money on the side this way: How can anybody live on $25K/year??" and, "If you investigated every Staff Ass on the Hill, I am sure you would find out some freaky shit. No way can anybody live on such a low salary. I am convinced that the Congressional offices are full of [drug] dealers and hos."[8] Later, she told her readers that she had been financially assisted by a "married man who pays me for sex" who was "chief of staff at one of the gov agencies, appointed by Bush." When Washingtonienne was outed as one Jessica Cutler, a twenty-four-year-old international relations major from Syracuse University working in the office of Republican Congressman Mike DeWine of Ohio, she was fired for "unacceptable use of Senate computers."[9] To no one's surprise, she followed up on her national exposure by writing a tell-all book.

2003–2004: The Election Cycle of the Blog

Blogs made the news in 2003 and 2004 for a number of reasons. For example, Eason Jordan, head of CNN news, resigned after weeks of attacks by right-wing bloggers over remarks he made at a speech which seemed to imply that the U.S. military had targeted journalists for death in Iraq.[10] But blogs became big news in 2004 because of the role they played (or were represented as playing) in the fall election.

Indeed, by any measure, 2004 was the year blogs arrived notably in Washington and everywhere else. Google added a blogsearch to its search menus. Merriam-Webster.com's most searched-for definition of the year was *blog*.

Certainly, notoriety is not necessarily a measure of popularity. But one way to measure the ascent of blogs is to assess their media prominence, or how much attention is paid to them not directly through blog reading or posting but through other media. Such a metric has a quantitative aspect: how many times stories in the mainstream press (newspapers, magazines) or television news mentioned blogs. Also, we can simply look around us and see blogs and discussions about blogs—blogmania—almost everywhere online. But blog prominence is often tied to major events that allow blogthroughs, where blogs, due to their unique qualities, come into increased press and public attention and thus further enhance their status as the latest new thing in media.

You discover an interesting pattern when plotting blogthroughs over time, in the relationship between blogs and the actual numbers of mainstream news stories about blogs during the crucial period of blog growth from the earliest days through spring 2007. Blogs were not an instant hit in the marketplace nor a big story in the news, as Misti McDaniel and Nathan Rodriguez, students of mine, found when we studied the quantitative history of news coverage of the terms *weblog, web log,* and *blog* across nine years and tens of thousands of hits in mainstream media (from newspapers, magazines, and television; see Figure 3.1).[11]

Blogthroughs—events that are commonly ascribed as having propelled blogs to media attention—included:

- Lottgate (controversial pro-Dixiecrat remarks by Senator Trent Lott)
- U.S. invasion of Iraq
- Howard Dean's rise and fall as frontrunner in the Democratic Party primary contest
- The Democratic Party Presidential Nominating Convention
- Swift Boat Veterans versus John Kerry battle (played out initially on television but then in blogs)
- Dan Rather and Memogate
- Presidential election and exit poll controversies
- Southeast Asia tsunamis
- Senator Dick Durbin's Guantánamo remarks
- London 7/7 bombings
- Hurricane Katrina
- Antiwar protests and antiwar gold star mother Cindy Sheehan
- Iraq prowar–antiwar debate

Crucially, as the presidential primary season kicked off in 2003, strategists for ex-Vermont Governor Howard Dean pioneered the

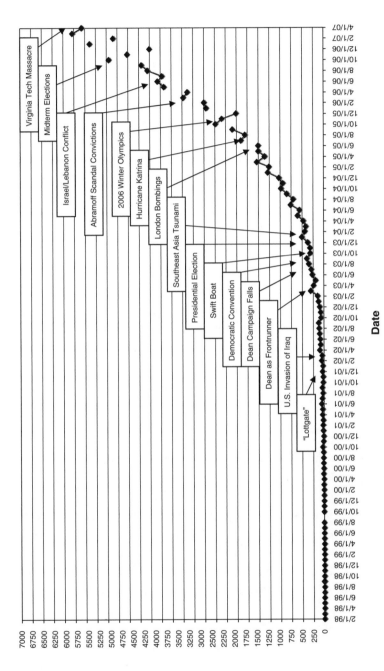

Figure 3.1. Growth of mainstream media stories about blogs, 1998–2007.

use of blogs and created their own blog site during the campaign. Joe Trippi, Dean's technology-savvy campaign manager, encouraged both the public and the press to visit the Dean Nation campaign Web site and its blogs. Trippi allowed users to post messages to other users and created a networking ability for them to meet for events. Jerome Armstrong, another Internet pioneer, started building a blog-friendly Internet apparatus that all campaigns today emulate and add upon. Supporters were encouraged to decentralize and start up their own Dean Web sites and even fund-raise through their blogs. There was a good deal of mythmaking about Dean's decentralization and interactivity (which I address later), but he did propel blogs into the political mainstream.

In turn, Wesley Clark cited a very bloglike Draft Wes Clark Web site's popularity and supportive blog comments as a reason to get in the race. Blogs were thus a legitimate story; political elites were deeming them important, and journalists saw them as a new way to hear the voice of the people. Blogs were also listed prominently by mainstream media in the fiasco of Harriet Miers's nomination to the Supreme Court. SCOTUSblog apprised readers about the Supreme Court and Miers's rise and fall; another anonymous blog, reported to be by Miers herself, included many entries portraying her as a mindless ninny.

But we found something interesting in the data. Ask people in the bloglands why blogs became so popular and most will say, "9/11," "Dan Rather and Memogate," or some happenstance that enhanced the celebrity of weblogs and the number of blog hits. But where is the 9/11 bump for blogs? It's not there; the mainstream media barely acknowledged blogs in their post-9/11 coverage. During September 2001, there were only seventeen references to blogs in all the major American print and broadcast press. The following months contained even fewer stories—seven in October and seven in November. Blogs apparently were growing in popularity as an alternative to news among Internet users (as the foregoing data show), but the news industry was not yet paying full attention to the upstarts. Our tracking suggests a different scenario for how blogs became so celebrated. Famous blog-covered events marked the path of blogs *exploiting* their powers and climbing steadily in power and prominence.

In short, nobody handed blogs their success; blogs thrive due to their adaptability and innovation. Bloggers' personal style, the technology, the use of open-end sourcing, and the ability to obtain and disseminate information and speculation quickly enable this new medium to go around the clunky logistical trails and cumbersome leadership—what economists call the "structural rigidity"—of the old media. *ABC News'* Peter Jennings, for example, could not break onto the air moments after the *60 Minutes II* program ended (dealing with George Bush's National Guard service) and proclaim, "There's something screwy about a story on CBS." And when a few bloggers had an idea about how to speed up and collate information about tsunami victims and survivors, they were not obliged to wait for an okay from senior editors or management. After Hurricane Katrina hit the Gulf Coast in fall 2005, a number of bloggers unaffiliated with any national aid organizations were instrumental in coordinating fund-raising and relief efforts.[12]

Likewise with politics as unusual. In July 2004, for example, the Democratic National Convention, held in Boston, credentialed thirty-five bloggers to cover the event. Although 15,000 traditional journalists were also given press passes, attention remained focused on the "bloggerati."[13] In a slow news month and during a dull convention, managing editors found blogs an interesting topic on which to focus. Blogs and bloggers were hot. Ana Marie Cox recalled being invited to the Republican Convention in September 2004: "This was a ridiculous period—there were more stories about bloggers covering the convention than [there] were things for us to write about. [The] reporters are starving for anything they can claim is different from four years ago. So it became 'bloggers are here!' I'm sure that as soon as they can figure out how to get podcasters on TV, bloggers will disappear."[14] (Indeed, 2005's most looked-up word via online dictionaries was *podcast*.)

One blog battle of the year 2004 was fought between blogger champions of John Kerry and the Swift Boat Veterans for Truth. When the vets raised charges that Kerry had exaggerated or faked part of his war record, two top Kerry advisers insisted, as Evan Thomas of *Newsweek* reported, that "the campaign didn't need to give the Swift Boat vets any more attention than they were already getting" and so for several weeks did not respond aggressively.[15] But that was old-media think. As one of my students, Joel Massey, documented in his research, the right blogs were already giving the issue so much attention that big media could not ignore it, which hurt Kerry's poll numbers in the short run. In turn, when left bloggers learned of Sinclair Media's plan to order its sixty-two stations to air a documentary that accused Senator John Kerry of betraying American prisoners during the Vietnam War, they organized letter-writing campaigns and boycotts. In the heat of protest, Sinclair Media's stock dropped, and the company backed off airing the documentary in its entirety.

In a sign of times to come, political blogging for hire became an issue in 2004 as well. Zephyr Teachout, Internet Outreach Director for Howard Dean's campaign, stated after the race was over that Kos and Armstrong had been subsidized: "On Dean's campaign we paid [them] as consultants largely in order to ensure that they said positive things about Dean."[16] Was this an ethical breach *if* it was in fact the buying of a mind? First, Teachout's accusation/admission is hotly disputed: I now believe that in fact, Kos and others were paid not for opinions but for tech consulting—no ethical problem or even issue there. But the question of paying bloggers is an important one, becoming more so in every campaign cycle. Certainly, it would have been a firing offense for a *Los Angeles Times* reporter to accept money from a campaign, for any reason, but most bloggers believe they live in a different land where judgment from their peers and readers is what counts. Kos himself stated, "My God, if I was a journalist, I'd be breaking half the canon of journalistic ethics. . . . I am the epitome of conflict of interest, but at least I don't pretend otherwise."[17] Armstrong, in his defense, took down his blog when he was working for Dean. And as Talkleft blog itemized, a host of print and electronic news stories in the mainstream press *had* reported Kos's ties to Dean; they were not a secret.[18] In addition, Kos—as of summer 2003—put a disclaimer on his site: "I do some technical work for Howard Dean." The alleged transgression was therefore not a legal or ethical infraction at all.

By one popular argument, blogs do not abide by the same standards as news organizations because they are, in microcosm, what Bill Gates claimed about the possibilities for the wider Internet, "the realization of Adam Smith's perfect market, at last,"[19] where the "invisible hand" of the blogosphere will "out" error. John Hinderaker of powerlineblog, for example, claimed that blogs "have mechanisms for self-correction. If somebody makes a mistake, readers are all over it, other bloggers are all over it."[20] Another blogger commented more colorfully during a debate on this subject at cyberjounalist.com, "I question the need for a code of ethics. The blogosphere will typically 'fact-check your a*'' if needed. Bad info and continued lies calls your credibility into doubt, which makes your blog a lot less worth reading. Sort of a self-correcting phenomenon."[21] Pamela, editor of the blog Atlas Shrugs, remarked to me, "The blogosphere has already established its code of ethics. We have smart, knowledgeable viewers that call us out on any inaccuracy. . . . Vetted by all Americans, blogs are forums in which to correct and speak out. No inaccuracy goes unpunished!"

Dating Howard Dean: The Blog

The rise of bloggers as part of modern politics has no precise start date, but it does have an origins myth: the run of Howard Dean for the Democratic nomination for the presidency in 2003 to 2004. Merely mention "Dean and blogs" in any political gathering and many opinions surface, some problog and others antiblog. To many "Deaniacs" (not a pejorative term to them), the "Sleepless Summer of Dean" was a golden time before the evil party bosses and press elites threw down their champion in the winter snows of Iowa and New Hampshire. In the opinion of a number of those party and journalism professionals, the Dean blog efforts were a crock that actually hurt the candidate. (Now, however, many such folks are blogging themselves.) Although blogs would no doubt have achieved their present popularity, prominence, and power even if Howard Dean had never run for president, no one drama had so powerful a magnifying role in telling ordinary Americans and political professionals and journalists that blogs had arrived. Dean would later claim that his campaign had "changed the country."

He was right, or rather, he changed the country's politics, perhaps forever. We live today in the confusing aftermath.

The Myth of Dean and the Blogs

The myth of Dean, as articulated by his campaign manager Joe Trippi, a longtime Democratic Party worker, dotcom guru, and Internet aficionado, runs as follows: Howard Dean, former governor of Vermont, was the only true nonestablishment candidate for president in 2003–2004. He was honest, spoke his mind, was beholden to no special interests or party factions, and was unconnected to the old-boy networks and compromising party leadership affiliations; he was in fact a man of the people from the Green Mountains. Gathering a loyal and dedicated staff, Trippi and Dean agreed that they would take their message directly to the electorate and embolden a people's army to march on Iowa, New Hampshire, and ultimately, to Washington. Via the Internet in general and blogs specifically, millions of ordinary people spontaneously organized themselves to support Dean's crusade. The Dean campaign worked synergistically with them, treating the blog constituency as campaign advisers in a sort of virtually democratic campaign. In fact, the relationship was so close that many in the campaign, most notably Zephyr Teachout, the Internet coordinator, compared it to "dating" the candidate (i.e., formally, "Dean Dates" via DeanLink software).

Such idealism was part of the Dean bloggers' self-promotion according to Trippi. But to the historian's eye, the central genius behind Howard Dean's blogging efforts, and someone who can justly be called the father of professional political blogging, was Jerome Armstrong, who in 2002–2003 was a blogger on his own MyDD.com. From the early beginning of a possible Dean run for the presidency, Armstrong was on record as a supporter. In 2003, he became associated with the campaign and eventually began work during the summer at the Burlington, Vermont, headquarters where he "directed Internet advertising, helped coordinate blogger outreach, built and administrated Dean's ForumForAmerica.com community website, among other campaign tasks."[22]

Armstrong had been a longtime participant in political forums and, as a liberal activist and Internet worker, strongly felt that up through the 2000 election conservatives and Republican groups had dominated online campaigning. He thus saw Howard Dean's independent run for

the presidency as an opportunity to reinvent and reinvigorate political campaigns through the new venue and medium of blogs and also
seize back the initiative online for leftists, progressives, and Democrats.
In particular, he felt that Dean was attractive to progressives because
"of his straightforward manner of speaking, which especially trans-
lated well in the black-and-white world of Internet print format. His
statements of contrast and opposition against Bush were enough to
make me stand up and be counted as his supporter from very early in
the presidential cycle."[23] In his memoirs of the campaign, Armstrong
states that he thought Dean was a long shot but that a few thousand
supporters unified by the Web could form a community that would
give voice to many disaffected Democrats and others on the left. He
describes Dean as responding positively to his pitch of the importance
of the online outreach to a candidature that had none of the traditional
accoutrements of power, such as money, staffing, and endorsements: In
other words, "He got it."

It is incorrect and unjust to claim that all the success of Howard
Dean's online efforts were due to Armstrong and others and that Trippi
was responsible for the failures. However, although Dean's campaign
did not succeed in electing their candidate to president, the effort was
innovative, even pioneering. It is the sad fate of innovators everywhere,
from Christopher Columbus to Charles Goodyear, that they often
failed to reap the immediate profits of their genius.*

In the beginning, the newly created DeanforAmerica site's "About
Me" section described itself as a blog that was "a political action committee dedicated to supporting fiscally responsible, socially progressive
candidates at all levels of government." Trippi asserted the primacy of
the weblog in the revolution on a post zero that asked, rhetorically,
"Can Blogs Influence an Election?" and invited supporters to register
and vote for Dean on MoveOn.org's Internet primary.

---

* Blogging has continued to benefit Dean, Armstrong, and Trippi, however. Armstrong
has become a successful blogger, with his blogs among the most popular and his advice
and counsel sought by politicians and political consultants; Dean's election to chair of
the Democratic National Committee has often been ascribed to a huge swell of Internet
activism on his behalf; and Trippi has become the mainstream media guru of blogging.

This is the question the journalists and some campaigns have been asking. One of them was quoted as asking derisively "why does Joe Trippi waste so much time talking to obscure bloggers?"

Well with the MoveOn.org Primary, Bloggers have an opportunity to influence this election and change the electoral process in a profound way.

If you are a Blogger who supports Howard Dean – it is time to blog the importance of supporting Howard Dean by urging your readership to register for MoveOn.org's Presidential Primary and further urge your readers to vote for Howard Dean in the MoveOn Primary. If you have 50 readers or 10,000 readers your post could make the difference in this Primary – particularly if all Dean supporting blogs act in unity and begin to carry this message.

If you are an independent Blogger who has no stake in Howard Dean's candidacy, MoveOn's Primary is an historic moment in the history of the grassroots Internet. To point this out and to urge your readership to register and to participate no matter who they vote for is equally important.

Blogs can influence this election, and further the cause of citizen participation in choosing our next President – by sounding the clarion call to the nation's first Internet Primary. A Primary that because of its impact in terms of grassroots organization and large number of small contributions, can change the entire dynamic of the current Democratic Party Nomination Process.

This is truly an historic moment. Blogs can influence this election right now and do so in an historic way – come together for a few days – advocate to your readers that they participate in this moment by voting in the MoveOn Primary.

And I humbly request that a campaign that understands the reasons Blogs exist and should be supported – is a campaign that can at least ask that the Blogs that support Howard Dean say so – and ask their readers to consider supporting him in the MoveOn Primary.

Respectfully

Joe Trippi

Campaign Manager

Dean for America.

Urging bloggers to register to vote in what was essentially an early straw poll by MoveOn.org, the huge Web-based liberal political organization, was a dramatic declaration of bloggers being a sort of constituency that political groups and politicians could try to win over to their cause. Earlier, there had been blogswarms—groups of bloggers temporarily (and virtually) joining to comment on an issue or attack a public figure—but the notion of a long-standing (at least for the length of a political campaign) voluntary association of bloggers was novel. The idea that they would, at some point, forgo blogging to show up and vote in a primary, caucus, or eventually, a general election was speculative at the least. But it worked at one level insofar as thousands, perhaps hundreds of thousands, of people, most not bloggers but volunteering via Web sites, eventually joined the Dean crusade. Many were indeed excited by the possibility of being outsiders with a key to the inside. One of my students at the time, who started a local Dean blog, told me, "I worked on another campaign where I [was] worker bee number 712; with a blog I can rule [Baton Rouge] for Dean!"

Along the way to Iowa, the campaign seemed to function as promised, and its successes were measurable by any political yardstick. At its peak, DeanforAmerica.com registered about 100,000 unique visitors a month. In four months in 2003, BlogforAmerica (then DeanforAmerica) was able to raise $7.6 million, and the Dean campaign claimed to have accumulated $20 million through Web sources by January 2004. Other technologies allowed what might be called a date-and-planning book as well as a community Web site in MeetUp.com, where supporters could connect, discuss the Dean campaign, and organize themselves. More than 100,000 people posted letters of support for Dean before the primary season began in Iowa and New Hampshire.

Many Dean blog events were captivating and seemed to speak of a new world of horizontal democracy and the upsetting of old-boy, rich-man politics as usual. For example, Howard Dean sat in his headquarters in Burlington in July 2003 and, as he described,

> Dick Cheney was holding a $2,000 a plate fundraising lunch so we asked Americans all over the country to join me the same day for a lunch in front of their computers. It sparked a huge response, and, amazingly, the online contributions from that day matched what Cheney made from his fundraiser. . . . We treated [the Internet] as a community and we grew the community into something that has lasted long after the campaign ended. The Internet let us build that community in real time, on a massive scale, and that lunch helped us do that. The turkey sandwich wasn't bad either.[24]

The list of registered supporters eventually grew to *600,000.* (A Dean worker told me, "If only we could get them to move to New Hampshire!")

I must admit that I was genuinely excited by such happenings: A new era did seem to be nigh, where campaigns would be interactive in ways no one had grasped or attained before. The campaign ultimately raised over $50 million and shot Dean from near obscurity to celebrity. By the eve of the Iowa caucuses, the candidate was so clearly seen as the frontrunner that former President Jimmy Carter posed for a picture with him on the way to church (with Dean implying that this constituted an endorsement), and former vice president and 2000 Democratic presidential candidate Al Gore actually endorsed him. The people's crusade had marched to the gates of Jerusalem. As measured by two of my students, Michelle Geig and Josh Britton, the number of mainstream news stories about Dean and his blogs each month starting September 2003 reached in the *thousands.* In Ames, Iowa, where I visited for part of the campaign season, bloggers were a story, too. At one of the caucuses I attended, a reporter stood near the people shuffling in and repeatedly asked, "Any bloggers here I can talk to?"

One early event that eventually served to offer the visual and rhetorical metaphor—the "super optic," as political consultants term it—for the power of blogs in the Dean campaign was the famous Red Bat rally. On August 26, 2003, Dean held a campaign rally in New York City's Bryant Park that capped the Sleepless Summer tour of fund-raising, speeches, gatherings, and organization building throughout the country and, significantly, on the Internet. Among the most theatrical moments was Dean's appearance brandishing a red bat as a symbol of the army of bloggers who had been "swinging the bat" independently to raise funds for the campaign.[25] (The graphic for many organizations' fund-raising drives is a thermometer or some other visual symbol "filling," in red, to mark increasing contributions.) Joe Trippi himself described the incident in almost every recollection of the campaign he has offered since:

> At the Bryant Park Sleepless Summer Tour we were doing about
> a ten thousand people crowd, ten to fifteen thousand people
> in Bryant Park and we had a goal of raising a million dollars

by the time the governor hit the stage at Bryant Park with the contribution bat on our Internet website. Nicco Mele, our webmaster, calls me up and says, "Joe, there's this cool idea on the blog." . . . Now, what was going on at that moment was real ownership of the campaign by the grassroots. They knew who had made that suggestion forty-five minutes earlier on the blog. Our blog traffic was amazing that night.[26]

The red bat became a visual staple of Dean campaign posters to mark the achievement of fund-raising goals (see Figure 3.2).[27]

Note the catch phrase: "You're unbelievable!" Elsewhere, Trippi asserted, "This campaign was the first campaign owned, really owned, by the American people and now what we have to do is to build a movement that's owned by them."[28]

It was a great story.

Figure 3.2. Red bat graphic as Dean fundraising symbol.

Reality: Dean's Dilemma

Alas, as I was to observe watching the blogposts of DeanforAmerica and looking at the blog comments and subsequent campaign actions, the myth was not the reality. Two researchers, Andrea Baker and Jennifer Stromer-Galley, also formally studied the interactions, via the blog, of Dean's staff and supporters and came to the same conclusion.[29] For those who care to look, the tall tale of the red bat and of the entire Dean campaign is somewhat different.

First, the big picture. Dean was, like George McGovern in 1972 and Jimmy Carter in 1976, an extreme long shot in early 2003. Both McGovern and Carter adopted a "people's" strategy for the nomination. McGovern was greatly assisted by knowing (better than did the party bosses) the new rules of delegation selection and tapping into the huge cohort of young, antiestablishment and antiwar '60s activists. Carter doggedly spent more time (and earlier in the race) in Iowa and New Hampshire pressing the flesh and attending the pancake breakfasts than any candidate before him. (A joke in Iowa had a farmer, at dinner, hearing the doorbell ring. He tells his wife, "If it's Carter, tell him thanks but I don't need any more help with the plowing.") In early 2003, Dean's name recognition outside New England was negligible for regular voters. So, yes, the campaign embraced the Web and technology for various reasons, including the romance of horizontal democracy, but they *had* to; Dean "got" the pitch by Armstrong because there was no other option. The campaign could not engage in massive marketing efforts, nor could it call upon a host of political bosses and connected officeholders throughout the country. The alternative hope was to build a presidential campaign through viral marketing, with people talking to each other, motivating each other, and convincing each other to work for Dean.[30]

Second, there were personal and practical exigencies toward a blog-oriented campaign as well. Trippi was a dotcommer and so was naturally more open to new media than most other campaign managers. Although he was an experienced political professional, his main claim to fame was investments in Internet stocks in the 1990s. It would have been remarkable if in any campaign he joined he would not have consistently pushed for Web-based innovations and strategies. Of course, considering that Dean was an underfunded long shot in January 2003 and that Trippi was not a name player in the political consulting or managing game, it would be unlikely that any of the larger campaigns would have hired him or given him so much power. Trippi sums up the predicament well himself, although again deeming a necessity a virtue by saying of traditional campaigning that "politics [had] become a race for money, a race to own a one-way communications tool that would take the American people essentially out of the process. It was no longer about average Americans, it was about, 'How do I find a rich guy to write me a $2,000 check [the limit on individual donations to presidential candidates] and then how do I take that money and buy television with it?'"[31] So although a bottom-up approach was ideologically attractive, it must have seemed practical as well to anyone in Dean's war room.

Third, where and how else would Dean have tried to build a constituency? Richard Gephardt of Missouri was the "union candidate." John Kerry, Joe Lieberman, and John Edwards were all vying for established Democratic interest group and party boss support. Many of the early write-ups of Howard Dean dismissed him as less than a serious (i.e., not a fund-worthy) candidate. It is a law of politics that money follows money and that money follows success or perceptions of success. Dean's positions might win sympathy at Hollywood Democratic fund-raising parties, but the smart money questioned whether he was, to use a bluntly undemocratic phrase, "nationally viable." I recall a Democratic political consultant telling me in March or April 2003, "Dean is the kind of candidate who can win a lot of hearts, but he is not going to get anybody to part with $2,000. Okay, maybe Paul Newman would." Indeed, one previous study of the influence of both personal and impersonal fund-raising methods used on potential contributors of serious money (cumulative donations ranging from $201 to the cap) found that ideological candidates should be more willing to utilize direct mail or telemarketing to reach ordinary voters.[32] It follows that really ideological candidates like Dean should try to reach the maximum number of politically sympathetic voters, those people precisely who are political bloggers, on both left and right.

Fourth, there was one major, wealthy, influential, and "unattached" constituency in the left–liberal–Democratic interest group pool in 2002 that Dean worked hard to gain as his initial base. As the *Washington Post* reported, "With just one exception, every fundraiser Dean attended outside Vermont in 2002 was organized by gay men and lesbians, as were more than half the events in the first quarter of 2003, according to Dean advisers."[33] At one point, Dean remarked famously, "If Bill Clinton can be the first 'black president,' I can be our first 'gay president.'" Obviously, although gays and lesbians are one consequential constituency under the Democratic tent, basing a national campaign or even a primary run on only their support, and allowing it to become a consistent "optic" of the candidate, was not a politically viable option in 2003–2004. The result was the same as that for the blog constituency: Dean had no place to go but online.

In sum, it was not quite the case of a bold outsider, disgusted with smoke-filled-room politicians, big bosses, and corporate fat cats, going to the people. As Trippi himself put it in his memoir: "our only hope for winning now was to decentralize the campaign, ease control away from the candidate and his handlers in Vermont (myself included), and let the momentum and the decision making come from the people—stop trying to control the river . . . just open the flood gates and see where the current took us."

"GET DEAN A RED BAT!!!!!!!!!!"

But did Dean and Trippi fulfill such a promise? How interactive was DeanforAmerica? How important a role did bloggers play in the campaign? If it was not a case of bloggers "dating Howard Dean," then what was the nature of the relationship? Close scrutiny suggests some holes in the façade of horizontal democracy.

Let us return to the red bat. Was this a symbol of blog power, a blogger-driven innovation? The bat challenge for fund-raising, "going to the bat" or "swinging the bat" for Dean, had been a long-standing campaign slogan and metaphor. But who created the red bat as a physical symbol on stage that night? Starting three hours before the Bryant

Park rally, the following comment by one Nashvillebill appeared on the DeanforAmerica Web site:

> I know this is probably the last thing anyone has time to think about—but any chance of someone getting a real red bat and giving [it] to Dean on stage at NYC, to celebrate the million we're pretty sure to have by then? The crowd would go BERSERK.

Other bloggers concurred. Lali wrote: "Nashvillebill—[the idea for using a] red bat in NY on stage tonight is GREAT! Campaign staff—are you listening? This would really work!" JohnG commented, "Someone get Dean a red bat to hold on stage! This will be awesome!!!"

As the comments show, the bloggers were interacting on assorted topics from the weather in New York City that night to Dean fund-raising goals to coverage of Dean in other media. Online Deaniacs constituted the reality of the self-aggregating voluntary association, encouraging each other ("We Can Do It!") and accreting knowledge about campaign issues. They obviously felt they were stakeholders in DeanforAmerica: That was no myth. But apparently, no one from the campaign was listening at that hour, just before a major rally. Another blogger, Sam in San Diego, decided to call Dean headquarters in Burlington. Then he reported to his fellow bloggers,

> I just called HQ.
> They are going to call Clay [Johnson, a Dean staffer] who is updating the bat and in touch with the campaign and tell them to GET DEAN A RED BAT!!!!!!!!!!! before he goes on stage in NY. (One of the big plastic ones from the toy store.)
> Yeeeee HaWWWWW
> Bat Bat Bat Bat Bat Bat bat
> great idea whoever thought of it.

Thus, it was an old-fashioned phone call, not a blog comment, that actually got the attention of the campaign, although the impetus was indeed developed on the blog by bloggers. As I discuss more in the final chapter, blogs and other media can, as in this case, work well together.

In general, what the archives reveal is that it is not apparent to what extent the Dean campaign was listening to bloggers then or at any time and whether Dean/BlogforAmerica attained the level of interactivity, either in quality or quantity, for which its leaders strived. As far as we can tell, Trippi and the others who ritually quote him, while not lying, are instead offering the kind of fractured and collapsed memory that is guided more by principles and hopes than by an accurate transcript of the day's events. No one claims they scammed or conned bloggers, only that then (and now) no one had yet figured out a way to truly sustain a blogger-driven political campaign. They were often listening, but just as often could not respond in a timely fashion, or had nothing to say to people spouting off on irrelevancies.

As the campaign developed, and then buckled, part of the Dean interactivity myth cracked for many bloggers as well. The essence of blogging is the soapbox analogy: Bloggers do not blog because they are a herd of followers but rather because they feel they can offer a contribution. The Deaniacs were not fair-weather friends or sunshine progressives. But they were not willing to sit on the bleachers in silence, especially when (a) events were occurring that they objected to (as when the Dean campaign was faring badly); (b) they thought they had good ideas that the campaign should use; and (c) the repeated message of the campaign was "we listen," but the evidence on bloggers' screens was "we don't."

Indeed, after Dean's devastating loss in New Hampshire, Joe Rospars, a staffer and regular blogposter, wrote, "There's a lot to discuss tonight" and told readers to "use this thread to speak out—we're listening." But when one blogger posted a long comment titled "Give Us a Sign" full of advice for the campaign, there was no response. Earlier, after the loss in Iowa and the negative response to Dean's television ads there, many DeanNation bloggers made their own suggestions about problems with the ads or offered ideas for new ads; they were apparently ignored. Blogger parker commented,

> We really are the campaign. Look at what the campaign has done, and look at what we have done.
>
> We started the meetups, and I am now in Arizona canvassing with 40 people . . . Amazing. LAforDean came up with that not the campaign.

If you have an idea for getting the word out, GO FOR IT!! Dont wait for the campaign. We are so strong, it can barely keep up. We are fighting a battle on 2 fronts, while the other campaigns only have 1.

This post, as well, received no reply. There is no question that parker spoke for many of his/her compatriots when she/he stated, "We really are the campaign." That they *felt* like they were on the team was highlighted for Dean worker Natasha Chart (now of Pacific Views blog), who recalled to me that:

> it was the Dean campaign era itself that started blurring the term
> [blogger] to include people who just commented on another blog.
> I know myself that many of these people would never dream of
> writing a post themselves, let alone running a whole blog. . . . It's
> actually at that point in time, history if you will, that the term
> got fuzzy like that. You can imagine my surprise when I went to
> a bloggers' function in Iowa, a meal hosted by [Congressman
> Leonard] Boswell, to find a room full of people who only wrote in
> the comments at the Dean blog. Many of them were better known
> than I was, unsurprising, but it was still a briefly baffling shift to me.

The proprietary owners of the campaign, however, may or may not have known how to handle a large community of people feeling ownership. In almost all cases, when a blog commenter posted a message to the effect of "Are you listening?" there was either no response from the campaign staff or a corporate "Thank you for your thoughts" reply. At the same time, the messages from Dean HQ on the blogs were, "We care about you" and "You are the campaign." Reality and myth were colliding in blogland. Many posts expressed frustration at the system and the process. St wrote in January 23, 2004, to two of the top Dean Internet staffers,

> ****ATTENTION HEADQUARTERS****** . . .
> the washington post has made a fantastic short video clip about
> Dean yesterday in New Hampshire and his supporters.
> OFFICIALLY LINK that clip to the MAIN site ASAP and to the
> upper right hand of the blog.

It was made by the washington post, so it was independently done. it gives you huge credibility!!!

YOU MUST DO THIS. it is excellent. do NOT miss out on another opportunity to help yourselves.

LISTEN to us . . . WE on the blog get it more than YOUR OWN media people.

PLEASE link it now. This is better press than you are producing yourselves. you just saved a hundred grand.

The archives are full of similar "you must do this" cries from the wilderness. Said Lookup: "Come on! Give us the plan man, give us something to run with, rally the troops, or at least tell us you are hiring a military advisor." Free Spirit complained: "***GET LOCAL*** I've sent these suggestions in before. A few have been implemented, but most haven't. . . . "

In June 2003, when Dean's son was arrested for stealing alcohol and the candidate returned home for a short campaign break, a post from a Dean staffer appeared as follows: "We just arrived back [in Vermont], and I wanted to tell all of you how much your words of support and encouragement mean to the Gov. We had a layover in Detroit and I had a chance to read your comments on the blog. I told the Gov. about them and he really appreciates your kind thoughts." The implication to bloggers, who are close readers, was that Dean did not then (or ever?) actually read their comments.

Lessons: Interaction Should Be Interactive

Now, one can get carried away here with retroactive criticism of a losing campaign. First, in relative terms, the Dean team of 2003–2004 was vastly more interactive than the norm. Wendy Norris, who had volunteered or worked in voter canvassing since McGovern '72, recalled to me her efforts in Fort Dodge, Iowa, and Ohio for Dean:

Typically, most campaigns employ a very restrictive, canned approach that can often be counter-intuitive to the unique get-out-the-vote efforts of different communities with different

concerns and histories of voter disenfranchisement. . . . One of
the key elements of Dean for America's success in energizing
volunteers was the decentralized nature of the campaign. I had
a fair amount of autonomy to recruit fellow volunteers and
utilize their talents as needed within the scope and culture of the
community. For example, we began to conduct outreach with
African American and Latino voters in Cleveland nine months
before the Ohio primary date. That's unheard of in the 30 years I
have been a progressive political activist.

Likewise, no one I have talked to associated with Dean '04 has ever given
me the impression that the blogging component was a hoax or a stunt:
They really cared and wanted to expand the democratic experiment via
the new medium. Perhaps the problem was the nature of decentralizing
politics in cyberspace versus the practicalities of political campaigning
on the road. And for almost half the Dean Internet activists, virtual
commilito was built independently of higher management: The groups
and bonding forged online in the campaign stuck, and the participants
report remaining in contact with campaign-made friends more than
a year later.[34] One study of the campaign found that, unsurprisingly,
the blogs associated with it that had the most influence were those that
were the most interactive.[35]

It is also hard to imagine a political campaign—which demands
twenty-hour days for all the traditional activities—adding unlimited
other hours a day of blogposting, reading, and commenting to a *candidate*'s schedule. As Jerome Armstrong recounted to me: "Everyone
on the staff read comments that were posted on the blog, it was more
of a time & quality thing that changed it; as the campaign went from
spring to summer, staffers would obsessively read the comments; but
then in the fall and winter, they amassed and a lot of it degenerated
from spammers and just the huge volume." If thousands of bloggers
were set up to feel as though they were dating the candidate, the latter would inevitably end up disappointing them because he did not
have time for each suitor. Furthermore, although many bloggers were
told they were important and many had good suggestions and ideas
for the candidate, can one really run a disciplined political campaign

(or an army or a newspaper) as a democracy? For one thing, democracies imply disagreement; many "you must do this" suggestions by Dean commenters in fact contradicted each other. To adopt all of them or to execute even some of them to the satisfaction of the DeanNation in its entirety would have been impossible; to paraphrase, you can't please all the bloggers all the time. The Dean campaign, despite protestations of being different (i.e., lacking the structural rigidity of traditional campaigns), could not have revamped its entire Web site or changed its ad campaign completely on the recommendation of one blogger.

Many other suggestions as well fell under the category of "off message." For example, at one point, guyz suggested a music playlist for rallies: "not just theme songs, but a play list before and after the rallies. I'll start it off: Creedence Clearwater Revival—'Traveling Band' Creedence Clearwater Revival—'Who'll stop the Rain? and of course, Bob Dylan—'The Times they are a Changing?'" Not necessarily the advice a campaign would implement or even pay attention to.

Retrospective counsel might have included to somehow demonstrate to bloggers that the campaign was listening while at the same time explaining why not every suggestion would lead to a campaign policy shift or action. Should there have been staffers specifically dedicated to answering posts, engaging in dialogues with commenters? Departments of government regularly employ people whose job is to prepare briefing documents for candidates. Couldn't someone have prepared a daily blog brief for Dean and Trippi, with highlighted items that "we have to respond to"? (Even this may have been difficult because we now know that the top leadership—Dean, pollster Paul Maslin, and Trippi—were themselves not very interactive with each other.[36])

Finally, there is the great "nose piercing" issue concerning Dean and bloggers. A famous *New Yorker* cartoon showed a dog in front of a computer telling a fellow canine that, online, "Nobody knows I'm a dog." But what happens when the dogs go door to door to canvass for a political candidate? Is the result effective person-to-person persuasion or puzzlement? The campaign reported that upward of 100,000 supporters,[37] many of them motivated young folks from exotic places like Seattle and New York, flooded the Hawkeye State in late December and January before the caucuses. I saw a few in Ames, Iowa, during my time there. I did not meet any who actually displayed nose piercings, spiked hair, grunge kilts, or combat boots, but, on the other hand, some of the orange-hatted Deaniacs were, to put it charitably, not the best spokespeople to evangelize middle-country, middle-class Iowans, even those who might agree with Dean on some issues. A veteran political consultant working for Dean stated bluntly, "They looked alien." Yes, the grunge kid in an orange hat was a false stereotype: A large majority of Dean workers was indistinguishable from anybody you might see at a Target store in Des Moines. But the other campaigns pushed the alien motif to a press delighted to portray Dean's crew as flaky or immature. Perception is almost everything in politics, and the smear worked. In fact, the later evidence found that being a Dean Internet activist had a strong association with old-fashioned political participation: According to a Pew study, a huge majority of Dean online partisans voted in the November presidential election.[38] Stay-at-home slackers or sore losers they were not, but neither were they a well-honed machine. But whose fault was that? Ground war Deaniacs will often mention that they were ill-served by bad canvassing data from on high and unprofessional training.

In sum, the Dean campaign probably could have done a lot more to make bloggers feel listened to and have used them more effectively, but it is hard to imagine a political campaign operating, as Trippi's metaphor suggested, as a boat pushed by the current of a river of people. To extend the other popular metaphor for Dean-blog inter-activity, that of a dating relationship, can an institution credibly "give love" to a smart mob, especially when each individual seeks a distinc-tive relationship to the candidate? As noted, the essence of effective leadership via political communication, whether in war, city wards, or boardrooms, is for the leader to make the individual followers feel spoken to, listened to—that is, feel important. Blogs are one poten-tially fruitful venue for achieving such intimacy, but the very indi-vidualistic nature of blogs, blogging, and bloggers does not make it a simple or plug-and-play enterprise. The pre-Iowa Dean effort was indeed a miracle during which Armstrong and his colleagues made political history, but sometimes in war and politics, a miracle is not enough to win.

Dean's Rant: A Typical Political Blogpost

Howard Dean's caucus-night bellow is a case in point of the complicated nature of blogstyle. After the Iowa loss, Dean stood up in front
of a room full of dejected supporters, some in tears, most exhausted.
Commilito demands a rousing "we have only begun to fight" speech,
so Dean unleashed a combative, thumping, and actually quite self-
mockingly funny (if you view the *whole* tape) yell. As I understand
it from Dean supporters in the room, none of them were shocked or
appalled, and indeed, the applause is strongly audible in the video. As
one student of mine who was there put it, "He was [signifying], 'Okay,
team, we lost but we're gonna win next time. Let's go get 'em!' What's
crazy about that?"

Well, as many politicians have learned, crazy is what appears
crazy in the evening news or, now, on YouTube. It did not help that
(a) nobody set up Dean with the standard MULT box for his mike,
whereby the press gets a direct, clean audiofeed without distortion and
(b) the room was so noisy that anyone would have had to shout for
the crowd to hear him. The video that appeared on the news (or rather
the seven- to ten-second excerpts of it) showed Dean screeching like
a wounded animal, punching the air, and snarling with arteries bulg-
ing in his neck. The segment was played repeatedly on national and
international media; many Web sites posted it; late-night comedian
talk show hosts parodied it; there are cartoon and anime ripoffs of it.
Dean pollster Paul Maslin argued that "the follow-me rallying cry was
framed by the unsympathetic conservative and liberal press and pundits as psycho-babble. Dean's opponents, who still considered him a
threat after Iowa, were of course content to watch the lynch mob run
past them."[39] One Kerry worker recalled to me, "Was the national press
unfair to Dean? Yes. Did we take delight in it? Yes."

Dean's yell was overplayed, and many bloggers unfriendly to Dean
used the same medium that had helped him achieve prominence to create an echo chamber of ridicule by posting streaming video of the edited
cry and spicing it up with satirical music or commentary.[40] MSNBC
commentator Chris Matthews would say after Iowa, "Done with dating
[Howard Dean], the Democrats want the real deal: a candidate to beat

George Bush."[41] Many national reporters would offer the postmortem indicating that Iowans had "Dated Dean: Married Kerry." What struck me at the time was that the transcript of the "rant" read like an exclamation point–filled blogpost. This is perhaps why blogs are blogs and television is television and the two should not try to ape each other.

In the end, political blogs survived Dean's fall because they had little to do with it. The former governor possessed many problems as a candidate that would have doomed him without the existence of the Internet. Yes, many bloggers embraced Dean, and other people discovered blogging as a result of their enthusiasm for Dean; Dean likewise tried to embrace blogs. That the first such dating experiment did not fulfill all its promises was not surprising. Many technologies, from fire to the steam locomotive to the armored tank to e-mail, did not work perfectly on their initial appearance. Failure in politics, war, or commerce is part of improvement if you are willing to appreciate those failures and come to understand their causes. Blogs *had* arrived in the political world by 2004, and as I will make the case in the final chapter, they are here to stay. But Dean's example shows that (a) bloggers are a complex and unherdable constituency that will grow restive and even rebellious if they feel they are being ignored or conned, (b) blog constituencies do not necessarily become voting blocks, and (c) cybercommunities may not mix and match well offline.

Dan Rather and the Memos

Most bloggers I interviewed concurred that the Dean campaign was the political platform through which blogging entered mainstream campaigns and elections. Another blogthrough of the campaign season, however, seemed to confirm blogging's political potential as well. On September 8, 2004, on the long-running television magazine *60 Minutes II,* CBS's Dan Rather reported a story questioning President George W. Bush's 1970s service in the Alabama National Guard.[42] The program showed viewers alleged photocopies of military personnel evaluations written by then Lieutenant Bush's supervisor, Lieutenant

Colonel Jerry Killian, stating that the young fighter pilot had not fulfilled his Guard service requirements while working on an Alabama political campaign. As the segment ended, posters by the hundreds on the conservative Web site FreeRepublic started commenting. For example,

> Kerry was busy committing treason while Bush was in the Guard. How's that for a 5 star resume? X44? Nope.106 posted on 09/08/2004 5:18:56 PM PDT by Waco

One post that night proved to set in motion a huge scandal, literally putting blogs on the map, and shook the confidence of mainstream media.[43]

> WE NEED TO SEE THOSE MEMOS AGAIN!
> They are not in the style that we used when I came in to the USAF. They looked like the style and format we started using about 12 years ago (1992). Our signature blocks were left justified, now they are right of center . . . like the ones they just showed.
> Can we get a copy of those memos?
> 107 posted on 09/08/2004 5:19:00 PM PDT by TankerKC (R.I.P. Spc Trevor A. Win'E American Hero)

Others picked up on the observation:

> To: TankerKC
> They looked ODD, didn't they?
> Here is their web site, but I don't see it:
> http://www.cbsnews.com/stories/2004/09/06/politics/main641481.shtml
> 123 posted on 09/08/2004 5:22:00 PM PDT by Howlin (I'm mad as Zell)

To which TankerKC responded,

> If, and I mean if, these memos are genuine, then this is a very big deal. Interesting—CBS didn't emphasize the Barnes interview—but focused on the found documents.

This is a paper trail that might have legs.124 posted on 09/08/2004 5:22:13 PM PDT by pacocat
[Post Reply | Private Reply | To 1 | View Replies]

And Howlin laid down the accusation that would shake CBS for months to come:

The documents CBS used are FRAUDS!!!!!!!!
125 posted on 09/08/2004 5:22:34 PM PDT by Howlin (I'm mad as Zell) [Miller]

A paper trail that had legs indeed. Pushing the Rather Memogate story, bloggers simultaneously displayed their main virtue and vice: speedy deployment of unedited thought. As *Slate*'s most popular blogger, Mickey Kaus, noted,

> [T]he virtue of speed isn't simply, or even primarily, that you can scoop the competition. It's that you can post something and provoke a quick response and counter-response, as well as research by readers. The collective brain works faster, firing with more synapses. In theory, "faster" can mean "fast enough to have real-world consequences" that print journalism or even edited Web journalism can't have. [44]

Other right bloggers, such as Scott W. Johnson and John H. Hinderaker of powerlineblog, started focusing essays and items on the question of whether the memos were fake. Their post, "The Sixty-first Minute," was one of the most cited in the medium's history (and earned powerline the Blog of the Year award by *Time* magazine). Their conclusion that "60 Minutes is toast" ultimately became true for Dan Rather's career. Then Charles Johnson (no relation to Scott) of Little Green Footballs posted a modern Microsoft Word re-creation over CBS's version of the disputed memo. In the program, Dan Rather claimed that the Guard evaluation was typed manually in the early 1970s. LGF's leader saw that his Microsoft Word version, "typed in 2004, is an *exact match* for the documents trumpeted by *CBS News* as 'authentic.'"[45] Johnson said that he was unnerved as he typed the first sentences and found that all the lines were breaking identically. Hundreds of bloggers answered with their own sleuthing techniques, some superimposing the forgery over the Microsoft copy and finding exact matches. For their actions that day, LGF has been called "the Woodward and Bernstein of Rathergate."[46]

Within days, the story leapt from new media to the mainstream. For two weeks, *CBS News* stood by its reporting but then admitted that its document examiners could not verify the memos' authenticity. The network launched an investigation to determine how the material ended up on the air. Eventually, four people at CBS were blamed for the error. Rather, who had anchored the evening news for twenty-four years, announced his retirement in November and left his position in March 2005. Many bloggers rejoiced at their power to topple venerable institutions and puissant players. Freerepublic.com blogger Rrrod warned, "NOTE [*sic*] to old media scum. . . . We are just getting warmed up!" Many right posters would also probably agree with 10ksnooker's comment on PoliPundit: "The Internet has changed everything, and most importantly, the old media can't lie with impunity anymore—just ask Dan Rather."[47]

But Memogate was not in fact a battle between Davidblogs and MSMGoliaths. A number of liberal bloggers such as Hunter of DailyKos struck back with their own extensive blogswarm investigation of the history of fonts, typewriters, and military forms.[48] For example, one claim by LGF's Johnson was that "this typeface—Times New Roman—didn't exist in the early 1970s." Hunter responded,

> There are several problems with this theory. First, Times New Roman, as a typeface, was invented in 1931. Second, typewriters were indeed available with Times New Roman typefaces. And third, this isn't Times New Roman, at least not the Microsoft version. It's close. But it's not a match. For example, the "8" characters are decidedly different. The "4"s, as viewable on other memos, are completely different; one has an open top, the other is closed. So yes, we have proven that two typefaces that look similar to each other are indeed, um, similar. At least when each document is shrunk to 400–500 pixels wide . . . and you ignore some of the characters.

Johnson and other conservative bloggers responded. And so on. To this day, the memos remain, to use the verdict available to Scottish juries, "not proven."[49]

In retrospect, the Rathergate story was a fascinating insight into the old and new media world because the substantive argument about the documents went on between bloggers for many months in cyber-space. Interestingly, the left blogger case (by no means made by all prominent left bloggers) was largely ignored by mainstream media, even by reporters and commenters who, if they had read it, would have found much evidence for their own anti-Bush positions. Why was this so? I prefer to think that once the mainstream had picked up on the narrative frame of "indy bloggers versus big guys," that became the theme imposed which, after all, was more sensational and combustive than investigations of typefonts and nomenclature. That this sidetrack occurred is an indictment of big media, not of bloggers left and right, who performed a public service.

Whatever our opinion about the issue, thus, people trying to make sense of the controversy would have gotten a better understanding by clicking back and forth from powerlineblog to Little Green Footballs and DailyKos than they would have from reading their daily newspaper. Certainly, *CBS News* did not put as much effort, time, and expertise into researching their memos as did nonjournalist bloggers attempting to authenticate them. The bloggers may have been wrong or right, but at least they put all their arguments and evidence out there for everyone to review, and they didn't need management or shareholder approval to do so. Without bloggers, the "paper trail that might have legs" may not have been uncovered or fully debated by all sides.

Further, the Dan Rather Memogate incident illustrated how blogs acted to distribute intelligence; they were allowed to share knowledge quickly and easily.[50] No surprise to learn that *60 Minutes II*'s chief producer "acknowledged that the bloggers and other matters . . . had shaken his confidence" in the twenty-four hours following the airing of the story.[51] And indeed, from then on, blogs would be described, as the title of one examination of the relationship of blogs to journalism put it, as those who are "watching the watchdogs."[52] Political powers agree: One study of congressional staffers' opinions about blogs found that they believed watchdogging big media was blogging's main function.[53]

Election Exit Polls by Blog

Blogs, then, made political news even before the official start of the 2004 campaign, and that they were an object of intrigue to political professionals was evident. White House Internet Director Jimmy Orr commented in July 2004: "Bloggers are very instrumental. They are important. They can lead the news. And they've been underestimated."[54] But if blogs played various roles in the presidential campaign of 2003–2004, the culmination of their ascent to political media stardom and power player status came, appropriately, on Election Day. The consequences, however, would comprise both good and bad publicity for the blogging arts.

On November 2, 2004, early morning exit polls indicated that John Kerry held a lead over George Bush. When results were leaked to bloggers, and subsequently the Internet, the story became "Kerry headed to victory." As described by Matt Drudge, who was very cautious in his description of exit polls, "Exit poll mania spread through media and campaign circles Tuesday afternoon after first wave of morning data showed Kerry competitive in key states. . . . National Election Pool—representing six major news organizations—shows Kerry in striking distance." Jerome Armstrong and his MyDD marked the first blog-out of the numbers at about 2:00 pm EST but he cautioned his readers: "Now, mind that these are early numbers. And even if correct, they reflect the ones most wanting to vote, and it's still a long way to go." He told me afterward that the leak came "from workers inside MSNBC." Ana Marie Cox of Wonkette posted that a "Little Birdie Told Us" that John Kerry was winning Ohio by 4 points and Florida by 3 points. Another mainstay liberal blog posted "some of the early [polls show] OH Kerry 52 Bush 48 . . . FL Kerry 51 Bush 58."[55] The typo on Bush's Florida vote was perhaps prescient: In the postelection letdown and finger pointing, some avid Kerry supporters refused to concede defeat.[56] Blogs were a main outlet for such frustrations and suspicions of voter fraud and irregularities. SoCalDemocrat of Democraticunderground.com spoke for many when he posted: "Kerry is well ahead in exit polls, but still losing the counts. WTH is going on? Kerry is well ahead in Exit Polling in Ohio. We're being screwed."[57]

Some commenters blamed the new medium and its messengers for both the leaks and the resulting confusion. "Bloggers blew it," intoned *BusinessWeek* magazine, as did Frank Barnako of CBS.marketwatch.com.[58] Bloggers lacked the "restraint" of the mainstream media, chastened the *Los Angeles Times*.[59] "Bloggers Botch Election Call," headlined the *New York Sun*.[60] CBS's Eric Engberg charged blogs with misinforming their readers and further maintained, "One of the verdicts rendered by election night 2004 is that, given their lack of expertise, standards and, yes, humility, the chances of the bloggers replacing mainstream journalism are about as good as the parasite replacing the dog it fastens on."[61] A reporter for the *Toronto Star* likened political blogs to "a million keyboards" in the hands of "a million apes."[62] Blogs were also victims of a technical blowback: Some of the most popular crashed due to heavy site traffic.

But elites *were* paying attention to the blogs. Kerry managers and supporters, naturally wanting to create a sense of inevitability, started early celebrations; journalists began feeling herded to make some sort of comment that would not leave them out of what the "mob outside the window" was shouting to be a Kerry victory. In short, blogs pushed big media, but of course, big media were at fault in reporting speculation as fact and for ignoring their own experts and protocols.

Exit Polls: Facts and Fancies

In perspective, during all modern elections, news organizations sponsor exit polls, but campaigns almost never do so exhaustively and scientifically. In 2004, two private firms, Mitofsky International and Edison Media Research, conducted all exit polling for the National Election Pool (NEP), which includes ABC, CBS, CNN, FOX, NBC, and the Associated Press. The polls themselves consisted essentially of statistical sample-driven placements of polltakers outside randomly selected precincts throughout the country but concentrating in crucial swing states, including battlegrounds such as Florida and Ohio. In terms of sheer logistics, the task of conducting exit polls is huge. Mitofsky, Edison, and their subcontractors covered about 1,500 polling locations, conducted about 110,000 interviews, and processed about 77,000 questionnaires by the time the polls closed in each state.

The exit poller seeks information beyond for whom you voted. Questions solicit demographic and psychographic profiles, from how often someone went to religious services to his or her feelings about the character of the different candidates. Exit polling data are extraordinarily rich and are useful for journalists in writing postmortem stories of the election, especially in identifying critical voting constituencies and moods of the voters. Political scientists use exit poll data for decades after the elections, trying to understand different trends and phenomena associated with campaigns. The purchasing companies, in this case the media consortium, technically have an unofficial agreement with Congress not to release the data to the public until after the polls in a state close. This voluntary standard was initiated to forestall the possibility of congressional regulation of voter surveys or exit polling.

Of course, early exit poll numbers have always been leaked and become the subject of gossip and information trading on Election Day. In addition, journalists use exit polls to "inform my expertise" (this is the expression a reporter actually used to explain what he did on air). So a television journalist who makes a statement such as, "I have a feeling that we will see a bigger than expected turnout among Hispanics in west Texas," has been given (or leaked) exit poll data. Likewise, exit poll leaks stimulate both despair and elation at campaign headquarters. (In the documentary about the 1992 Clinton campaign, *The War Room*, Clinton adviser James Carville crows over some leaked exit poll numbers showing his candidate winning.) At some point after polls close, exit poll companies will call the contest in a particular state. They are almost always correct; in fact, their error rate in projecting winners at the time polls close is less than 1 percent. However, past prominent too-early calls of states that barely went the other way (using previous polling methods) led exit poll companies in the 2004 election to be even more conservative in announcing victory.

The key point is this: *Everyone who works in the polling business knows that it is dangerous to read too much too soon into early exit poll numbers.* The figures are not a sample of all voters but rather of voters who happened to vote by, say, 10 A.M. in Virginia or Ohio. Many factors, such as weather, lifestyle, and so on, can influence who votes when. In some states, like Washington, many people (75 percent in 2004) do not even vote on Election Day; they had previously mailed in their ballots. Some types of voters, from minority women to Republican men, for various reasons, are more likely to refuse to participate in exit polls. Exit pollers, just like political groups, must in most states keep a certain distance away from the voting area.* New voters, unfamiliar with the concept of the exit poll, may tend to be suspicious or surprised when someone in the parking lot asks them questions about whom they voted for. Exit poll response rates in fact have been roughly 50 to 55 percent in recent years. In their final report on the 2004 exit polls, the NEP group stated that, for whatever reasons, "Kerry voters were more likely to participate in the exit polls than Bush voters."[63]

Although some journalists made ritual statements such as, "We don't have any real numbers" or "these are just speculations," none, in my study of the transcripts, made the clear declaration of the truth: Exit polls are merely the pulse of the moment; they project who is voting when, not what the eventual outcome of the race will be prior to the polls closing. (Actually, because consortium buyers want results immediately after polls close, polling companies stop interviewing voters an hour before.) So, if Kerry had an exit poll lead by 1 point at 10 A.M., this is much like the Boston Red Sox being up by one run in the second inning; the score does not mean anything until the game is over. But the baseball analogy is faulty itself because sports scores do not have margins of error, which make all the difference in projecting close elections. If Kerry is ahead 51–49 in Ohio at 10 A.M., with a margin of error of 3 percentage points, it is equally possible that Kerry could be winning by 54–46 or that Bush is in fact ahead 52–48. In other words, as I remind my students in the public opinion and public affairs class I teach each year: If the numbers for two candidates are within the margin of error, the race really is too close to call.

And historically, there have been disparities between the exit poll numbers and the final actual vote above and beyond those explained by sampling error alone. As one pollster put it to me—off the record—"It's

---

* The demographic of the pollers themselves may play a role in who responds to them. It is a commonplace in the business that it's hard to hire anyone but senior citizens to do a good, honest job.

not something anybody wants to talk about. There are always a certain number of people who don't figure out the voting protocols for one reason or another. But nobody wants to say in a democracy that some people are too dumb or too addled to vote." For such reasons, today's statisticians at the polling companies and news organizations are extremely conservative in making the call that any state has, after the voting is finished, gone to one candidate or another. Finally, although not all polls are perfect (which is why they have margins of error), the plain fact was that no official call of any state for Kerry or Bush proved incorrect.

Mystery Pollster to the Rescue

The blogging of Election Day 2004 was more complicated than a story of amateur bloggers stumbling over their own innumeracy. First, the exit poll outers did not do so without any context. Blogs that posted the early exit poll numbers included caveats, although sometimes they hinted of conspiracy. MyDD told its readers: "Mind that these are early numbers. And even if correct, they reflect the ones most wanting to vote, and it's still a long way to go."[64] Buzzflash, another liberal blog, warned: "Note: Exit polls are iffy. Take them with the proverbial salt grains" and instructed, "Keep Voting and Don't Count Your Eggs Until the Chickens Come Home to Roost."[65] Wonkette printed what the "Little Birdie" said but then clearly stated, "In fact, the little birdie is really skittish and not exactly trustworthy in all cases. Please vote, even if you live in PA. These [exit poll numbers] could be total forgeries, designed to keep you from voting. As a friend put it, 'The Yankees always figure out a way to win.'"[66] Then, later, Cox even put an ideological spin on the decision to publish exit poll numbers as leaked: "My retrospective argument seems relevant: we had to publish exit polls in order to kill them."[67] In perspective, Wonkette, unlike most on-air pundits, was consistently admitting her own limitations and amending her musings as new information became available. Moreover, she was not a survey-method novice; she had worked for the Statistical Assessment Service (STATS) center at George Mason University.

Then there is the open-source argument. Kos himself said that his site was essentially just putting the numbers out there, letting the public see the same thing that politicians and journalistic and academic elites were already being leaked, and that open access was "all that matters."[68] Indeed, around every presidential election, those who know anybody in campaigns or parties can call and ask, "Heard anything from the exit polls?" Now, legally, exit polls are owned by the news organizations that pay for them. But too many people are privy to the incoming results for them to be kept secret until after polls close, although reforms instituted in 2006 almost achieved this goal.* The difference on November 2, 2004, was that blogs existed to "out" leaks to lots of folks who had no acquaintances among the media or political elite. Maybe instead of blaming bloggers for being ignorant about what polling numbers mean, we should do a better job of educating everyone, including CNN commentators, about what polling numbers mean.

Plenty of influential bloggers, such as Charles Johnson of Little Green Footballs, were denying the validity of the exit polls, at least the early ones, and Instapundit's Glenn Reynolds simply refused to publish them. Probably most important, the single wisest statement made about exit polls, which within hours propagated throughout the bloglands, was by a blogger himself, who was anything but an amateur. If you consider the circumstances of his posting—what might be ranked now among the ten or so "posts that shook the world"—he qualifies as a blog hero.

Mark Blumenthal's Mystery Pollster site was only two months old at the time, but he conscientiously explained to the blog nation that early exit polls are not meaningful and should not cause anyone to gloat

---

* The exit polling company in fact kept its staff compilers sequestered and claims that no leaks came from its organization. If that was the case, the leaks came, as they traditionally do, from the news groups receiving the data feed. According to one of the exit poll directors I interviewed: "In 2006 we instituted a 'quarantine room' in which only two people from each NEP member (twelve people total) were given restricted access to the early exit poll numbers before 5 p.m. EDT. The people in the 'Q-room' were required to give up all means of outside communication—cell phones, BlackBerries. As a result, no leaked data reached the Internet in 2006 until 5:30 p.m., just thirty minutes before the first polls started closing in Kentucky and Indiana."

or panic or, worse, fail to vote. Blumenthal worked for years in polling, mostly for Democratic candidates, and Mystery Pollster had become in a short time a source of credible information on polls and surveys. On Election Day, however, Blumenthal was busy; his son had been born three days earlier. He was in the hospital with the newborn, his wife, his parents, and his in-laws when he made the fateful statement: "Um, I have to go do some work; I'll be right back." He then sped to his office and "dashed off" (in his own description to me) the following post:

Exit Polls: What You Should Know

So sometime very soon, the traffic on certain web sites will hit astronomically high levels as the blogosphere goes in search of the latest leaked exit polls. The conventional wisdom on this is unshakable: The networks "know" who will win, but won't tell us. Lets take our own peek at results shared by those working at the networks today and get in on the secret.

Well, I hate to disappoint, but this site will not be a source of leaked "exits." However, I would like to take a moment and give you a bit of a reality check. Let me tell you a bit about what exit polls are and why you may want to take what you hear over the web with a giant grain of salt.

I have always been a fan of exit polls. Despite the occasional controversies, exit polls remain among the most sophisticated and reliable political surveys available. They will offer an unparalleled look at today's voters in a way that would be impossible without quality survey data. Having said that, they are still just random sample surveys, possessing the usual limitations plus some that are unique to exit polling (I also remain dubious about weighting telephone surveys to match them, but that is another **story** for another day).

A quick summary of how exit polls work: The exit pollster begins by drawing a random sampling of precincts within a state, selected so that the odds of any precinct being selected are proportionate to the number that typically vote in that precinct. The **National Election Pool Exit Poll**, which is conducting the exit polling for the six major networks today, will send exit pollsters to 1,495 precincts across the country.

One or sometimes two interviewers will report to each sampled precinct. They will stand outside and attempt to randomly select roughly 100 voters during the day as they exit from voting. The interviewer will accomplish this task by counting voters as they leave the polling place and selecting every voter at a specific interval (every 10th or 20th voter, for example). The interval is chosen so that approximately 100 interviews will be spread evenly over the course of the day.

When a voter refuses to participate, the interviewer records their gender, race and approximate age. This data allow the exit pollsters to do statistical corrections for any bias in gender, race and age that might result from refusals.

The interviewer will give respondents a 5 1/2 by 8 1/2 card to fill out that will include approximately 25 questions (see an example from the New Hampshire primary **here**). Respondents fill out the survey privately then put the completed survey in a clearly marked "ballot box" so they know their identities cannot be tracked and their answers remain confidential.

The biggest challenge to exit polls is logistical: How to transmit all the results to a central location quickly and accurately. In past elections, interviewers would take a 10 minute break every hour to tabulate responses. Interviewers would then call in tabulations at three approximate times during the day: 9:00 a.m., 3:00 p.m. and shortly before the polls close (disclaimer: I have no first hand knowledge of this year's procedures, which may be different).

Once the polls close, the interviewer will attempt to obtain actual turnout counts, and if possible, actual vote returns for their precinct. One of the unique aspects of the exit poll design is the way it gradually incorporates real turnout and vote data as it becomes available once the polls close. The exit poll designers have developed weighting schemes and algorithms to allow all sorts of comparisons to historical data that supports the networks as they decide whether to "call" a state for a particular candidate. When all of the votes have been counted, the exit poll is weighted by the vote to match the actual result.

So if this poll is so sophisticated, **why can't we rely on the leaked mid-day "numbers"** that will soon spread like wildfire across the web?

1) It is still just a survey – Even when complete, an exit poll still has the same random variation as any other survey. NEP **says** typical state exit polls will have a sampling error when complete of +/– 4% at a 95% confidence level, and +/– 3% for the national exit poll. Even if comparable to the final numbers – which they are decidedly not – the mid-day leaked numbers would have much greater error, perhaps +/– 7% or more.

2) The mid-day numbers do not reflect weighting by actual turnout – the end-of-day exit poll used to assist the networks in determining winners will be weighted by the actual turnout of voters at each selected precinct. The weighting will then be continuously updated to reflect turnout at comparable precincts. In the past, mid-day numbers have reflected a weighting based on past turnout, so the leaked mid-day numbers may tell us nothing about the impact of new registrants or the unique level of turnout this time.

One point needs emphasis here: even in past elections, networks never called an election based on raw exit poll numbers alone. They were first weighted by a tally of the full day's turnout at each sampled precinct. This end-of-day data is (obviously) not available at 12 noon.

3) Voting patterns may be different early in the day - People who work full time jobs typically vote more heavily before or after work. Even a perfect mid-day exit poll – and there is no such animal – may not be any better at picking a winner than the half-time scores in any given football game on Sunday. Also, despite what you may have heard on the West Wing, I know of no serious study showing a consistent

Democratic or Republican tilt to the morning or evening hours (if anyone does, please email me).

4) Early or absentee voting - As of last night, the ABC News **survey** estimated that 15% of all registered voters nationally had already cast absentee or early ballots. Obviously, these voters will not be available to interviewers standing outside polling places. To incorporate early voting, the **National Election Pool** is doing telephone interviewing in 13 states to sample the votes of those who voted early. Will these early votes be included in the mid-day leaked numbers? Who knows? I wouldn't count on it. (Good question, **Andrew**).

5) They could be fictional - Both sides have huge armies of field workers sweating it out in the streets right now. Field workers have been known to find creative ways to boost the morale of their own troops or demoralize the other side. Might someone start a rumor by sending made up numbers to a blog? Ya think? After all, the guy most web surfers turn to for leaked exits likes to say that the information he provides is only 80% accurate. What are the chances he could be, excuse the technical term, making shit up?

6) The people who do exit polls would rather you ignored them - OK, admittedly, that is a pretty wimpy reason, but they have a point. Exit polls provide a valuable resource for all of us. The will help us better understand who the voters are, why they vote the way they do and what the answers are to some of the debates that have raged for months that will not be resolved by vote returns alone. When someone leaks or broadcasts results of an exit poll (or telegraphs it by winking the way certain news networks tend to do about about 4 or 5 o'clock), calls are made to ban exit pollsters from polling places. That would be a very bad thing.

Listen, I understand human nature, and I'm not going to try to change it. We are all intensely curious about what is going to happen tonight, and most of us will find a way to peek at leaked exit polls at some point today. I just want you to know that those leaked exit polls really don't tell us much more about the outcome of the race than the telephone polls we were obsessing over just a few hours ago. Even if we wanted to call a race on unweighted, unfinished, mid-day exit polls alone (something the networks will not do), we would need to see differences of 10–15 points separating the candidates to be 95% certain of a winner.

So look at them if you must, but please, don't go plugging the numbers into spreadsheets and assume that your Electoral College "projections" have any special magic or scientific validity. Then don't. You might be better off flipping a coin to determine the outcomes of states like Ohio, Florida, Wisconsin, Iowa, etc.

I'll be back with more later in the day. If you have questions about exit polls that don't involve today's numbers, please sent them my way. You might also want to check the **Frequently Asked Questions** at the National Election Pool web site. See the jump page for offline sources this post.

P.S. I am leaving the comments section open, but with some very firm rules today. Absolutely NO POSTING OF LEAKED EXIT POLL NUMBERS. Anyone who chooses to ignore this admonition will have his or her message deleted and may be blocked from posting further. If I have to delete more than one or two messages, I will turn off comments for today. It may be the new Dad in me, but it's my blog: don't make me stop this car! ;-)

Embarrasing typos fixed 12:45 p.m. Points to anyone who caught "football dame." The MP needs some sleep.

"What You Should Know" is a marvel of clarity, accuracy,* and economy done, again, on the fly and under pressure. It would rightly become one of the most trackbacked, hat-tipped, cited, and quoted blogposts of all time. Wonkette herself posted shortly after her "Little Birdie" revelations: "A FURTHER NOTE ON EXITS/EARLY POLLING: Mystery Pollster has an excellent post on early numbers, as well as a vow to not post them himself. He's a bigger man than we are. . . ."[69]

"What You Should Know" was also a good example of one way bloggers have changed politics. Whether or not you believe there was chicanery involved in the 2004 election, Blumenthal provided a much-needed perspective on the basics of exit polling, which the news anchors did not. And he did it in a style that built the *personal* trust so important to blogging politics. The "MP needs some sleep" indeed, and he deserved, to use Churchill's famous praise, to sleep the sleep of "victorious peace."

The drama of exit poll 2004, then, was neither a failure of blogging nor one of the imperfect art and science of polling. What the exit poll mess showed in fact was the need for *more* discussion of polling by everyone, what Blumenthal later called "an Open-Source Methodology."[70] Yes, if you read only one or two selective blogs, you would have been misinformed, frustrated, or cut off when their servers crashed. But if you consulted a variety of leading blogs, including Instapundit, Andrew Sullivan, TalkingPointsMemo, Wonkette, National Review Online's the Corner, MyDD (the comments section), Hugh Hewitt, Command Post, or the Volokh Conspiracy, you would have gotten many perspectives and eventually much wisdom. Can the viewers of network news say the same?

---

* The post contains a few minor errors: Exit polls were taken at slightly fewer precincts than scheduled because some young polltakers did not show up; respondents fill out an 8½-by-11-inch questionnaire, not a card; the earliest report to the media consortium was made at about 10:15 A.M., not 9 A.M.

Fatally, I believe, as someone who teaches courses on public opinion, pollsters themselves have bought into the star system. As Wonkette herself wrote eight months earlier in an essay about luminaries among the "pollster pundits,"

> Pollsters typically present their poll results in press releases that do little to educate journalists as to the meaning of the numbers they contain. In Wisconsin, the pollsters trumpeted the apparent Kerry landslide with the same confident aplomb that voters would see in any newspaper: "Kerry On Pace To Carry Wisconsin [Primary], New Reuters/MSNBC/Zogby Poll Reveals"! Or, according to AMG: "Kerry in Commanding Lead Among Democratic Primary Voters in Wisconsin." These are hardly the messages of institutions that wish their results to be treated with caution.[71]

Amen. The rise of star journalists eager to abuse the system to make themselves appear prescient as well as omniscient, and star pollsters who sought to drive elections and not just to appraise them, had corrupted the system long before bloggers arrived on the scene.*

Toward 2006: Getting Serious

By the winter of 2004–2005, whether it was the London bombings or contested Supreme Court nominations, blogs were part of every major news event, commenting ("chewing") on them, generating them or at least complementing them, and being consulted by mass media as a

---

* Starting in 2006, the NEP members intended to withhold distribution of exit poll numbers—even internally to reporters, pundits, and anchors—until 6 P.M. EDT. The English model for achieving such secrecy is one possibility (in England, strict measures are taken to avoid leaks of exit polls to bookies taking wagers on political contests). Statistical decision makers from the consortium members sit in one room. None are allowed any private communication devices, including cell phones. Each is watched by his or her own handler who, literally, monitors them all day, even during trips to the bathroom. In all, then, Wonkette and her comrades did not kill the exit poll, but in a way, they did prompt much-needed reforms.

sort of online "man on the street," as a pulse taker of the Internet, or even as experts. Political blogs, especially, were no longer treated as just "a hip latest new thing" or, as Mickey Kaus put it, "queens for a day," and many researchers were trying to explore the nature of blogging politics. More research found that about 28 percent of American blog readers had engaged in some sort of political activity prompted by a blog.[72] As that paladin of the old media, Tom Brokaw, summed up the situation on Election Day, "There's a large and ever-expanding universe, a new universe in American political dialogue, the bloggers."[73] At the same time, polling data suggested caution about deeming the blog phenomenon deep and widespread. The month of the election, a Pew study found 62 percent of "online Americans" unable to identify what a blog was.[74] Others wondered whether blogs could keep up their pace of audience growth in a dearth of hot political events: The top political blogs saw their audience dip by as much as half by February 2005.[75] But behind these numbers, after the bombast and oversell of blogs and the 2004 election, blogging was professionalizing, becoming part of politics, and many innovative folk were finding ways for blogs to fit in the system while trying to retain their unique capabilities.

Thus, the year blogs arrived was 2004, and in the 2006 election, blogs became full-time players in the game; 2008 will be the year political professionals thoroughly explore what blogs can do in all political races, including the run for the White House. In 2006, blogs became diversified so that we now speak of them as among their sister technologies—like YouTube, which at the time of the 2006 voting saw political clips take up *half* of its online library.[76] Politicians learned, from the example of George Allen, that the "citizen journalist" with a cause and camera should not be ignored. Allen's "macaca moment" (when, at a campaign rally, the former Virginia senator singled out a videotaping volunteer for his opponent's campaign with a racial slur) would have been a local story or even no story, but via YouTube it received upward of 400,000 viewings in weeks. Left and liberal blogs acted as force multipliers, as they often do, talking about the video, focusing on its significance, spreading links to ever wider audiences, and of course, drawing in traditional media; a virus vlog (video blog or log) had conquered, and every politician giving a speech anywhere knew they were fair game.

There is no way to confirm that a single video blog affected a race for the Senate in terms of actual votes, but we do know that Allen's poll number went flat and then dipped as the controversy churned and burned. Also, the allegation prompted follow-up stories in mainstream media of alleged racial incidents in Allen's past. So, yes, we can say that one vlog made a difference out of all proportion to its actual costs as media; further, Allen lost his race for reelection by a few thousand votes, and the Democrats gained the Senate by one seat. The disparity of effort and money struck not a few observers as the real lesson of vlogs, YouTube, and blogging technologies and sociologies. The costs of making and disseminating the video were negligible, but millions of dollars in traditional television advertising could not heal the wound it inflicted.

Money, that proverbial mother's milk of politics, would be another key story in the blogization of politics. Blogs were large money funnelers for Allen's victorious opponent, James Webb. In fact, the left blogs seemed to have their stars better aligned. In several close House races. fund-raising by collations of left blogs such as the ActBlue network— the self-styled "eBay of online fundraising for Democrats"—became a player. The blog Eschaton alone raised $23,489 for the close victory of Patrick Murphy (Eighth District, Pennsylvania).[77] The actual breakdown of monies raised is laid out in Table. 3.1.

On the other hand, in 2006, half the Senate candidates who operated a blog won, not proving blog power in either direction.[78] But sometimes, viewed as a national chess match of allocation of monies and resources, politics is about forcing your game on your opponent. Mcjoan of DailyKos points out that blog fund-raising in the midterm election

wasn't just about winning. We weren't intending to win with some of those seats we specifically endorsed and raised money for—we were expanding the playing field and forcing the Republicans to defend seats that they hadn't had to defend in years, or sometimes decades. Case(s) in point Larry Grant in Idaho-01, Gary Trauner in Wyoming, and Scott Kleeb in Nebraska-03. The Club for Growth and the GOP put much, much more money into those races than they would have if we

Table 3.1.
Netroots Candidates 2006 by MyDD, DailyKos, and the Swing State Project

Politician	State	Running for	Donors	Total $	All Pages
Ned Lamont	Connecticut	Senate	5,770	$180,586.02	$452,867.04
James Webb	Virginia	Senate	5,557	$193,248.85	$893,180.68
Jon Tester	Montana	Senate	5,472	$157,007.24	$343,023.52
Joseph Sestak, Jr.	Pennsylvania	House	3,617	$133,573.07	$866,810.54
Jerry McNerney	California	House	3,456	$101,504.65	$206,560.70
Darcy Burner	Washington	House	3,414	$79,906.67	$223,523.75
Patrick Murphy	Pennsylvania	House	3,063	$63,882.67	$165,855.27
Eric Massa	New York	House	2,878	$58,950.15	$415,300.13
Larry Kissell	North Carolina	House	2,868	$62,234.13	$170,680.21
Jay Fawcett	Colorado	House	2,644	$50,432.09	$63,696.90
Larry Grant	Idaho	House	2,625	$60,622.53	$72,103.63
Gary Trauner	Wyoming	House	2,568	$55,779.44	$275,779.24
Paul Hodes	New Hampshire	House	2,562	$53,900.18	$87,247.61
Linda Stender	New Jersey	House	2,549	$48,578.17	$64,603.64
John Courage	Texas	House	2,377	$40,239.87	$72,152.11
Dan Seals	Illinois	House	2,341	$41,961.62	$538,608.62
Blog PAC	—	—	2,250	$40,422.23	$83,475.36
Tim Walz	Minnesota	House	2,164	$44,972.42	$53,306.68
Francine Busby	California	House	1,409	$54,453.00	$124,380.99
Ciro Rodriguez	Texas	House	508	$21,789.15	$154,346.01
Totals			14,437	$1,544,044.15	$5,327,502.63

Source: Adapted from http://www.actblue.com/page/netrootscandidates, by Nathan Rodriguez

hadn't brought national attention to those races. Both Grant and Kleeb did get national attention, including in the *Washington Post* and *The New York Times*. Bush and Cheney were forced to make appearances in these districts. Trauner came within about 1,000 votes of winning. In that sense, we were changing the entire dynamics of the entire race.

Or, as Markos put it: "we absolutely helped expand the playing field." Joel Connelly of the *Seattle Post-Intelligencer* observed, "The 'net roots' of the Democratic Party jump-started challenges to seemingly entrenched Republican incumbents." So not only do new opportunities arise when local politics becomes national blog politics, blogging also opens up the money game to individuals who have a new idea. For example, in the spring of 2007, one Barack Obama supporter, of apparently modest means, started up a South Asians for Obama Web site to bundle contributions from friends and fellow ethnics nationwide.[79] That, too, is the Web cash advantage: The donors organize themselves. The smart money was paying attention. By the start of the 2008 preseason, nobody in politics or the political press ignored the interactive venue and style of campaign communication and organization. The real question was not whether blogs could play a role in politics but how and, more important, *predictably* how.

4

Mercuries and Wisebots: External Political Roles of Bloggers

I have made the case so far in *Blogwars* that

- There are many variations of political blogs, and although they have some similarities, they should not be overpraised, overdenigrated, or categorized as fitting into neat stereotypes.
- Events have not driven or thrust fame upon blogs, but rather, bloggers, blogs, and blogging have been able to exploit a confluence of developments in mass media, technology, and daily life to achieve power, prominence, and popularity.
- The Dean campaign showed the potentials and pitfalls of political blogging—the most central being that "going to the blogs" means more than just pasting statements on a Web site and inviting comments without truly interacting with the blog constituency. In an IDS (Internet-digital-satellite-selfcasting) age, interactivity has to be more than a slogan.
- Blogs are getting down to business, and serious political folk, ignoring the all-or-nothing hype, are exploring what blogs can do practically for covering politics as well as for serving politicians and political causes.

I hope these two remaining chapters function as a menu of options for nonpolitically employed citizens as well. Consulting blogs can help all of us become better consumers of political information.

In this chapter, I show how blogs have infiltrated the *external* mainstream of politics and public affairs: the people who give us information with which to make our political decisions but who don't actually run campaigns or govern us and make policy. My focus is not only on high-profile blogthroughs but also on the unsung yet critical ways political bloggers are taking on new roles within the political system. I call them by familiar names: expert, educator, analyst, and others. But the ways bloggers are assuming these duties are wholly novel and could not have been possible in any previous era.

Blogger as Compiler of Political Information

Bloggers can serve the public as informants, investigators, collators and compilers, and revisers and extenders of political information.

The Internet has been described as a giant shipwreck of information, containing debris and muck but also troves of gold doubloons. Most search terms get tens of thousands of hits; Google seeks out and rates sites by the number of times they are cited within other sites. Their algorithm is much more complicated than that, but—and here is a key point to why political blogs are consulted by political workers—in the words of tech columnist John Hiler, "Google Loves Weblogs."[1] What he meant, in part, was that the Google search engine's "insatiable appetite for fresh content spilled over to any frequently updated websites, including Weblogs." Those seeking to bump their sites up the list can try to manipulate the system. (Among the many spams I got when I started blogging were offers from porn and gambling sites to list my blog in theirs in exchange for the same.) That is why, for me, Web searching is actual *searching*, rooting around, refining search terms, and looking down hit lists. When I lack the time to do it myself, I, like most college professors at research universities, employ "wisebots," intelligent humans reared on the Web who are capable of a systematic survey for just the right piece of information. They are not just "smart" as in smart bombs but wise in thinking about what they want to look for and how to get it. The technical term for these searching sojourners is *graduate students.*

Blogs began as a way to tell people what is out there. Tim Berners-Lee, Jorn Barger, and others initiated truncated posts about items they saw on the Web. Yes, a majority of blogposts run something like "Piece in *Chicago Tribune* on Hillary Clinton's Speech on Thursday. Biased trash!" or "Read this great story on Republican fundraising for a presidential run." Current Twitter technology, which allows users to text message short (no more than 140 characters) passages to their Web site, produces eerily similar outcomes: Barack Obama will twitter, for example, "In Chicago, walking picket line with hotel workers at the Congress Hotel. For more info visit http://www.congresshotelstrike. info/" or "Enjoying an ice cream social with residents of Sunapee, New Hampshire."

The importance of simple "check this out" posts should not be underestimated. In the early days of the Internet, most of us had no idea what was where: People who found after investigation or just stumbled on interesting stuff and told us about it were helpful indeed. *For many reporters and media elites, blogs are the wisebot scouts searching for newsworthy (or titillation worthy) items on the Web.* There may even be another interlocutor in this process for the higher status political elite: Younger staffers at media and political organizations are blog friendly, and they pass on blogged material to their superiors. Ari Rabin-Havt, director of online communications for Senator Harry Reid (D-Nevada) and the Democratic Caucus, explained to one of my students, "The Senator isn't [a] computer programmer or graphic designer. . . . Sometimes I give him stuff to read from blogs; sometimes I know he's reading blogs himself because he'll print something out or e-mail me and say take a look at this."[2]

Bloggers thus perform the service of providing political content for journalists and government and political workers and the rest of us in several dimensions.

Blogger as Informant in a Political Marketplace

Retired political correspondent Richard Benedetto once told me that he originally became a reporter because he liked the idea of "traveling to places that other people couldn't go to and then coming back and reporting" what he had seen and heard. I have found no more succinct definition of foreign correspondents. Bloggers can also report from the scene in the "I was there and this is what I want to show you" style of Edward R. Murrow's "This Is London" 101. We see them, as said, as the citizen journalists in every breaking news event, such as the London 7/7 bombings or Virginia Tech shootings, where bloggers reported what they saw, firsthand, close to the events, and even uploaded pictures, typically taken with cell phone cameras. Patrick Hynes, of the conservative blog AnkleBitingPundits and a blogging adviser to John McCain, lives in New Hampshire, the first presidential primary state and target of the visits of many would-be commanders-in-chief; he regularly uploads his own videos of visiting presidential contenders because, as he told me: "I want everyone in the country to get to see what we people here see of them." Likewise, an increasing number of local bloggers focus on events within their own community. They supplement (and sometimes supplant) regular reporters; they also report events that, for one reason or another, print and electronic journalists did not cover at all.

Sometimes, the reporting is a straightforward eyewitness account of an event within the blogger's community. Pamela, the exuberant super-right mistress of Atlas Shrugs, for example, offered this description of a lecture by the great Italian journalist Oriana Fallaci:

> I went to see Oriana Fallaci this evening in what will most likely be her last speech. . . . The crowd to my surprise, was small. . . . She is dying from cancer. No photos allowed. And while she could not have been more than 85 lbs, she railed away at Radical Islamo Fascism, the treasonous left and the impotent right as if she was taking on Goliath. . . . The following remarks are from my fierce scribbling. In a word, *Fallaci was wild*. Smart, determined, and intent on getting the message out there that we are underestimating the enemy. . . .[3]

Pamela, as her loyal readers know, produces much "fierce scribbling." As with many right bloggers, one of her motivations for creating alternative media was her perception that big media were being too politically correct in covering (or rather not covering) the Islamic origins of international terrorism. (Conversely, many left bloggers say George W. Bush's election was their inspiration for blogging.) But both her opinion and that of Fallaci's deserve a stall at the marketplace of ideas, however you might try to avoid them. Thus, bloggers can go places where there is a small crowd and add volume to a frail voice. That blogs are a remarkable modern vehicle to empower nonmedia elites is a matter of some historical context worth exploring here.

Blogs as "Scribbling Mercuries"

The blog is possible through the convergence of many new technologies of the IDS (Internet-digital-satellite-selfcasting) age: revolutions in human communication that were both tipping points (of ideas) and points of the tip (of new things). In parallel, more than half a millennium ago (1452–1454/1455), Johann Gutenberg printed his two-volume, 1,282-page, forty-two-line-per-page Bible in Mainz, Germany. He produced 180 copies (150 on paper and, it is believed, 30 on parchment), using about twenty assistants in the process. His innovations included a screw press (a converted wine press) and movable type with individual elements (periods, upper- and lowercase letters). Interestingly, the small number of Bibles hardly represented mass communication, but one of Gutenberg's follow-up projects did. To raise money to pay for a crusade against Muslim Turks, the Roman Catholic Church contracted with Gutenberg to print thousands of letters of indulgence—certificates the Catholic faithful could buy for cash, absolving them of their sins. The practice was among the chief of the ninety-five complaints a young German monk named Martin Luther nailed to the door of the Wittenberg Cathedral, signaling the beginning of the Reformation. It is hard to imagine that such heresy could have spread so widely and so quickly in an era before movable type. In fact, Luther's theses would have become only sketchily known by word of mouth (and probably easily suppressed before they became too widespread). But in the developed print works of Germany, the "Disputation of Doctor Martin Luther on the Power and Efficacy of Indulgences" would become a mass-disseminated document. New technology allowed Luther to proclaim to everyone who could read or be read to, not just those he could talk to personally.

Unlike in China or Korea, which had invented printing earlier but were unified countries with established ruling classes, the print world of Gutenberg and his philosophical heirs was the free-for-all arena of ideologies and political partisanship of western Europe. Printing, therefore, became an instrument of both orthodoxy and revolution. During the religious wars of the sixteenth century, for instance, each side would prepare innumerable books and pamphlets that propagandized their cause and demonized the enemy. Crucially, however, few people supported a free and open dispute of ideas. In areas under stable church or government control, censorship of what people could print and what they could read was the norm. (In any case, the literacy rate was not generally that high, but many people were read to by the literate in a community, the influentials of the time.) In Henry VIII's England, for example, printing a book without the king's license was punishable by death.

Many philosophers of the Enlightenment era rebelled against royal control. The principles they crafted in their writings during the period highly influenced the founders of America and the framers of the Constitution. Freedom of the press, for instance, assumes that presses will be in competition with each other as bulwarks against government abuse, ensuring freedom from monopoly by any single power. One of the originators of such a concept was John Milton, the seventeenth-century English poet, who published a pamphlet in 1644 titled *Areopagitia* (subtitled *A Speech for the Liberty of Unlicenc'd Printing*) in which he insisted that open debate freed the mind to find truth.

> Well knows he who uses to consider, that our faith and knowledge thrives by exercise, as well as our limbs and complexion. Truth is compared in Scripture to a streaming fountain; if her waters flow not in a perpetual progression, they sicken into a muddy pool of conformity and tradition.

In American history, the principle of the "marketplace of ideas" became set as a value of both journalism and society. Justice Oliver Wendell Holmes Jr. wrote in a decision in a First Amendment case (*Abrams v. United States*, 250 U.S. 616, 630) in 1919,

> [W]hen men have realized that time has upset many fighting faiths, they may come to believe even more than they believe the very foundations of their own conduct that the ultimate good desired is better reached by free trade in ideas—that the best test of truth is the power of the thought to get itself accepted in the competition of the market, and that truth is the only ground upon which their wishes safely can be carried out. That at any rate is the theory of our Constitution.

By Holmes's time, the mechanics of that marketplace had changed to an industrial model of the press. The principle remains with us to this day, however, and blogs and those who embrace blogging as a democratic revolution in media often call the phenomenon the best incarnation of the perfect marketplace of ideas.

Not by coincidence, those times of great political upheaval and even revolution were when the marketplace seemed at its utmost fury of competition. The great flowering of the printing press in England as an expression of countervailing political ideas came during Milton's day. The mid-seventeenth century saw struggles between King Charles I and the English Parliament, followed by several civil wars, the execution of Charles, the rise of Oliver Cromwell and his Puritan faction to supremacy in England, and then the death of Cromwell and the restoration of the monarchy under Charles's son.[4] Newspapers of the era were known as "news books"; most of them carried the forename "Mercurius," a reference to the Roman messenger god, Mercury, today commonly drawn with a winged cap or winged feet. It was a good metaphor for these news books, holding titles such as *Mercurius Aulicus* (a Royalist periodical) and *Mercurius Britannicus* (a vehicle of the anti-Royalist Roundheads).

The mercuries were bloglike in that (a) they represented the opinions of diverse political factions; (b) they were the direct creations of a few individuals, either independently or representing factional interests; (c) they required some expense to publish and distribute, but they were not beyond the means of individuals; and (d) they were often scathing in their attacks on political figures and others. For example, *Mercurius Impartialis* blamed "the ruines both of King and people" on "the Pulpit and the Presse" and charged further that "his Majesties Subjects [have] beene Poysoned with Principles of Heresie, Schisme, Faction, Sedition, Blasphemy, Apostacie, Rebellion, Treason, Sacriledge, Murther, Rapine, Robbery, and all" the other "enormous Crimes, and detestable Villanies, with which this Kingdome hath of later times swarmed."[5] But the partisan mercurian newspapers could vilify in either direction. Oliver Cromwell, the executioner of the king, complained, "My very face and nose are weekly maligned and scandalized by those scribbling mercuries."[6]

Among the most celebrated editors of the many regularly published pamphlets put out, along with periodically published news books, was Milton himself, an adoring supporter of Cromwell and the antimonarchist government. One of his most famous pamphlets reads like a Renaissance blogpost title: "The Tenure of Kings and Magistrates: Proving that it is lawful and Hath been Held so through All Ages, for Any who Have the Power, to Call to Account a Tyrant or Wicked King, and after Due Conviction to Depose and put him to death." Milton was "posting" in reply to arguments made by the more moderate faction in Parliament (the Presbyterians) who were arguing for a retention of the monarchy and the sparing of the king's life. Milton was later appointed by the government to be Secretary to Foreign Tongues where, again bloggerlike, he ended up doing most of his work from his own home. Milton advocated "liberty of unlicenc'd printing" despite the fact that he held very powerful (i.e., partisan) political convictions.

In sum, many folk saw the basis of free society as the free exchange of ideas, but nobody promised that these disputations would be pretty or without rancor.[7] (We also hold such a combative tenet to be the basis of our legal system.) Like Churchill's famous characterization of democracy as the worst form of government but without rival, a free press (small, medium, or large), although sometimes repugnant, has no palatable alternative.

Bloggers as Correspondents

A basic localized political role of bloggers, to paraphrase Richard Benedetto, is simply to go places we cannot. On-the-scene bloggers have a singular opportunity to create new connections because they can visit the archives up the street or attend the City Hall meeting downtown. In fact, a reasonable prediction about the future of political blogs is that they will have much more measurable political impact at the local level than in national campaigns. Larry Handlin, the graduate student who edits ArchPundit (a reference to the St. Louis Gateway Arch), a blog that focuses on Missouri and Illinois politics, pointed out to me in an interview:

> Given our lives are most affected by state and local governments, from school boards to state legislatures, it seems strange that information about them is the most lacking. I hope that in Illinois, and to a lesser extent in Missouri, my coverage offers insight into those levels of government. I don't have any pretensions that my site is able to do this all by itself, but I think it may be one of the first to really address those issues and hopefully be a starting point for others.

Indeed, in the future, the greatest growth in political blogging may be around the corner and *about* the corner. For example, Charles Kuffner, whose blog OfftheKuff deals largely with Texas regional politics, pioneered the blogger as interviewer, not just posting comments on what other people said but also asking the questions himself. In December 2003, he helped define a new subgenre of blog content by holding an extensive interview—the first—with a Democrat planning to challenge Tom Delay, then Republican speaker of the House, for his seat in Congress. Kuffner, thus, was adding value to blogging and to politics by taking up one of the duties of reporting: asking questions of politicians.

More exotic are foreign correspondents who blog. Christopher Allbritton successfully set up a personal Web site and asked readers to make online donations to finance his travels to Iraq.[8] The so-called PayPal journalist calls his work "pure, individual journalism using a laptop and a satellite phone,"[9] done without the protection of the Department of Defense embedding program or a bulletproof vest. Other bloggers who travel abroad and report back what they see from the front lines of war include Michael Totten, Bill Roggio, and Michael Yon. The last is an interesting case of the indy blogger changing the rules of war reporting. The independent journalist-blogger in Iraq so outrages some in the military power structure for his critiques of the war and his conduct with soldiers in the field that one general allegedly, during the spring of 2007, sought to expel him from the country. Yon—who is both pro-war and a severe critic of the tactics of the Pentagon—is a particularly galling flea to brass elephants because of his credentials: He is a former Green Beret. He is on site, he is an expert, and he blogs. The combination can be lethal to the powers-that-be.

Blogging also allows foreigners to be foreign correspondents, something unusual in the American tradition. For example, it was one Iraqi, Salam Pax (a pseudonym), who became a media star for his daily dispatches from Baghdad covering events in the city up to the start of the war and for a short time later.[10] Peter Maass, a foreign correspondent writing for *Slate* magazine, praised Pax's work: "His lively and acerbic blog was far better than the stuff pumped out by the army of foreign correspondents in the country."[11] More familiar to Americans is the proverbial army of milbloggers, men and women like CaptB (now Major Pain), who, M-16A2 rifle in hand and laptop in knapsack, are telling us what they see and hear and feel and smell from wars in Iraq and Afghanistan.

Blogger as Collector and Collator

Bloggers don't simply locate a political item and run to tell us about it; they can also be thought of as librarians and annotators of a kind. They help seek out knowledge and organize it, create cross-links, and uncover and present information that we might have never found otherwise. Blog commenters add to the process through "you might want to also look at" contributions to threads of discussion and debate. Good bloggers thus help readers via the collection and collation of information.

For example, one of my student political bloggers, Jessica Tucker (then a campus leader at Louisiana State University) created a short-lived blog, TheNewNewOrleans, to examine the immediate aftermath of Hurricane Katrina. In one posting she told us what was going on (or failing to) at the front lines of the salvation and reconstruction effort, and, more important, the political machinations behind the scenes. Some of Jessica's rich political data came from the newspapers, and others from simply calling people up and asking questions; she also got tips or leaks from friends in state government and in political parties. But Jessica was the collector, organizer, deployer, and exhibitor of those many interconnected tidbits that affect the future of Louisiana's political power structure. She thus created a synthesis that adds value to her blog beyond references to published material.

Blogger as Reviser and Extender of Big Media

Another way bloggers can create new content is to revise and extend, to add value to existing big media publications. The space and time bloggers accord to their endeavor and their passion and focus, which other people call partisanship, allow them to literally go beyond the news. For example, on May 30, 2005, the *New York Times* published a story titled "In Rising Numbers, Lawyers Head for Guantanamo Bay."[12] Among those quoted in the story was "Michael Ratner, president of the Center for Constitutional Rights, *a group based in New York* [italics mine] [who] is coordinating the assigning of lawyers to prisoners." Now, if I had seen that sentence in a student paper, I would have flagged it as problematic. The *Times* should have told us more about the CCR; in fact, because the group plays such a prominent role in the Gitmo story, the *Times* should have profiled the organization in a sidebar. Journalism school basic training holds that, within the limits of space, you give readers, listeners, or viewers the background and context of sources, from individual experts to groups. (Stories on the Web, of course, possess virtually unlimited space.)

Why identify the people you quote or mention in a story? Because it is important to know who holds what political perspective, who is on whose payroll, and who is a front for whom. As noted, readers and viewers should be made aware, for example, that certain former government officials or politicians are on the payroll of foreign countries like China or Saudi Arabia but who editorialize or who are quoted in stories about trade policy or Middle East politics. The explosion of advocacy compounds the necessity of transparency, especially for industry front groups with uplifting or patriotic buzz titles like People for Freedom or People for Motherhood and Apple Pie. Before the advent of blogs, I would have made this point to my students and then moved on because there was nothing we could, after the fact, do about it. Big media stop for no viewer or reader.

Enter, stage right, Rocco DiPippo, a building contractor in Providence, Rhode Island. His blog, antiprotester, is largely devoted to "the background of war protestors that the liberal media hide from us." His take on the CCR was, he told me, the product of "about ten hours of work" and was in far more depth than the *Times* piece, listing in detail a history of the CCR, biographies of its founders, and much more. One may disagree with his about 5,800(!) words—a left blog, for example, might offer a different set of views—but the *Times* should have provided *some* information about the CCR. One should know whether a group has a history of supporting left- or right-wing causes or is staffed by lawyers from the oil industry or Greenpeace. Revelation of possible agendas and biases does not discount what anyone says or does; it simply puts the information into perspective for the public. If journalists will not do it, then partisan bloggers will, to the benefit of us all.

Bloggers can also go where big media herds are otherwise too distracted to venture. During 2005, for example, a great game was under way, largely below the radar of much media and most citizens. The journalist Arthur Hadley wittily called the lengthy interim between one presidential election contest and the first actual votes of real convention delegates for the next "the invisible primary."[13] During this period, potential candidates for president explore their options, and many witnesses, from political bosses to big donors to political journalists, judge their viability to run for president at all. Among the activities that generally escape front-page newspaper reporting are the following: the formation of direct and indirect campaign committees; the jostling to hire the best staff; fund-raising and campaign appearances on behalf of local candidates throughout the country to build up IOUs for their own run; working concentrations of donors; sending out policy papers and materials; and perhaps writing books to enhance a résumé as a statesperson. And of course, most notoriously, despite denials such as, "I'm not thinking about the presidency; I'm just focusing my attention on the people of New Jersey as their governor," there is also pressing the flesh at party political functions in the nation's first caucus state, Iowa, and first primary state, New Hampshire. Big media cover such events sometimes, but local bloggers are there almost all the time.

Even though no votes are cast during the invisible primary, the consequences for the future primary season are huge. Since the 1970s, it has been a rule that strong primary candidates do not arrive on the scene late; rather, they surface early.[14] Furthermore, early fund-raising success almost always translates to the ability to wage and eventually win a sustained campaign despite initial upsets.[15] Studies have found, for example, that nearly half and as much as two thirds of the money that candidates raise for their campaigns is gathered during this time.[16]

But now blogs may be serving both as extensions of media, covering invisible primary events missed or intentionally ignored by the giants, and as providers of in-depth information that might eventually affect our future votes. Whether you like it or not, the preprimary period is a lot less invisible thanks to the Internet and blogs. For example, blogger-only meetings are common for candidates and are becoming even more so. When former North Carolina senator and 2004 vice-presidential candidate John Edwards spoke at the University of Texas, Austin, in late October 2005, blogger Neal Sinhababu, a UT student and editor of the blog Ethical Werewolf, recounted "the John Edwards experience." I reprint it in full here because it shows the kind of old-fashioned, cynicism-free cheeriness a young blogger can have about meeting a candidate and telling us about it.

> Over the last few years, I've developed an incapacity to properly listen to political speeches. I generally approach them in some kind of meta way, analyzing how the speaker's rhetorical moves and mannerisms contribute or detract from the effect he

is trying to create, and considering how they play into a broader political context. It doesn't usually matter whether I support the speaker or not – it happens as much with Democrats as with Republicans.

That's not what happened today. For most of John Edwards' talk on poverty here on the UT campus, I was naively absorbed in what he said. This is partly because of my great Edwards enthusiasm, and partly because Edwards' speech—the stated purpose of which was to encourage students to join a campus volunteer group—didn't fit within a narrowly political context. It's also because Edwards is an truly amazing speaker. Everything seemed completely natural, off-the-cuff, and conversational and yet it fit together—often uncannily—into a well-organized speech. (There's a reason for this— much of the speech is **here**. Ezra linked to it a long time ago, but I never got around to reading the whole thing.) The following reflections are, almost without exception, ex post facto.

Edwards' anecdotes about poverty didn't fit the "here's an example to obviously fit my point" rubric that disposes unsympathetic listeners to immediately think up counterarguments. In the aftermath of Katrina, Edwards met a man who had lived and worked for 23 years in New Orleans, but whose workplace had been destroyed by flooding and wouldn't reopen. A truck came by the shelter he was staying at to pick up day laborers for work at 5 AM some mornings. He had stood there for 10 days trying to be among those chosen for work, without success. He told Edwards, "So far, it hasn't happened, but I want to go to work." The anecdote segued him from talking about Katrina to talking about general poverty issues, and I only realized later that it defused the stereotype of poor people as indolent and lazy. Some of the less tendentious Lakoff framing principles are operative here – when you want your audience to think "A", and you know they have some degree of credence in "not-A", don't say "not not A". Give them evidence for "A", and give it in such a way that people won't even remember that "not-A" has some appeal to them. One of the major roadblocks to antipoverty spending – the worry, primarily of middle-class whites, that they'll be supporting lazy blacks – is thus neatly avoided. Does stable belief-change actually result? Perhaps not immediately. But I'm guessing that it would successfully push people towards liking policy proposals premised on "A", even if "not-A" also has some grip on them. And once people get in the habit of nodding along to "A", their attachment to "not-A" may fade away.

"Some of you might remember I'm the son of a mill worker" was successfully played for laughs, and that made me happy. Not only because it's good to see that Edwards knows what he's repeated *ad nauseam*, but because it's good (even in a fairly tuned-in crowd) to see that he's established his poor-boy upbringing enough that the joke works.

Now for the really awesome part: After the speech, I and a few other local reporters and bloggers were invited to a media session in which we could ask him questions. First I asked about his plans for providing health care coverage to more uninsured people, and asked if he had any particular reflections on single-payer plans to offer us. He didn't come out and offer any particular positive proposals, though he did talk about the necessity and inevitability of universal coverage, and went briskly through the flaws of the current system. He also had a nice bureacracy anecdote – when Elizabeth was undergoing cancer treatment, he had to fill out a whole bunch of paperwork that he simply couldn't understand, despite being a former lawyer and Senator. I'm wondering whether Elizabeth Edwards cancer-treatment anecdotes will someday play an effective rhetorical role in bringing us closer to a decent health care system.

The end of his speech had discussed the need for American leadership in combatting global poverty, which I was very happy to hear him bring up, especially since there was no real reason why he had to talk about it. So I asked him about that too. He expressed support for more foreign aid spending, and discussed Bush Administration failures of leadership on climate change and a host of other issues.

For the last question, someone asked about whether he'd be running in 2008, and he had some kind of genial non-response, starting with "I can't believe we got this far without hearing that one!" Nobody asked him about Iraq, though he had a few offhand negative remarks about the situation. At one point, he talked about the need for Democrats to have "big ideas" instead of merely targetting their tax cuts a little lower than Republicans target theirs. He was wearing a white "Make Poverty History" bracelet of the Lance Armstrong variety that a student had given him in another town.

At the end I got my **picture** taken with him and some other folks. I told him that I'd volunteered for him, and that it was good to finally meet him. As I left the Union, simple walking proved too mundane for my emotional state. I leapt onto a long elevated piece of concrete that people often use as a bench and walked on it. A girl passing by broke into a smile as she saw me, and I realized that my enthusiasm was more obvious than I thought.

Indeed, the post and the event are smile-worthy: I like hearing from a younger person that somebody or something in politics, as opposed to sports or music, is "awesome." Blogging is not just ranting; it can be an exhortation for hope, about one candidate and about democracy itself.

But the Ethical Werewolf did not haphazardly stumble upon the Edwards talk; he was invited. Edwards is probably the most blog-aware of the 2008 contenders. As he did in each proto-campaign stop, Edwards met after the speech with a number of bloggers, including Phillip Martin of BurntOrangeReport and bloggers from PinkDome and InthePinkTexas. Martin then reprinted the text of the exchange, Edwards's speech in a post, and a question he asked Edwards. Edwards continued his blogging friendliness throughout his precampaign and beyond. Before announcing that he was in the race, he bought ads on blogs, gave interviews to bloggers, and of course, posted a YouTube video.[17]

Bloggers, thus, have made this crucial time in the quadrennial building of a presidential campaign much less invisible. Blogging now constitutes a complicated, amorphous protoprimary in itself, if not quite the "new Iowa" then at least a testing ground, constituency, and benchmark for the invisible primary. That engagement allows the creation of original blog content by the citizen blogger and now by the politician who blogs as well.

Blogger as Investigative Reporter

A final method of creating original content for blogs is perhaps the most respected form of political journalism: investigative reporting. Obviously, the individual blogger, not a political or media player, who is blogging as a hobby, without access to independent funding, commands few resources for classic muckraking. Investigative reporting on blogs typically is either Google driven or source based. Of course, as resources for blogging increase and more professionals, including investigative reporters, blog, we will no doubt see an increase in this subgenre of blogging; at the local level, the enterprise is more logistically practicable. One man who established a model is Christopher Frankonis (aka The One True b!X), "the writer, editor, and publisher of *Portland Communiqué*" (communique.portland.or.us). Since he started his blog in December 2002, Frankonis has offered thousands of posts on Portland issues and events as politically important as "Who's Coordinating the Money in the Fight over Measure 36." A local journalist described b!X's mission as follows:

> Unlike most bloggers, who typically link to previously reported material and then offer their own analysis, b!X is unusual because he's going out and doing his own legwork. Armed with a black spiral notebook, a laptop and a homemade press pass . . . [he] has become a familiar face at City Council hearings, county task force meetings and news conference crushes, quietly forging something that is one step beyond the Fourth Estate.[18]

Frankonis is a true independent who supports himself with donations. He covers issues that interest him, which often are not reported at all or not in depth by the corporate press. He was one of the few reporters who followed a Portland city council race; the local newspapers were more interested in the higher profile mayor's race. And his digging is not dull stuff. It is difficult to imagine that hobbyist bloggers with a day job could follow Frankonis's lead. It is certain there will be more and more snooping b!Xs in the future. Blogs allow junior and journeyman investigators to both deploy their findings quickly, easily, and widely and to gain support directly from the public.

Independent investigative blogging at the national level is much more difficult and costly, and thus rarer, but it does exist. Dave Neiwert is an investigative journalist with a long résumé of respected articles and books mainly focusing on the activities of far-right extremist groups. He turned to political blogging through his Orcinus blog as a way to express his opinions, thoughts, and insights that did not lend themselves to traditional long-term investigative reporting or newspaper essays. One 2003 piece concerned itself with "Whistleblowers and the DoD" and looked at the treatment of those who uncovered and made public allegations of fraud, waste, and corruption in the Pentagon. Neiwert took months to research the post. As he commented to me, "Writing is hard enough work, but reporting requires another level of work. Most of the time, if I'm uncovering original information, I'm likely to take it to a media outlet. But the blog is an easy way to do early drafts of such work." As blogs and bloggers develop, we will see more such "early drafts" and more open-source investigations. Reward systems for bloggers, such as PayPal contributions, awards, and prizes, will perhaps act as incentives to invest hard work into blogging as investigative reporting. Again, the parallel to the cash-supported partisan press of the early republic is self-evident. A huge majority of bloggers, however, still make little or no money from the act of blogging.

Blogger as Political Analyst and Critic

Bloggers themselves, via "open-source expertise," have overturned the convention of who is an expert source "mediafit" to offer commentary on political and public affairs issues and events.

You can read blogs not just to gauge what's in the news but also for revelations on the development of news coverage itself. For example, Eriposte of the Left Coaster blog created a multipart series that examines the "liberal media myth." Its installments include "tone" of media coverage, "catch-phrases" like "right-wing extremist" versus "left-wing extremist," "newspaper headlines," "topics" covered, "think-tank" citations, journalist ideology or voting preferences, public opinion polls on media bias, and unintentional errors in news reports.[19] One post studied the creation of the "'liberal media' myth using *surveys of journalist ideology or voting preferences*." Its hyperlinks, citations, and references run into the hundreds; it is a tour de force of both comprehensiveness and succinctness, worth reading if you care about the bias of the media, right or left. Whether or not you agree with bloggers, you can still find value in reading and thinking about and further investigating their analyses. In the forced marketplace of the classroom, I ask my students to read Eriposte *and* "the media are biased to the left" criticism on good, literate right-wing blogs like Oxblog and Oh, That Left Wing Media.

Nevertheless, the common stereotype of blogger, held both by blogging's champions and its denigrators, is blogger as amateur, outsider, nonelite. To those who cheer for blogs, not being a political, media, or corporate insider is a badge of honor: You are not part of the corrupt self-serving power structure; you are a true tribune of the people. To blogging's enemies, the "basement blogger" is at best a Calvinesque ignoramus and loudmouth, at worst a Lonesome Rhodes demagogue with a Web site. Again, with tens of millions of blogs to choose from, tens of thousands of examples could be produced to support either portrait of an average political blogger. But bloggers can be, unequivocally, experts in public affairs and policy. Some have earned that expertise the old-fashioned way by traditional measures. Some have achieved expertise by their own labors outside academia or the professions. More and more, such "nonexpert" experts are becoming accepted information sources.[20] At the end of the day, the difference between the species of experts is immaterial if they are both perceived to add knowledge worthy of attention (hyperlinking) and source referencing (hat tipping or "h/t").

Who comprise *authentic* credentialed experts? That depends on one's perspective. Influentials are influential in the eye and ear of the beholder. When I was blogging, I became angry when commenters disagreed with my opinions. My academic ego was pricked: How dare people who, I presumed, had no doctorate and no shelf of books and articles to their credit challenge my studied positions? On the conference panel and in faculty meetings, I accepted such situations: I expect give-and-take and believe that other credentialed peers can offer wisdom. But blogging was different, perhaps because the commenters were calling me a moron and a monster as well as opposing my political stances.

But how do we define expertise? Mass communication researcher Lawrence Soley coined the term *Golden Rolodex* to delineate the bank of chosen discourse elites who are called upon to speak in mass media.[21] I am a minor member of the group; my main research area of politics and news images puts me in the call list for networks and newspapers when there is some hot photo icon in the media stream. But I do not think the system serves the public interest well. Part of my sour regard for "expert-sourcing" is based on several cold facts.

First, many "experts" are hardly objective observers. In a previous book,[22] I looked at American newsmagazine coverage of China over several decades. I noted that, in print, "old China hands" would be frequently quoted. But the reader would not be told that these sage observers were on the payroll of China, Taiwan, or some multinational conglomerate that profited from trade with either country. For example, by the 1990s, many luminaries such as Henry Kissinger worked as "consultants" for China while also writing (in big media) and lobbying on China policy.[23] (In September 1989, after months of writing about China policy, urging against harsh sanctions after the Tiananmen crackdown, Kissinger was embarrassed when the *Wall Street Journal* revealed that he was involved in business deals including a $75 million China partnership.) Emotional bias was also evident in China expertise. A host of scholars, journalists, and others who had visited, pictured, or studied China in the rapprochement era were *lao peng you*—"old friends" of China—although the relationship was not based on direct subsidies. The same holds true in trusting assertions by so-called Middle East policy gurus, many perhaps underwritten by the Saudis. How many respected foreign policy commentators receive monies from foreign governments or are beholden to foreign interests for material reasons? We don't often find out. But it seems odd that a blogger accepting a politician's stipend constitutes a scandal, whereas a former secretary of state on a foreign government's payroll playing the sagacious talking head on CNN does not.

Second, there does not seem to be a real correlation between expertise and accuracy. Witness Victor S. Navasky and Christopher Cerf's *The Experts Speak: The Definitive Compendium of Authoritative Misinformation*.[24] The scientific, social, political, and cultural sages are so often wrong, they enumerate, that one wonders whether rolls of the dice or fortune cookies would produce better results. To wit, we social scientists are pretty good redictors (we can explain what happened in the past), but our record of prognostication is manifestly awful. A prime example: Almost no Soviet studies expert, of the thousands in 1990, predicted the collapse of the Soviet Union in 1991. It is also difficult to overlook the fact that eminent statesmen and intellectuals, well-schooled generals and mighty CEOs, the proverbial best and the brightest were responsible for many of the disasters of the policymaking past. It was not semiliterate, ill-informed amateurs who led the nations into World War I, unleashed communism, created the Depression, and allowed Hitler to rise to power in Germany; furthermore, it was the "best and the brightest" who ushered us into (and mismanaged) the tragedies of Korea and Vietnam. "Experts" have much blood on their hands.

Yet, it is incorrect to assert that all bloggers with no press or political background bring nothing to their postings besides free time and passion. Beldarblog, which often addresses legal issues, is run by a lawyer; SCOTUSblog, which deals with legal issues, and its sister Supreme Court Nomination blog are written by attorneys at a law firm; a Marine captain who served a year in Baghdad publishes the blog Iraqnow; Juan Cole, a professor specializing in Shi'ite Islam, blogs on Middle East issues. And as noted, a number of uberblogs are written by professional media elites; Andrew Sullivan, for example, was a respected writer and editor before starting AndrewSullivan.com.

There are other experts who are thoughtful, careful, and talented writers who don't happen to be in the golden Rolodex of reporters seeking sources to quote.

Nontraditional Experts Who Blog

Blogging gives voice to nontraditional experts. For example, mainstream stories about prescription drug issues and the politics, costs, and efficacies of medical therapies tend to feature the usual suspects of reps from drug companies, politicians pushing legislation, doctors (typically at major university hospitals), and heads of advocacy groups. One does not think to contact twenty-something Lindsay Beyerstein, philosophy MA, who "eventually [hopes] to enroll in a PhD program, but for the time being I support my contemplative lifestyle as a freelance pharmaceutical writer." To find out her opinion, click her blog majikthise. typepad.com (named for a "philosopher [who] is a minor character in Douglas Adams' *Hitchhiker's Guide to the Galaxy*)."

I chanced upon her blog when an acquaintance of mine whose child is autistic asked me about a relevant political controversy. Robert F. Kennedy Jr., the assassinated senator's son, now an attorney for the Natural Resources Defense Council, wrote an article on *Salon,* the Internet magazine, and claimed that "a mercury-based preservative in [some] vaccines—thimerosal—appeared to be responsible for a dramatic increase in autism and a host of other neurological disorders among children."[25] Further, Kennedy charged that the Food and Drug Administration was complicit with pharmaceutical companies in covering up this disaster. If correct, this would be a sensational item with huge impact not only for thousands of families but also for federal policy.

Ms. Beyerstein wrote two long posts on this issue. She is a liberal blogger who would normally agree with someone like RFK Jr., but she also appreciates the truth.[26] She made the case that the great weight of scientific and medical evidence held that there was no association between thimerosal and increased rates of autism. It was fascinating, well-written stuff and, again, as far as my students and I can tell, all factual.

Nonmediafit Experts Who Blog

There are other experts who indeed possess the résumé of expertise but who just do not happen to be in the golden Rolodex for one reason or another, including that they are not *mediafit*; that is, their look, sound, manner, or ways of delivering information "don't fit the need of today's journalism." That last description is an actual quote from a cable news producer who was reacting to a foreign policy expert who had appeared on his program. The producer lamented, "He just didn't know how to speak in bursts"—that is, sound bites, the pithy seven-second ripostes that pass for debate on television. The expert in question was also—and this really made him untelevisual—not confrontational. So, when facing an aggressive think tank attack dog, he came off as diffident and, well, wimpy. Unfortunately, good analysis is hard to compact into seven seconds for broadcast or in a ten-word quote for the papers. In my case, when a print reporter arranges an interview with me on a given topic or when I am scheduled to appear on a news program, I must prepare several hours to be "spontaneous" with my sound bites of choice.

There are thousands of authentic experts on many news topics who go uncalled, untapped, and unheard (apart from their peers in academe or government bureaus). Hence, for the purposes of debating or illuminating political and public affairs, they are unavailable. One example in the bloglands is John Burgess, a retired State Department foreign service officer who edits the blog CrossRoadsArabia specializing in the kingdom of Saudi Arabia. So when, in late July 2005, King Fahd of Saudi Arabia died, I clicked Burgess's blog first. He was my wisebot: a compiler and collator of news about the event and its effects on the Western and Muslim worlds. In post after post, he offered background about the king, his successors, Saudi policymaking, and many other interesting observations. He also deftly dissected the problems with many media accounts that were inaccurate in either facts or analysis. For example, he once posted on one of the most challenging problems in trying to understand the Middle East: the basic translation of Arabic.

Again, the blogger cannot only act like an expert, but he or she can verifiably be one. Before blogs, the ungolden ones had no channel through which to enter the marketplace to make their voices heard.

Burgess himself began blogging near the end of his diplomatic career because, as he describes,

> My thought was (and continues to be) that first-hand, on-the-ground reporting of just what an officer—usually a junior officer—was doing, day-to-day, would provide a more accurate and more compelling story of what was going right or wrong. Then I found that was a step too far in decentralizing authority. State, alas, remains one of the most hierarchical bureaucracies in the U.S. government. The thought of public dissemination of uncleared information, written by non-senior officers, led to apoplexy. And the death of the project.

Only retirement and blogging allowed him to revive his idea, to our gain. Again, before blogs, what recourse would a frustrated John Burgess have had: griping to fellow retirees, perhaps writing a little-read "look back in anger" book, or even starting a small-circulation newsletter? A blog became his outlet and our resource.

A crucial factor in the blogstyle of CrossRoadsArabia is that Burgess does not pontificate but rather discusses with us, his readers. He invites us to become *part* of his expertise, not to kneel at his feet. Television newsman Brian Williams once lamented that journalists—"professional ones"—had to compete "on an equal footing with someone in a bathroom with a modem."[27] But few good bloggers blog alone: They employ and deploy their blog readers. Again, beyond "producer" and "receiver" the term *interactor* seems to fit—to construct, not just announce, expertise on a subject. Blogging's interactivity allows the commenter to try, and often to succeed at, not just being a passive participant in expertise on a subject, event, or issue but to contribute to it: the promise and the ideal of the Howard Dean campaign. In helping accrete wisdom, we gain a stake in it and thus are much more likely to perceive that the resulting insight is indeed expertise.

Most big media, with the exception of call-in talk shows, allow no such interactions. In the mainstream, the mediafit expert speaks, writes, or interacts with other mediafit experts, and we are witnesses. Their expertise, thus, is static: We can accept or reject it, but we cannot *build on it*. Blogs, on the other hand, can redefine who is an expert on politics or any other area, and over time, we can judge for ourselves whether we wish to join with the bloggers in creating an expertise of which we are part, to our own mutual enrichment or folly.

Blogger as Political Watchdog

Bloggers can serve as watchdogs over the actions of government and big media—and each other.

I have argued that we have had bloglike forms in human communication for quite some time; thus, too many news and information blogs read, as does Drudge, like reporters' notes before what was called "going to press." The relationship is a symbiotic one, not just of form but of function. "Journalism," famously spoke *Washington Post* publisher Philip Graham, is the "first draft of history"; blogs could be considered, as one researcher put it, the "first draft of journalism."[28] In some ways, blogs look and sound like rough drafts of what might be more polished news stories and columns.

Yet, part of the propaganda of commercial media is that they keep us in touch with, as one slogan goes, "the news you need"; one network program even promises, "Give us twenty-three minutes and we'll give you the world." But the world we tend to see in mainstream media is narrow, selective, episodic, and torn from context. I illustrate this fact by asking my students to name more than two wars going on in the world today. Most can cite conflicts in Iraq and Afghanistan. But in fact, there are about forty wars raging in various parts of the planet. Some objectively are huge news stories—1 million dead in the Sudan, 3.3 million killed in the Congo—but they receive scant or spotty attention, while others are given saturation coverage. Why? The reasons are complex,[29] but the result is that the herd follows itself. If Iraq is the big story, then all the lenses go to Iraq, Congo be damned. Meanwhile, the U.S. mainstream media herd diverts into issues that we would all agree are quite trivial in the scope of the economy or world peace—the Michael Jackson trial, the disposition of Anna Nicole Smith's corpse, or the jail conditions for Paris Hilton, for example.

The blowback for such inattention can be fatal on a grand scale. On August 24, 2001, I wrote an editorial printed on the MSNBC Web site about the then wall-to-wall coverage of the missing intern from then California Congressman Gary Condit's office, Chandra Levy.[30] I pointed out that a Nielsen-estimated 24 million Americans had watched Connie Chung's interview with Condit. I contrasted this immensity of news coverage with the fact that, according to United Nations reports, up to 60 million female children are "missing"—that is, presumed killed by parents who don't want daughters. I wondered if we couldn't find some way to escape from the spiral of silliness, triviality, and celebrity sensation that had become the news business or at least instill a sense of relativity. A few weeks later, on September 11, 2001, we were all reminded that important events and issues occurring in distant lands can explode in our backyard (or downtown) if we ignore them. Who can cheerlead for such a system of selecting "what is news"? Who will mourn its passing? Again, blogs may not be the answer, but the mainstream media are the problem, and the many good, conscientious, honest reporters trapped within the system know it.

Then there is the issue of accuracy. Time and again, my students and I have found the proverbial "first draft of history" to be riddled with errors. In a number of studies we have conducted of the Tiananmen events of 1989, for example, we found that almost *all* initial news stories, as reported by the major networks from the field, proved later to be factually incorrect. If anything, the Web has exacerbated the tendency of traditional journalists to first publish and *then* verify.

In my own case, while writing this book, my life and everyone else's in southern Louisiana (then my residence) was disrupted by hurricanes Katrina and Rita. I was without electricity at home and so was not witness to the first live media reports from New Orleans. But unsurprisingly, within a month afterward, my students and I, colleagues around the country, and journalistic critique groups like seconddraft. org found that nearly every single major report and fact offered to the American public for the first week after Hurricane Katrina was later proved outright false, contextually misleading, or wholly exaggerated. In other words, although there are many journalists who try hard and are successful in reporting the truth as they see it, journalism as a craft is in deep trouble in perception and in reality.

If big media are not giving us the complete story or are getting the facts wrong too often, then blogs can serve another important function in the political-media system: watchdogs of all the powers that be, including the press itself and, of course, other blogs.[31] They can raise a hue and cry over questionable actions and utterances by government or big media or any powers that might otherwise seem immune to constructive criticism.

Case Study: City Planning via Blog

Government, it is said, is run by the people who show up to vote or to the city council meeting. But most of us do not really pay attention to what government is doing until it immediately impacts our lives, unless good journalists call attention to issues that should concern us, whether down the street or halfway around the world. It is a stereotype that blogs, bloggers, and blogging are obsessed with high-profile issues such as war and peace, abortion, media bias, and so on. There are many other bloggers who focus on issues of practical and local importance. Consider Bill Callahan of Cleveland, who blogs Callahan's Cleveland Diary (first at cleveland_diary.blogspot.com then http://www.callahansclevelanddiary.com/). Many of his posts concern city politics and city planning issues. A lot of his content is clearly written and wittily observed, but you won't see it being argued about on *The O'Reilly Factor* or getting top billing on CNN's *The Situation Room*. But the items and Callahan's analysis are important to people where he lives. In other words, the *Diary* deals with "hard news" and nonherd journalism, where "undiscussed issues" are scrutinized. Take one unsensational 2005 item about abandoning neighborhood retail strips:

> One of the many undiscussed issues surrounding the Steelyard Commons project is the shift it signals in City Hall's neighborhood commercial development policy. In hitching its policy to a megabox "power center" featuring a Wal-Mart SuperCenter, the Campbell Administration is abandoning a twenty-year strategic commitment to neighborhood retail strips – nodes of small and mid-sized stores serving households within a mile or two.

This **caught Tuesday by Jeff Hess**, makes the whole thing pretty clear. SYC is a "regional power center serving an untapped trade area with no competition . . . This development will create a new regional trade area in a previously underserved and impenetrable market."

What's this "untapped trade area with no competition" . . . this "impenetrable market"? For the answer, take a look at this city neighborhood map [not shown] with a three-mile circle drawn around SYC, represented, naturally, by a frownie-face.

You can see that this circle includes all or most of nine neighborhoods (not counting downtown and the Industrial Valley). Each of these neighborhoods (Old Brooklyn, Brooklyn Centre, Stockyards, Detroit-Shoreway, Ohio City, Clark-Fulton, Central, North Broadway and South Broadway) has its own community development corporation, or shares a CDC with the area next door. Each of these CDCs has a longstanding commercial development program focussed on preserving and expanding local shopping opportunities in one or more retail nodes. In most of these programs, neighborhood food markets – i.e. small to mid-sized supermarkets – play an essential role as local amenities and anchors for other local shopping.

The little colored squares on the map are those food markets. Blue squares are Dave's Supermarkets, green squares are Tops Markets, brown squares are independents. The orange square in Ohio City is the West Side Market. I haven't included discount groceries like Aldi's, but Brooklyn Centre, Detroit-Shoreway and Broadway have those, as well. The square with the "x" in Clark-Fulton is the recently closed Tops on Clark Avenue – which would be the subject of a neighborhood crusade right now, if it wasn't for the Wal-Mart SuperCenter looming just over the hill. Where you see a colored square, there is almost certainly a larger "local retail" node that's been nursed, marketed and invested in – by the local CDC, by the City, by the foundations through Neighborhood Progress – for ten, fifteen or even twenty years.

The business plan of Steelyard Commons is to pull lots of the local customers away from neighborhood retail nodes, effectively wiping them out. That's not scare talk . . . it's a simple statement of obvious fact. SYC's big anchor is Wal-Mart, and Wal-Mart wouldn't play unless it could sell food. The principal market area for a SuperCenter is generally described as two miles around for food, and five miles around for other goods (that's why so many small cities are seeing one built at each end of town). Who are the "untapped, impenetrable" customers for Wal-Mart in that magic circle? They're the people now shopping at Dave's, the Bi-Rite on Fulton, Gillombardo's Tops on Broadway – the local shoppers who make those local retail strips sustainable.

By supporting – pushing, celebrating – this SYC/Wal-Mart business plan, the Campbell Administration is abandoning the City's twenty-year commitment to food-anchored neighborhood shopping districts in these and (eventually) other neighborhoods. The Mayor will hotly deny this, of course, but there's really no other rational interpretation that fits the facts.

The circle on the map is a retail blast zone, and City Hall is escorting Wal-Mart to the launch button.

Why is this not a fighting issue for even one of Campbell's opponents? There you have the great mystery of this election year.

In style and substance, the post is blogging at its best: detailed, well-researched, full of facts, adding value beyond what exists within the discourse of regular media and political speech, and *richly local* as well as analytical. It is also good watch-blogging, a blogger discoursing on stories people should know.

So, certainly, *all political blogging is global* in the technical sense: What is posted on an Iowa blog need not stay in Iowa; it is available to interested Internet-connected parties in Beijing and Timbuktu. Of course, macaca moments will comprise some items of local vlogging gone big. The common coin of such a global town meeting has tended to be big-ticket blogthroughs. Taking on the New Hampshire primary and Supreme Court nominations has compelled many people to blog and has brought blogging substantial media attention. But a healthy ongoing trend is that more and more blogs are local; they deal with the potholes, the city council races, and the school bond measures. And local blogs can just as well build associations nationally: Colorado Confidential is a megablog that focuses on state issues in partnership with local journalists. Its model has been so successful that it spawned similar enterprises in Minnesota and Iowa. In the long run, such blogs will provide more lasting information of value than will endless debates in the bloglands about the sexier national issues.

Case Study: Blogswarming Virginia State House Bill No. 1677

In December 2005, William Cosgrove, a Republican member of the State House of Representatives in Virginia, introduced House Bill No. 1677, which, as originally written, was "relating to reports of fetal deaths." Among its provisions was that

> when a fetal death occurs without medical attendance upon the woman [mother] at or after the delivery or abortion or when inquiry or investigation by a medical examiner is required, the medical examiner shall investigate the cause of fetal death and shall complete and sign the medical certification portion of the fetal death report within 24 hours after being notified of a fetal death.[32]

The bill was evidently an attempt to have the legislature officially recognize—and a woman facing an abortion confront—the fact that an abortion resulted in the death of a fetus, a basic argument of the anti-abortion, or pro-life, movement. Such a bill would in itself be controversial, but a further issue was that the penalty for failing to comply with the law would have been a "Class 1 misdemeanor."

First to take note of the bill was the group blog Democracy for Virginia, which features a "legislative sentry email list." Blogger Maura in Virginia—Maura Kearney, a former Howard Dean activist (of DemocracyforAmerica)—offered a major analytical (and incensed) post on the story. In response, more than *100* blogs, with trackbacks and quotes and hat tips in the thousands, picked up the story. Maura's post was also featured on DailyKos. DemocracyforVirginia received about 70,000 hits in twenty-four hours. Left-blog headlines sum up their attitudes toward the proposed legislation and its outcomes:

BitchPhd: "Miscarry? That's a crime."

Pharyngula: "Virginia is for hateful loons."

Apostropher: "All Your Baby are Belong [*sic*] to Us"

Pharyngula: "Another brilliant piece of medieval legislation."

Echonyc: " . . . if you're as angry about this as I am, please take the suggestions Maura gives at the end of the article."

At least *500* people wrote Representative Cosgrove e-mails about the bill, and almost all were negative.[33] Notably, Maura's post was also picked up by Web sites devoted to pregnancy, fertility, and midwife concerns.

Cosgrove felt the heat. He e-mailed Maura who, to her great credit as an honest citizen and blogger, published the e-mail he sent her explaining that the original intent of the legislation "was indeed not to criminalize miscarriage but attack the problem of abandoned or 'trashcan' babies . . . full term babies who were abandoned shortly after birth." He added, "However, after discussing the bill again with our legislative services lawyers, I have decided to include language that will define the bill to apply only to those babies that are claimed to have been stillborn and that are abandoned as stated above."[34] Maura responded,

> For now, Delegate Cosgrove, if you're reading, the most important thing I want to say is thank you for listening to the concerns of so many people, even those who expressed their concern angrily or even abusively. I am heartened to hear that you plan [to] narrow the scope of HB1677 to more closely fit your stated intent.

The exchange and the blog link became nationally famous when Cosgrove was invited on *Nightline* to talk about the bill and the blogswarm. He eventually agreed to withdraw the bill altogether, and it was withdrawn by unanimous vote of the committee in charge. The *Virginian-Pilot* of Norfolk commented that "it was a tough introduction for the Republican to the brave new world of Internet 'blogs.'"[35] Dave Addis, a columnist for the paper, noted that the affair "created a beautiful illustration of how the 'old media' and the 'new media' can combine to give fits and headaches to the old guard who rule us."[36]

And they should. Blogs, right or left, serving as watchdogs can help us, whatever our opinions or passions, engage in that most important political behavior, speaking to government about its proposals to rule us. Think about that classic Norman Rockwell painting of the ordinary man getting up to speak at a New England town meeting. In his pocket is a piece of proposed local legislation (that we assume he and everyone else in the room have actually read). His fellow citizens (including, no doubt, the mayor and the town council) await his opinion. Maybe he will end up on the losing side of a vote, but at least the local powers-that-be got to hear him. Rockwell created the icon to illustrate one of Franklin Roosevelt's "Four Freedoms," in this case, speech. But we cannot "speak" effectively to government if, as is often the case, we have no idea what it is up to. Once upon a time, in the small villages, we could engage in face-to-face interaction with our legislators. In my own town, the former mayor and current city commissioner owns a barbershop where, if I wanted to, I could get a trim and discuss the public parks budget. Many Americans, however, do not have such an option. Most rely on somebody else, the press or now bloggers, to keep informed on what the powers that be are concocting. We are all better served the more seriously big and small media take the role of political watchdog, locally, nationally, and globally.

Blogger as Political Educator

I argued in the first chapter that although many blogs performed their political education function by factional partisanship, there were others that took a moderate approach. Some blogs add value to the political experience. Gregg Birnbaum, political editor of the *New York Post*, made his independent JustHillary a one-click stop for Hillary Clinton information. There is also Watchblog, which describes itself as "a multiple-editor weblog broken up into three major political affiliations, each with its own blog: the Democrats, the Republicans and the Third Party (covering everything outside the two major parties)." The creators of the blog explain, "Let's face it, politics is confusing. Sometimes it's difficult to know who to believe, who to listen to and who to support. We're here to help. Posting on a regular basis are editors representing each major party. Stay informed." Each of the two major parties and the third party are accorded their own section within the blog. Watchblog is a wonderful teaching tool that I use because of its compare-and-contrast format, a true shared market of ideas.

In the future, there will be more blogs that serve as political educators and more big media coverage of that function. But one of the immediate political education services that blogs can perform is to speak to their own readers about the realities of politics and political communication. People who pay attention only to blogposts that are on the attack fail to note all the blogposts that contain internal political critiques—that is, political education.

One ongoing case study is the antiwar movement. Right now, blogs are playing a critical role in the battle to define not only the war in Iraq but the political and symbolic struggle over the war at home. It is very easy to be simplistic about this and say that the sides fall into

- Right-wing, conservative Republican, or promilitary bloggers who believe and find evidence that the mainstream press is negatively distorting the war in Iraq, stressing failures, casualties, terrorist attacks, and so on, and ignoring the overall good news of the defeats of genocidal tyranny, material reconstruction, the lack of violence in many areas of Iraq, and the building of democracy.
- Left bloggers who believe that the mainstream media failed to sufficiently watchdog the administration's buildup of rationalizations and reasons for invading Iraq in the first place and that right bloggers who support the war are perpetuating a disaster out of motivations that include racism, militarism, patriotic arrogance, and refusal to admit that Iraq is a quagmire.

Neither of the characterizations offered above operate in the real blog-lands cleanly and neatly. There are conservative bloggers who oppose the war and excoriate Bush and liberal bloggers who support the war and question the motives of the war's opponents.

In particular, the role of bloggers as political educators is apparent not only in antiwar blogs attacking the right and right blogs attacking the antiwar left but in a critical conversation going on *within* left blogs themselves. Here it is worth reviewing some basic research on antiwar movements of the past. As I have noted in some other writings, during the 1960s and early 1970s, a large majority of the public, when surveyed, reacted negatively to anti–Vietnam War protesters.[37] At the same time, an increasing number of Americans registered antiwar sentiments them-selves while the war was fought, ranging from the hawkish "we should go all out to win" to the dovish "we should make peace at any price." The theatrical (and media-attracting) tactics of antiwar protesters who were on the streets surely influenced their public image. As opinion researcher John Mueller noted, "[O]pposition to the war in Vietnam came to be associated with rioting, disruption, and bomb throwing, and war pro-testors, as a group, enjoyed negative popularity ratings to an almost unparalleled degree."[38] Similarly, political scientist George Herring argued, "Public opinion polls make abundantly clear . . . that a majority of Americans found the anti-war movement, particularly its radical and 'hippie' elements, more obnoxious than the war itself."[39] After the 1968 protests at the Democratic National Convention, opinion polls saw over 80 percent of Americans siding with the police against the (beaten-up) demonstrators.

As of 2005–2007, a similar process was occurring in relation to protests against the Iraq war. In fact, as I type these words, it is interesting to note that the majority of the American public is antiwar (although not in favor of an immediate pullout) but that an antiwar movement seems visible only on blogs and other kinds of Web sites. Most Americans, whatever their moral or political stance, will not rally 'round the flag of war protest if it is partially occluded by banners proclaiming "Free Mumia," "Anarchy Now," "9/11 Was an Inside Job," and "Castrate Cheney" held by outlandishly dressed (or undressed) protesters. Proving that all blogging is global, the picture-blog Zombietime[40] specializes in posting photographs taken at antiwar and anti-Bush protests, mainly in the San Francisco area. Images of men and women parading as skeletons, as suicide bombers, bare breasted or in drag, and sporting signs such as "Queers for Palestine," "I Love NY Even More Without the World Trade Center," "Death to America," and "George Bush Is the Anti-Christ: Embrace Love Now" find gleeful reposting or hyperlinking throughout the conservative bloglands. Perhaps once upon a time, a group of naked old people marching in San Francisco in support of "breasts, not bombs" would have attracted little or no press attention except locally. (This particular demonstration was indeed covered only in the alternative left press of San Francisco.) Among right blogs, however, these images are repeated, discussed, and referred to as decisive visual evidence of, as one right blogger put it, "the freaks and kooks" that make up the antiwar movement.

Many on the left recognize the problem. They worry that their antiwar message—which is essentially "support the troops by not killing them in an illegal, unneeded, and hopeless war"—is being diluted, hijacked, trivialized, obscured, or just plain shouted out by the wrong messengers. Consequently, within the left bloglands are serious discussions about what an antiwar movement should say and not say, do and not do, and look like and not look like. A sober example of such political education via blog is offered by Erin Rosa (EmRosa), a writer for alternative magazines and a blogger who also posts on DailyKos. Her "Do's and Dont's for Anti-War Rally" post was a classic piece of candid, reflective, and realistic strategizing. Among her advice to her comrades-against-arms:

> Don't have a hippy drum circle:
>
> There are few things more annoying and irrelevant than a bunch of dreadlocked Boulderites banging on drums while dancing around with erect nipples under their hemp shirts.
>
> Don't have a gothic pagan chorus on the stage talking about mermaids:
>
> This actually happened at the last November 3rd movement rally. It has nothing to do with the overall point of the protest. Rather it is just an opportunity for superficial hipsters to whine about "mother earth". They then leave to go get coffee and don't stay for the rally.
>
> Don't talk about gay rights or other issues that have little to do with the Iraqi invasion:
>
> Believe it our not, all of the protesters do not see eye to eye. Although Palestine and gay rights are very important issues (and yes, I do realize that there are parallels between imperialism with Palestine and Iraq) that does not mean we should have speakers that talk for 30 minutes on the subjects. It is sloppy and off message to the united coalition of organizations and individuals against the Iraq war to talk about different issues that they may not agree with. Stay with a poignant message and prosper.

And so on. As one might imagine, the comments in reaction to the various postings and pickups of EmRosa's manifesto were numerous and often heated, but they did start an important conversation. Again, EmRosa's "cred" on such matters is significant: She was not some political scientist lecturing antiwarriors or a conservative columnist ridiculing them. She was one of them ("I've been to too many Denver anti-war protests to keep my mouth shut"), and no one could deny that she was speaking from the heart ("I'm not trying to be holier than thou, or say that I know all the answers. . . . But I just can't take it anymore"). In short, she was a blogger, she was personally involved in the issue, she was practical, and she was educational. Right and left blogging needs such agents of internal self-scrutiny and debate; they advance democracy, whatever their political colors. And the conversation continues, as it should.

EmRosa thus joins her virtual peers, from John Burgess to Eriposte to Bill Callahan, in not being inside players (or not anymore, in Burgess's case) in government and politics. But their digging, sorting, and thinking help us learn more about our political world.

Blogs as Wisebots of Politics and Policy

Over the years of teaching media analysis, I have found that students tend to resist "stopping" media. They don't like it when I freeze a frame of film to examine its mise-en-scène (the arrangement of its visual elements) or factually verify and stylistically critique the text of a news story word by word. I understand their unease. Our modern mediated world—a unique and recent development of our species—presents a superlatively dense visual environment, such as the magazine page, the neon-lit city street with billboards, and the television screen. Moreover, there has been a progression toward greater and greater visual density and complexity. A modern, modular Bloomberg news screen, for example, contains as many as seven layers of pictures within pictures, streamies, charts, graphs, and banners, some of them in constant motion and all updated quickly. An MTV video is a riot of cuts and action compared to a John Ford film of the 1940s. Such data stuffing, hyperactivity, high kinetic content, and quicker pacing decrease the possibility of quick comprehension. (Watch *Casablanca* followed by *Bad Boys II* to appreciate the difference in movie pacing then and now.) Everything is *Faster*,[41] as James Gleick summed up in his book, and thus comprises an information-glutted "data smog," as David Shenk put it.[42] The computer screen showing an Internet page might also contain innumerable banners, pop-ups, hyperlinks, pictures, text boxes, and so on; all of us have at some point been lost in click-through hell, unsure in cyberspace where we are, were, or want to be. Those who hope to reach audiences with particular pictures or messages face vast clutter composed of other people's competing, screeching, and blinking items and messages.

Yet, the evidence from research on the mind-brain suggests that our cognitive skills adapt out of cognitive education; that is, if your brain is raised on MTV, fast cuts and jerky cameras make much more sense than if you were raised reading Victorian fiction and watching opera.*

---

* I was amused recently by the complaint of a local comic book store owner that "kids today" do not have the attention span to read his merchandise!

But I think tech optimists like Stephen Johnson are plain wrong when they claim that the faster processing skills of kinetic-media watchers, our children, make them smarter and thus potentially wiser. From the prejudice of someone who tries to teach those same young people to observe media *critically*, I find that our and their instinct is just to go along for the ride. We want the Michael Bay action movie, the episode of *Entourage,* the Xbox game of Halo 2, and even the evening news to flow: Close visual and textual analyses are unnatural. Nor do I see any evidence in the psychological research on attention or in the classroom that simply being able to multitask means we become better at doing each of those tasks well.

Bloggers, however, for politics as well as for other topics, offer an alternative, something very subversive in the roller-coaster media culture: They freeze-frame media content and scrutinize it closely. Take the editor of rantingprofs.com, Dr. Cori Dauber, an associate professor of communication studies (and of peace, war, and defense) at the University of North Carolina at Chapel Hill. Her area of scholarship is the way the media represent war and the military. Here is her analysis of the coverage of some fighting in Afghanistan by the *New York Times.* It is worth repeating in full because its copiousness demonstrates that blogging does not just have to be short bursts of chewing:

More Fun with Headlines

An opening paragraph can certainly serve to frame a story, but the headline is critical; it is the combination of the two that matters.

Let me give you an example from the front page (above the fold) of today's New York Times. (No peeking, don't look at your paper, don't go to the web site, for now just look at the pull quote here.)

The story begins:

GAZEK KULA, Afghanistan - *For weeks, sightings of Taliban fighters were being reported all over the rugged mountains here. But when Staff Sgt. Patrick Brannan and his team of scouts drove into a nearby village to investigate a complaint of a beating, they had no idea that they were stumbling into the biggest battle of their lives.*

On May 3, joined by 10 local policemen and an interpreter, the scouts turned up at a kind of Taliban convention - of some 60 to 80 fighters - and were greeted by rockets and gunfire. The sergeant called for reinforcements and was told to keep the Taliban engaged until they arrived. "I've only got six men," he remembers saying.

For the next two and a half hours, he and his small squad, who had a year of experience in Iraq, cut off a Taliban escape. Nearly 40 Taliban and one Afghan policeman were killed. "It's not supposed to be like that here," said Capt. Mike Adamski, a battalion intelligence officer. "It's the hardest fight I saw, even after Iraq."

Wow.

Damn.

I mean, really.

A squad of only *6 men* held off perhaps as many as 80. Didn't just hold them off either, but killed 40. With the help of only 10 Afghan police (that's police, not Army.)

I'd say that's a pretty spectacular good news story. Almost writes its own headline, doesn't it?

You betcha.

"<u>Despite Years of US Pressure, Taliban Fight on in Jagged Hills</u>"

Sigh.

Well, here's the argument:

During the last six months, American and Afghan officials have predicted the collapse of the Taliban, the hard-line Islamists thrown out of power by American forces in 2001, citing their failure to disrupt the presidential election last October and a lack of activity last winter.

Aah, <u>the old spring thaw theory</u>.

But, there's still fighting in this neck of the woods, she says, 100 square miles of valleys, proving they're still vibrant and financed.

The May 3 battle was part of an almost forgotten war in the most remote corners of Afghanistan, a strange and dangerous campaign that is part cat-and-mouse game against Taliban forces and part public relations blitz to win over wary villagers still largely sympathetic to the Taliban.

That annoys me no end. Ms. Gall has been a full time stringer for the Times in Afghanistan at least since 2001, perhaps earlier (**her family has connections to <u>Afghanistan</u>**.) I'm sure she's unhappy that she can't get her work in the paper more often (not in a careerist sense, but in the sense that she no doubt cares about what's going on around her.) But her beef is with her editors and she should be sniping directly at them. As for the effort to win over the population of the country, it is a bit more, with stakes a bit higher, than a "pr" blitz, which is nothing more than a cheap shot.

Now, this is new and important:

An Afghan informer, who did not want his name used for fear of retribution, has told American forces that the Taliban ranks have been rapidly replenished by recruits who slipped in from Pakistan. For every one of the Taliban killed on May 3, judging by his account, another has arrived to take his place.

With a ready source of men, and apparently plentiful weapons, the Taliban may not be able to hold ground, but they can continue their insurgency indefinitely, attacking the fledgling Afghan government, scaring away aid groups and leaving the province ungovernable, some Afghan and American officials say.

But notice that it isn't directly a story about progress in Afghanistan – that's a story about trouble in Pakistan. Doesn't make the story less important, and doesn't it make it less relevant to progress in the war in Afghanistan, because she's right, it will impact progress of reconstruction and the stability of the government. **But if they're forced to import all their recruits from Pakistan, it suggests that we *are* making progress in the hearts and minds campaign in Afghanistan.** The problem is that Musharef isn't getting the job done in the Northwest area, and that he continues to alienate his population, not that our forces aren't getting the job done against the Taliban inside Afghanistan proper.

She continues:

Still, the former commander of United States forces in Afghanistan, Lt. Gen. David Barno, described the insurgency as in decline in an interview on April 26 and predicted that a government amnesty offer would fatally split the Taliban in coming months.

Having not teased out the implication of her "they just keep coming" quote, that looks like classic Pollyanna, but if you stop and think about it isn't crazy at all. But of course, that wasn't on the front page.

Here's something else that gets buried deep in the article:

*In April and May, **in a new push to flush out and end the insurgency, American forces began probing the final bastions of Taliban control** in this unforgiving landscape. **They have succeeded in provoking some of the heaviest combat in Afghanistan in the last three years,** killing more than 60 Taliban fighters in April and May, by one United States military estimate.* (My emph.)

Hey, that's not too important as context goes**. Why, in other words, is the fighting heavy now? Because *we're starting it*,** by stirring the hornet's nest to push this to a conclusion. **Yes, the fighting is heavy – but it's on *our* terms.** In that sense that little episode that starts the article is a bit atypical, apparently.

And, oh, speaking of that little episode, **look at what detail didn't make the front page**:

The Taliban fought to within 150 yards of American positions and later hit one of two armored Humvees with a volley of rocket-propelled grenades that set it on fire, Sergeant Brannan said. Specialist Joseph Leatham, in the turret, kept firing as the vehicle burned, allowing his comrades to get out alive.

By the way, **here's a question: the Taliban reinforcements are crossing over on short notice from Pakistan on incitement from their mullahs, without weapons, then given weapons somewhere in the area and put into the fight**.

Anybody know how well trained these guys are compared to the fighters who were lost? Anybody ask?

Meanwhile, it sounds as if the Taliban may have a hearts and minds problem of their own. While the Americans were in that village for awhile, the Taliban came for one night.

Twenty days ago there were 10 Taliban in this room," a former policeman, Abdul Matin, 40, told the Americans sitting on the floor over a glass of tea in his home.

They came in a group of 100, he said, and spread out around the village. They had satellite phones and plenty of money, offering one man $2,000 to work as an informer. They were gone before dawn and have not been back since, Mr. Matin said.

"The people support the Taliban because they don't loot and they respect the women," he said. But he added, "The whole district wants to help the Americans, because our country is destroyed."

So, yes indeed, they do keep fighting. Yes, indeed, they keep getting reinforcements from Pakistan, which means this fight could keep going for quite some time.

Having been through the entire article, does it strike you that that's the single most salient fact to pull out?

Posted on June 04, 2005 at 11:23 AM | **Permalink**

You may disagree with her, but at least she is *conducting* close, line-by-line analysis, which is something sorely missing from professional press "criticism." Much news, to take Bill Keller at his word, *needs* to be "chewed" on. And Dr. Dauber is, with humility, inviting others to respond, an expert freely opening her own expertise to open sourcing. Unless you are willing to accept everything you read, listen to, or see in the media at face value, then you should, whatever your ideological inclination, be reading media texts critically and thoroughly.

Bloggers can tell us how to do that. On December 1, 2005, the Associated Press released a news photo that it described as showing the following: "A protester watches a presidential helicopter fly overhead in Baltimore, Maryland." In the image, we see the back of the head of a protester who, presciently, has his sign facing the camera reading "STAY WHAT COURSE?" (we presume he means in Iraq) while looking up at a large helicopter that appears to be flying off. Although the caption does not specify, it does imply that President George W. Bush is in the helicopter. And the caption was employed to illustrate stories, like that displayed on CNN.com, headlined "POLL: MOST DOUBT BUSH HAS PLAN FOR IRAQ VICTORY." In metaphorical terms, Bush is "leaving" (Iraq?) in an uncertain direction. This is good photo symbolism; I would teach students in an advanced photo class to seek those kinds of shots.

But factual accuracy is a necessary precursor to great journalism of any kind. So I am gratified to see blogs engaging in pictorial skepticism.

An example from the right comes from Bob Owens, aka confederate-yankee (http://confederateyankee.mu.nu/), who noted in a post titled "Which President Were They Protesting?":

> I have a simple question for CNN and the Associated Press . . . president of what? The helicopter pictured above is a CH-46 Sea Knight, which doesn't even remotely look like the Sikorsky VH-3D flown by Marine Helicopter Squadron One and used to transport President Bush. . . . The helicopter in the CNN/AP photo has twin main rotors. Marine One, the helicopter used in presidential transport, has one main rotor, with a much smaller tail rotor.

Again, you can agree (or disagree), but whatever your opinion about the war, good reporting requires labeling something for what it actually is. Bloggers can help us assess the news if news organizations can't or won't.

In sum, we need blogs and bloggers out there, prowling around, in person or Web searching, coming back and telling us what they found, saw, or heard. Just like professors who learn that a good graduate assistant is worth her weight in research funding, anyone who seeks political information needs to find a squad of trustworthy, enterprising bloggers (preferably flying varying political flags) to consult. If you are feeling both overwhelmed and underinformed about the world, you have not found the best wisebots yet. Start looking; they are out there blogging.

5

"My Fellow Blogging Americans": Internal Political Roles of Bloggers

The final evolution of that feisty, raucous newcomer to the halls of power in political communication, public affairs, public opinion, and policymaking is for bloggers not only to report, investigate, and comment on politics but to *be* political players. The transition from blogger as curious outsider to that of powered insider, however, is not proceeding without growing pains and ethical recriminations. Further, if it is true that many of us are not *mediafit*—that is, speaking, writing, or looking like what is required to be political players on television or in print—it is also true that some politicians will find they cannot (or should not) become *blogfit*—that is, adapting to the style and content requirements of effective political blogging.

Certainly, the big bloggers can sound, if not like party bosses of yore, like people who feel their time to wield power has come, although they often express this sentiment with wry self-deprecation. Kos himself described his role in national politics in this fashion: "I wouldn't want to be a senator or congressman. I'm able to influence politics much more effectively doing what I do. Now I can shape the national political debate. The only way I could exert more influence would be if I were president. But I'd never want that guy's job. Never."[1] Such advances, however, are not achieved without blowbacks and battles. Kos and Jerome Armstrong are regularly called upon to give political advice. Sometimes they are paid; reportedly, though, Markos has not worked as a political consultant since the 2004 election. Both are, dare we say it, political professionals who also blog as well as bloggers who sometimes get paid for their wisdom about politics. For that they have been criticized both by other bloggers (mostly from the right) and by mainstream journalists and columnists. But the successful political blogger is rarely one to duck and cover from a fight. Markos Moulitsas blogged while Armstrong was being attacked for working as a consultant for possible 2008 Democratic presidential candidate Governor Mark Warner of Virginia:

> Just a quick reminder as the media nip at our heels—We didn't get here because of them. They can praise us, they can trash us, they can ignore us, and ultimately none of that will matter as long as we keep doing what we've been doing. Whether we succeed or not will depend on our own efforts. Not those of anyone else.[2]

Furthermore, they can claim, just as most political consultants do, that they only represent clients in whom they *believe*. No scandal there, just the birth pangs of a new industry.

What is more relevant, as Dr. James Joyner (outsidethebeltway. com) pointed out to me, is "transparency." As an example, in the 2004 South Dakota U.S. Senate race between Democrat Tom Daschle and Republican John Thune, two prominent conservative local blog authors who had attacked the former and the state's largest newspaper supporting him turned out to have been paid by the Thune campaign. The payouts were known to the Daschle campaign and the press, but were not well publicized until after the election itself.[3] One of the bloggers, then University of South Dakota history professor Jon Lauck, is reported to have received $27,000 for his efforts; the other, lawyer Jason van Beek, received $8,000. Although both had small audiences, a number of their postings were picked up in the media. In a November 5, 2004, article by Kathryn Jean Lopez, editor of the *National Review*, Lauck's blog is quoted as pointing to a Daschle flip-flop on abortion.[4] Similarly, on July 8, 2004, the neoconservative flagship journal the *Weekly Standard* reported that "local bloggers are going to make [Tom Daschle's] reelection fight tougher" and referred to a number of "great blogs covering the . . . Senate race—coverage that is necessary. . . ."[5] One of them is van Beek's blog. The effect of such so-called hitblogs cannot be measured in terms of public opinion, but Thune eventually won the election by only some 4,400 votes.*

The Thune blog issue—a blogola scandal according to some Democrats—has been dutifully reported in almost every source, including my own previous writings.[6] But over time, some complexities have emerged, as they always seem to do in any blog-related narrative involving politics.

First, although he did not mention it on his Web site, Lauck was working for Thune concurrently with teaching at the university.[7] Second, the payments became an issue only after Daschle lost and his campaign operatives brought it to wider attention. During the campaign, Daschle's communications advisers had consistently avoided raising the profile of the conservative blogs because they didn't want to drive more readers to their sites. (Such a dilemma is now common among campaigns attacked by bloggers and the outcome in South Dakota suggests that aggressive response, a rule in countering TV attack ads, should often be applied to a blog-snipering.)

Last, Lauck had been pro-Thune and anti-Daschle for many years, so he had established a track record for his beliefs. Lauck told me in an interview, "It's a very small state. . . . The notion that I was a 'secret' Thune supporter is ridiculous." It was clearly not a case of his being paid to think (and report) one way or another any more than Kos has or was. In addition, conservatives in South Dakota had long felt that the state's main newspapers—especially the Sioux Falls *Argus Leader*—were too liberal and too pro-Daschle. (Lauck is now working for Thune full time, an example of blogs serving as a ladder to professional political

---

* Blog subsidies are the subject of much mirth in the bloglands. The editor of Righting Wisconsin jokes with his readers (I think he is joking) by reciting a line from the movie *Miller's Crossing:* "If you want me to keep my mouth shut, it's gonna cost you some dough. I figure a thousand bucks is reasonable, so I want two."

work.) The Thune blogs and others then, as I discuss later, could be seen as analogues of Roosevelt's fireside chats: When one medium seems to have fallen short as a successful method of communication or persuasion, try another.

In terms of transparency, part of a blogger's code should be to state up front (via a visible disclaimer on her or his entry Web page) that he or she is receiving subsidies or funds from someone in particular. But to demand (or legislate) such a step from bloggers is unreasonable. Blogging is getting down to business, and it is still in the flux of developing codes of ethics, even debating within itself whether there should be codes of ethics besides those demanded of the marketplace. As one of my students, Mary Schoen, and I found when we researched blogger ethics codes in 2005, most did not have one, at least not one with stated principles.[8] Bloggers who reveal that another blogger has been subsidized are to be commended, but the bloggers receiving subsidies should not necessarily be unseated. If bloggers seek to be political kingmakers, they cannot do so from a position of poverty. They must, however, find some formula for transparently explaining to their readers why they took the king's shilling and why they support the king. As noted earlier, many mainstream experts and commentators are much more clearly in violation of the transparency ethic.

The key factor in blogger–reader relations is personal trust. My students one semester assessed twenty blogs by elected officials. Almost always, those they liked the most—that is, were interested in and appreciated reading—deftly integrated the roles of statesperson and intimate confidant. As one student put it, "I liked [one politician's] blog because he talked about issues of the day but he also got personal and gave us his way of seeing things, not just somebody from Washington mailing us information." Likewise, Senator Barack Obama's (D-Illinois) blog won the highest cross-party praise for its almost lyrical balance of erudition, thoughtfulness, and candor. Blogs that put my students off were too intimate, those that felt more like a diary or a solipsistic journey into minutiae, or blogs that were too third personlike. Reacting to one such blog, a student stated, "They call it a blog but they might as well just print his speeches on the Web." Of another, a student wrote, "Reads like it was written by staff." It is a considerable accomplishment to pull off a blog style and present blog content that both sounds heartfelt and also offers government policies that make sense. Moreover, the politician who blogs faces more than a few perils in taking on the latest new thing in personal mass political communication.

What Do Politicians Want? Searching for Mass Commilito

To repeat, from time immemorial, *successful mass political communication is that which best approximates successful personal communication.* The necessity of intimacy is not accidental but is rather the result of hardwiring. For millions of years, for small bands of hunter-gatherers, political persuasion was face to face: "I am the best hunter! I will give you more meat! I should lead the clan!" or "We must go south. The weather here is bad for the children's health." These were political decisions that circumscribed the life and death of a gene pool; bad leadership or poor cooperation spelled extinction. In that sense, there is no evidence in the archeological record of a "war of all against all." Rather, from the start, groups of humans cooperated with each other, although often for the purpose of fighting the neighbors. The smallest unit of humanity is the group, not the individual.

In historical ages, battle was recognized as the keenest test of human leadership and group solidarity. This is no contradiction that war, our species' most extreme form of physical violence (politics seems to subsume the most extreme form of *rhetorical* violence), is also the time of greatest bonding. It follows that, as sociologist Georg Simmel pointed out, in contradiction to those who saw conflict as antisocial, conflict can be an "integrative force in the group."[9] A body of people finding themselves in a situation of actual or perceived danger often bonds closer—the "circle-the-wagons" effect. The bond of the reference group is reinforced if all its members are "in the same boat" facing a common enemy.[10] In wartime, research has shown, soldiers are motivated to work, fight, kill, and even die not as much for patriotism or abstract motives as for loyalty to their immediate reference group of "buddies."[11] Indeed, the "comrades of the trenches" is a suitable visual metaphor for group solidarity in the face of external threat.[12] Groups in conflict will maximize the group-centric differences between the groups; therefore, events will be reinterpreted as justifying the virtue of the affiliated group and the villainy of the "other."[13] Such oppositions are mitigated by innumerable factors; however, it is equally obvious that in times of life-and-death struggles (e.g., war, rebellion, disaster) between groups, the "black-and-white" (or in America today, red vs. blue) distinctions will be the sharpest and bitterest.[14]

For would-be lords of war and men, how to build and maintain such fellowship under the strain of battle became a subject of great interest. The Romans, those great masons of stones and society, called *commilito* ("fellow soldiership") the bond that was inculcated among men facing death in war and also that forged with the charismatic war leader. A famous practitioner of the arts of superlative commilito was Trajan (r. 98–117), labeled by Edward Gibbon as one of the "five good emperors" of Rome. The administrator Pliny the Younger wrote in his *Panegyric* to his ruler, "It was your habit to inspect [the soldiers'] tents before you retired to your own; the last man must go off duty before you would take a rest yourself."[15] In short, Trajan was careful to make every legionary feel "special and cared for," in today's language of human resource management. (One of my students, a major in the U.S. Army, commented after I referred him to these passages: "That's what my men expect of me, too.") "Nothing escaped your direction or your observant eye. . . . You can call nearly all your soldiers by name, and know the deeds of bravery of each one, while they need not recount the wounds they received in their country's service, since you were there to witness and applaud," continued Pliny. The historian Dio Cassius recounts that the emperor personally expressed concern for wounded soldiers, gave medals to the brave, and spoke in the name of the fallen.[16] Again, in managerial speak, Trajan was "hands on," "visionary," and possessed that magical "personal touch."

Still today, in war, business, politics, and practically every realm of human endeavor, we tend to judge our leaders by the standards of the caves and the legions. Studies of leadership within armies, businesses, and politics argue that one vital quality possessed by superior leaders is their ability to establish a personal connection with subordinates, even if they do so via a medium of some kind. Hence, as legendary Democratic political consultant Ray Strother affirmed, "In any campaign the most important message is the candidate." Accordingly, the politicians we deem great communicators (or great emoters) seem to have mastered the art of transforming mass communication into interpersonal communication. The most sought-after praise by viewers of a televised speech is, for example, "I felt as if he were talking to me personally" or "I felt she was concerned about my problems" or "I felt I could trust him to look out for me." Political consultants stay up nights searching for ways to build up such impressions about their clients. The goal of the thirty-second political ad is not to expound in detail or complication about any particular issue but, through a medley of sounds, images, associations, metaphors, and above all key words and images, to help define the candidate as someone who "shares the viewers' own concerns about issues and feelings and aspirations."[17]

Blogs would seem to be the perfect venue or medium through which politicians could achieve commilito with voters or constituents or at least with political bloggers. Writing in the first person, employing personal pronouns, describing eyewitnessed events but also commenting on issues, events, and ideas of the day—those are the essence of blogging. Again, in survey after survey of my students, I have found that the blogs they consult most frequently for serious political information are those they found credible and creditable: They "like the blogger," "trust him or her," and "really connect with her or his outlook." What I discovered when I probed such responses was that merely agreeing with the partisanship of a political blog was not enough. Yes, students who described themselves as liberal Democrats found more to please the eye and ear at DailyKos and Pacific Views than at Oxblog and Redstate. Considering the blog informative, entertaining, or both was important, as was the fact that the blogger advocated positions they held strongly and even attacked heartily enemies of those positions. But to select and describe a "favorite," a "go-to" political blog, my students used the language of intimacy, not policy analysis.

As one conservative sophomore put it, "I love Atlas Shrugs [the blog] because she [editor Pamela] likes the same people and things I like, hates [the same] people and things I hate. We agree on most issues, she is funny, and well, I like [her] a lot." The interactive element is key because at its core blogging is both a monologue and a conversation. Students who posted comments on blogs rated highest those blogs in which the blog editor responded not necessarily in the affirmative but with respect and with attentiveness. As another student described a blogger's rapid and extensive responses to her comments: "She wants to hear me; she doesn't have some sort of computer [-generated] 'Thank you for writing' message; she really thinks about what commenters post up." Of course, the blog editor need not be the only one providing such intimacy; one can thread with other commenters. Another student declared, "Eileen of Inthepinktexas is fun to read but she attracts a really [witty] group too—I like to dive into it with them in comments."

How can a *politician* create such connections? Is virtual commilito possible? Can we duplicate the firesides and battle camps via an impersonal electronic box? It turns out that this question has been asked—and answered in the affirmative—in the previous century, the era of mass electronic media, for as we have noted, radio and television were new media at one time. Before we examine how today's political professionals use blogs in their quest for mass commilito, it is worth reviewing how it was accomplished by their predecessors.

Case 1: FDR as Radio Blogger

Most political consultants concur that the great paradox of contemporary political communication is that we still judge political candidates by their ability to project a personal connection but have only impersonal technology available to do so.[18] One major example of a successful strategy to convert mass communication into interpersonal communication, straddling the high–low divide, and finding channels of unfiltered media exposition was enacted by the nation's first "mass media" president, Franklin Delano Roosevelt. In early 1933, shortly after taking office, he faced a largely hostile press environment. A majority of newspaper publishers opposed, editorially at least, the new president and the New Deal.[19] The administration's solution was brilliant: to use a new medium exploding in popularity, radio, to bypass traditional media and directly persuade the American people to support Roosevelt and his polices.[20] During a March 13 broadcast, the president began a series of fireside chats with the nation. His opening words were simple and clear, employing that personal touch heretofore restricted to the speech hall or the campground,

> I want to talk for a few minutes with the people of the United States about banking—with the comparatively few who understand the mechanics of banking but more particularly with the overwhelming majority who use banks for the making of deposits and the drawing of checks. I want to tell you what has been done in the last few days, why it was done, and what the next steps are going to be.[21]

"I want to tell you" was the secret of interpersonal interaction with Roosevelt's audience.

Indeed, talented in style, voice, and manner, Roosevelt's renowned charms were well suited for the airwaves, as even his worst enemies had to admit.* *Barron's* magazine, no friend of the New Deal, described the first chat as suffused "with a technique that would have made the best 'announcers' tear their hair in impotent envy. If there be any 'voice' better upon the air than that of the President, it has not yet been heard."[22] An antagonistic but awed political columnist wrote, "If the President's addresses were delivered in the Czechoslovakian tongue they would be listened to with pleasure. He could recite the Polish alphabet and it would be accepted as an eloquent plea for disarmament."[23] Another commentator praised FDR's "ability to create a feeling of intimacy between himself and his listeners, his skill in placing emphasis on key words, [and] his adroitness in presenting complicated matters in simple terms that the man on the street could understand."[24] Several speech scholars of the time asserted that "the cues in Franklin D. Roosevelt's voice—the voice alone—inspired confidence."[25] Ordinary

---

*From the president's cadre of left critics, the anticonscription folk minstrels The Almanac Singers lamented in a song, "Franklin Roosevelt told the people how he felt and we damn near believed what he said."

listeners, when asked, tended to agree: "The calm tone of the address in the face of great world emotion, as well as the logic of the speech, were truly remarkable."[26] Among Roosevelt's techniques was that while he remained presidential he was not patronizing, and he freely used idioms of mass and folk culture.[27] FDR thwarted his enemies by being mediafit with a new method of communication.

Case 2: Eisenhower Answers America

Radio did not die as a political tool after Roosevelt. Today, drive-time radio ads are still part of many (mostly local) political campaigns, talk radio remains a powerful force in political discourse, and George W. Bush gives radio addresses. But a few years after Roosevelt's death, another medium arrived that seemed to offer more possibilities for establishing the personal connections that politicians sought while at the same time reaching huge audiences. Roosevelt, after all, used words to create intimacy, trust, and personal connection. People knew what he looked like—although not from the waist down, an illustration of that previous era of political-media gentlemen's agreements when reporters refrained from mentioning that the president was confined to a wheelchair. But what would happen when politicians could reach into our homes via a mass medium that was seen as well as heard?

It was Dwight D. Eisenhower who inaugurated the new age of the personalization of mass political communication when he became the first presidential candidate to hire an advertising agency, BBD&O, to produce a television commercial. The results included the famous "You like Ike! I like Ike! Everybody likes Ike!" musical animation. But the ad that probably most typified the televisual approach to leader–public interaction was "Eisenhower Answers America," in which the candidate seems to engage in a question-and-answer session with various ordinary citizens. Actually, this was an illusion of editing: Eisenhower and the questioners were filmed separately.[28] In response, Democratic presidential candidate Adlai Stevenson launched the first attack on political ads, which would serve as the medium's common critique to this day. He ridiculed the "high-powered hucksters of Madison Avenue" for selling Eisenhower "in precisely the way they sell soup, ammoniated toothpaste, hair tonic, or bubble gum."[29] (Nevertheless, the Stevenson camp eventually bought television airtime for their candidate's speeches.)

Notably, Eisenhower was not mediafit for television, and he did not relish engaging the media. He once commented to reporters at the start of a press conference: "I will mount the usual weekly cross and let you drive the nails."[30] His homey manner and banality-prone speech caused him to be less than eloquent, even while he was a convincing president.[31] But Eisenhower, the supreme allied commander during World War II, was credible; people believed he said what he meant and meant what he said. As one historian described, "The one quality that most distinguished Eisenhower's speaking was sincerity. It was a personal quality that said as much about the man as the subject matter, a quality that would manifest itself throughout his career."[32] For presidents of the Depression, war, and postwar eras, possessing individual qualities that made listeners or viewers feel a personal connection was as important as using different venues to bypass the mainstream press. Commilito by television worked if the man *looked, sounded,* and *felt* like he was up to the job.

Case 3: JFK's Press Conference Bypass

John F. Kennedy became known as the "first television president" (although Franklin Roosevelt was the first chief executive to appear on television at the 1939 New York World's Fair, and on Sept. 4, 1951, Harry Truman was featured in the first transcontinental TV broadcast). But Kennedy, more than his predecessors, *looked* like he was cast for the visual medium. His tanned, rested, and ready performance in the debate with Richard Nixon established the principle that the modern politician must be camera friendly. As one scholar notes, "Not only did television become a consequential factor in the 1960 election, but it established itself as the primary vehicle of information in presidential politics—supplanting newspapers, magazines, and radio and quickly burying newsreels for all time."[33] Kennedy was also, like Roosevelt, facing a print press that had mostly supported his opponent. It was Press Secretary Pierre Salinger who argued—despite skepticism from other aides—that the president should use the press to get directly to the people.[34] JFK, who had studied Roosevelt's example, agreed.[35] His most direct means of media manipulation was the presidential speech and news conference, where his extemporaneous eloquence, easy confidence, and quick wit were all on display. The press was cooperative as well in providing free airtime and refraining from open antagonism in its questioning. Yes, some old-line folk fumed: The *Chicago Tribune* called the Kennedy performances "government by public relations." But the administration successfully pioneered manipulations of media common these days: one-on-one candid conversations with compliant interviewers, live viewings of the president and his aides discussing weighty issues, and foreign visits run like stage-managed photo-ops.[36]

Case 4: Nixon's China Show

During the Nixon presidency, bypassing and manipulating media by creating televisually attractive media events became routine. An exemplar for such orchestration was the president's historic trip to China. On July 15, 1971, after secret negotiations by his top China aide, Henry Kissinger, the president, without explaining to anyone in Congress or the press beforehand, spoke on TV to the American people, stating: "I have requested this television time tonight to announce a major development in our efforts to build a lasting peace in the world. . . . It is in this spirit that I will undertake what I deeply hope will become a journey [to China] for peace, peace not just for our generation but for future generations on this earth we share together."[37] It was, as Kissinger put it, "The announcement that shook the world."[38] The backdoor and back channel took everyone from China scholars to news editors by surprise. Even after the announcement, Nixon simply told congressional leaders that they should let him work unimpeded.[39] Members of his own government, like Secretary of State William P. Rogers, were mocked for not being "in the loop."

The planning for the China trip on both sides was extraordinary although, to the initial chagrin of both Kissinger and the Chinese, Nixon's advisers quickly concocted elaborate proposals to make the trip, as one aide put it, "one of the most exciting events in TV history."[40] As print journalists would later complain, the entire visit was a visual spectacle for the tube, and cooperation with the major TV networks was close.[41] Moreover, this was *Nixon's* trip to China: All focus was on the commander in chief as superstar.

Nixon arrived in Beijing on February 21, 1972, the first American president to visit China. His glee was obvious as he descended from the *Spirit of '76* presidential jet with his wife, Pat, to shake the hand of Chinese Premier Zhou Enlai.[42] (Nixon had ordered his entourage to stay inside the plane so that the television spotlight at that moment would be solely on the pair.[43]) So began, as Nixon put it, "the week that changed the world."[44] The president and his wife visited what now comprise the standard tourist targets in Beijing: the Ming Tombs, the Great Wall, Tiananmen Square, and the museums. Although there was an inevitable posttrip letdown, the China visit was a milestone in media bypass or, rather, manipulating media into a conduit for direct contact with the people.

Searching for Commilito via New Technology

Nixon's fall ended what has been called the "golden age of presidential television."[45] At the time, new venues and opportunities for either manipulating or bypassing the press, expressing a version of Roosevelt's "I want to tell you," multiplied. Faxes, direct mail, and telephone calls became subindustries of political campaigning and issue advocacy; candidates could lobby the people directly through paid media. Free media venues also opened up, with the development of satellite television links. In the late 1970s, for example, satellites facilitated the coverage of campaigns by local television outlets (which tended to be less critical and more eager to fill airtime) with live interviews and statements by candidates. Videotape offered campaigns a way to produce video news releases, essentially packaged stories on the candidates that local media could plug and play with minimal editing and scant notation of their propaganda genesis. As *Newsweek* commented at the time, the tapes were useful in many ways:

> Scores of congressmen pipe self-serving cable TV programs
> to their districts. Another favorite scheme is to videotape

committee meetings, then transmit by satellite craftily-edited, 30-second sound-bites to the local "Eyewitness News" program. This technique works particularly well for the more than 150 subcommittee heads on Capitol Hill, who can show themselves being addressed impressively as Mr. Chairman.[46]

Advances in video editing, such as computerized, nonlinear editing software packages, along with lighter, technologically superior cameras, allowed the presentation of stories in a more visually exciting, action-filled style, including an increased use of "live" reports that provided new opportunities for candidates to acquire airtime.

There were also more commercial channels and greater numbers of news programs with the rise of cable television. C-SPAN, starting in 1979, resurrected the political speech, allowing members of Congress and later candidates on the stump to give full, unedited, and uncommented-upon presentations.[47] At the same time, C-SPAN speeches, committee hearings, and sparring on the floors of Congress and the Senate might spur greater attention by mainstream media.[48] The parallel of the blog audience to C-SPAN watchers is an interesting one. Republican leader Newt Gingrich and his allies became masters of the "special order" speech, delivered at night to an almost empty House chamber. The events flew under the radar of most political analysts because the C-SPAN audience was tiny; it was also thought that modern audiences were too inattentive to sit through long speeches. But the C-SPAN audience in fact (like bloggers today) was keenly interested in political public affairs—influentials of the time. Indeed, Gingrich believed his C-SPAN offensive helped his party to win control of Congress in 1994.

Radio and television talk shows also opened an entirely new arena of political commentary, often allowing candidates to address viewers or listeners directly, with supportive hosts and "amen" audiences. Bill Clinton was a master of the emoting visual stand-up, whether with Arsenio Hall or Larry King.[49] Candidates also innovated other ways to virtualize public speech and interaction such as the "electronic town meeting" made famous by maverick billionaire H. Ross Perot.[50] More important, politicians could coordinate publicity campaigns with friendly media and bypass less receptive media. Journalists Dan Balz and Ronald Brownstein describe the alliances that assisted in the Republican takeover of Congress:

> Technology enabled the Republicans to cement their new relationship with the talk show hosts. The key was the fax, which allowed the party to communicate with hundreds of shows—instantly. That speed revolutionized political argument. Republicans couldn't match Clinton's access to the network news, but even without such a national platform, the "blast fax" to hundreds of talk show hosts, other media outlets, and sympathetic grassroots groups allowed them to shower their response to his initiatives across the country as soon as he announced them—and sometimes before.[51]

Among the partners in this campaign were Gingrich and talk show host Rush Limbaugh. The precedent is significant: In the future, politicians will almost certainly not only blog themselves but also build blogging alliances and coordinated blogging campaigns, most likely with major bloggers. Voluntary associations do not tend to restrict themselves to one medium.

Becoming a Business: Blogger as Political Consultant

The political professionalization of blogging began with Howard Dean hiring people to manage his blogs and others (bloggers) as consultants; it will end with all political consulting firms, campaigns, and parties retaining staff bloggers and employing independent bloggers. Such an evolution, from independent outsider to professional insider, is familiar and universal. In 1964, a sociologist wrote a seminal article titled "The Professionalization of Everybody."[52] He noted that almost everyone now claims to be a professional (e.g., instead of garbage collectors, we have sanitation engineers and so on). Indeed, I surprise my students when I remind them that it was only in the twentieth century that some innovators—mostly newspaper publishers interested in creating a stable, professional workforce—concocted what seemed at the time the crazy idea that people should attend school to learn how to be journalists. In the early republic, journalism schools were more than a hundred years away as a concept or a fact.[53]

An interesting outcome of the explosion of blog politics and the adoption of them by professionals is that it has created a reverse status hierarchy for most new media, especially for blogs. As one political consultant described to me, "After 2004, it was clear that we had to have some blog presence within [my] firm. I have to admit, I wasn't quite sure what we needed, but every client was asking me, 'What about blogs?' So I had to be able to trot someone out and say, 'This is Melissa, our blogmaster. She'll blog you up.'" The "expert" in this case was twenty-two years old. That is the promise of a fringe medium's arrival into the mainstream: The sages have literally skipped the decades of training normally required to inspire trust with other campaign and election functions such as fund-raising, writing scripts for TV ads, booking media time, or speechwriting. In each of those instances, my students would start work with a congressman's office, a political consulting firm, or a political party and spend years working as apprentices, watching the master guildsmen, so to speak, the veteran political professionals, and learning their craft. Day-to-day political work is for the young—campaigns burn people out quickly—but the bloggers who are becoming professional political consultants and workers are, as another political consultant put it, "about as pink-cheeked as you can get." (This is literally true as well; the vast majority are white.)

As I tell my students, the opportunity for them is huge. In what other business, except entertainment, can they be featured as a master craftsperson or star two weeks out of college? Twenty-one-year-old Neil Sroka, for example, got a job with Trippi & Associates based on his obvious smarts and a single undergraduate paper on political blogging. He told me that his previous political experience was with the teen advisory board of his local congressman in Ohio.

Then there is Byron LaMasters, who as of this writing works for Tyson.org, a Democratic GOTV (get out the vote) firm run by political consultant Gerry Tyson in Texas. Tyson has worked in politics for thirty years and has a bipartisan reputation for efficiency and success in many traditional aspects of electioneering such as generating voter turnout and organizing precinct workers. Through the '80s and '90s, his toolkit included direct mail, door-to-door canvassing and solicitation, live and automated phone calling, and increasingly in the '90s and at the turn of the millennium, Web sites.

LaMasters is a former president of the College Democrats at the University of Texas–Austin. I first noticed Byron because some students of mine and I had been creating a list of local political blogs in various states, including Texas. Byron's BurntOrangeReport was one of those that impressed us most. His entry into blogging is a typical story. He had been reading blogs, mostly left liberal and Democratic ones like Dailykos.com and MyDD.com and also Offthekuff.com, another Texas-centered Democratic blog. Byron's main involvement had been posting comments. In April 2003, after a brainstorming session with a friend, he set up his first blog via LiveJournal and then, within months, had created the independent BurntOrangeReport through Movable Type software and hosting. Byron explains,

> Blogging was an attractive means of communication to me for
> many reasons. As a political science major and political activist,
> I wanted an outlet to express my political thoughts and writings.
> As the BurntOrangeReport grew, I realized that we provided a
> specific niche that made us attractive to readers—we covered
> Texas politics from a Democratic (student) perspective.

BurntOrangeReport was a success, especially because Byron started his focus when the 2004 election cycle was heating up. Texas was not competitive in the presidential contest, but the state was home to a number of congressional races that gained national attention.

Byron was not just commenting; he was providing that added value to his readers that wins bloggers respect—creating new information, not just reacting to that of others. He would interview campaign staffers and candidates, attend speeches and events, and generally act as an amateur, but very professional-sounding, political reporter. He could also point out what he perceived to be mistakes in big media. In several cases, he trumped national and local media by uncovering new facts. Byron's blog became a go-to blog for political activists. In one case, he corrected and got a retraction from a mainstream newspaper for a factual error in one of its articles. As an inroad into political work, of course, Byron's blogging and his engagement were invaluable and led directly to his being hired by Tyson.org. Other young bloggers have and will follow his lead, learning political work through their online activities as well as their fieldwork. We can predict that blog writing will be the portal through which many future political power players enter politics; that may be blogging's single most important contribution to the style, methods, and business of politics in America.

Tailgate the Candidate: Vlogging as Political Media

Another young expert has helped pioneer an innovation within the innovation of blogs: the potentially politically significant medium of the video log, or vlog. Since the late 1990s, political campaigns have experimented with putting videos—usually their campaign commercials originally broadcast or simulcast on television or their candidate's speeches and appearances—on their Web sites. I and a group of my graduate students conducted a survey of some of these attempts in the late 1990s. Anyone who remembers the problems of "Web TV" at that time will understand why the results were often disappointing. Choppy, blurry, postage-stamp sized as they were, it was hard to envision at that time how Web videos would add much to campaign communication. Increasing broadband access, high-definition cameras, improved media-playing software, and various other technical developments have greatly upgraded Web video. For example, the Bush–Cheney campaign in 2004 created more than forty Web-only videos for its campaign Web site. If you include Webcast television commercials, perusers of the site, whether ordinary information-seeking voters or journalists, had access to more than 100 campaign videos covering every conceivable subject and issue. Now, with YouTube, RocketBoom, and other user-generated video sites, national distribution of the videos is effortless and ubiquitous.

The early Web videos were of terrible quality, but this is not in itself a defeat of persuasion; many campaigns in the past have attempted to approximate the documentary or cinema verité genre by employing black-and-white film, overexposing the film, and causing the camera to shake. Experiments I have done show that audiences do perceive a greater quality of authenticity in such campaign commercials versus the slicker, brighter, full-color ads. Campaign Web ads have not developed fully enough for us to know through research whether or not they may be more persuasive because of their *lower* production values. Has, for example, the popularity of reality TV, camera phones, and YouTube low-res homemade video actually lowered audience expectations about what used to be called "broadcast quality"? We don't know—yet.

Political consultants have learned that Web ads work best when they (a) are used to test-market content and (b) have a homier, more *personal* feel than the thirty-second TV spot. Hence the video log. Justin Germany, one of my students who produced Web campaign ads for Bush–Cheney 2004 and who now works for Campaign Solutions, a Republican campaign consulting firm creating vlogs and Web ads for clients like John McCain, comments, "The main difference between a vlog and a regular Web video is that the vlog has the candidate speaking directly to the camera. This is organic; it's reality Web-video and it allows a more direct feeling of communication between the candidate and the voter."

Here is where a vlog may indeed constitute persuasive innovation. Political ads—or for that matter, ads for cat food or bedsheets—have many enemies. People with digital video recorders, VCRs, TiVo, or just a TV remote are likely to skip them or flash past them. We also live in an immensely cluttered visual world, with many images and words vying for our attention. Ad makers are thus forever seeking something new to catch our eye. Shocking or salacious content is one approach, but another way to entice our overstressed neurons is by creating advertising that is stylistically different. Computer animation and amazing special effects may fulfill this requirement, but vlogs offer something else. We are acutely aware when watching a TV ad that, although we may be alone in our living room, we share that experience at that moment with millions of others. But just like posting a comment on a blog gives me a momentary frisson of empowerment—my medium, my choice, my words, my space—so does hyperlinking to the vlog. Their lower scale look and their directness—a candidate talking face-on to the viewer, the potential voter who (and this is an important component of the interaction) has initiated the contact—feel different to me and to the classes of students to which I have shown them.

An example is a vlog set up by Justin for the unsuccessful candidacy of Lynn Swann for governor of my home state of Pennsylvania in 2006. As mentioned previously, campaign fund-raising was one of the major Web breakthroughs of the 2000 election, with John McCain's campaign pioneering the Web site as an instant and efficient cash machine. The Dean campaign also raised a great deal of money, partly with his famous $5 online fund-raising "lunch" virtually participated in by hundreds of thousands of bloggers, in purposeful mockery of an old-fashioned $2,000/plate dinner in a swanky hotel with the Republican vice president. As an innovation, Justin and the Campaign Solutions team set up a donation page for candidate Swann that had an integrated vlog. Swann, a former star receiver for the Pittsburgh Steelers, has a magnetic camera presence, and it does feel like he is talking to us. (Think about the interactive soap opera characters in the film version of *Fahrenheit 451* who "break the fourth wall" toward the at-home viewer.) In a longer vlog, Justin shot Swann "on the scene" at a Steelers football game tailgate working the crowd (Figure 5.1). This is an example of the oldest type of campaign event covered by the newest medium.

Figure 5.1. Lynn Swann, "Penn State Tailgate" (Justin Germany, Campaign Solutions, video blog)

It is difficult to translate the "feel" of such vlogs via an illustration in a book. Furthermore, vlogs are so new that the form's innovators are still writing rules that they may later break. But again, the essential goals are to create an image of the candidate that (a) is personalized, that is "speaking to me," (b) has the style of the first-person narrative or the spontaneous observation, and (c) does not look like packaged talking points made into video.

Blogger as Politician

In American politics, perhaps the most significant role of bloggers may be that of political elites who themselves take up the medium. All over the world, political leaders of very different statures and styles are doing so. The deposed king of Cambodia, Norodom Sihanouk, for example, has his own blog. In his own 2004 reelection campaign, British Prime Minister Tony Blair led potential voters through his Web site with a series of video blogs that followed him in various campaign stops. This allowed him to show commilito both with voters on the scene and virtually with his Web constituency. There are now, according to a recent count conducted by one of my PhD students, as many as a thousand blogs "hosted" by federal and state officials in the United States. The variety of blogs, bloglike diaries, and other new media employed by current sitting U.S. senators is both spotty and impressive in total, as shown in Table 5.1.

By the time this book is published, the number will probably rise to the tens of thousands of pols blogging or *professing* to blog. The pretense issue—that is, whether or not a blog is written by the signed or implied author—is one of uncertain significance but ancient lineage. According to the Roman historian Tacitus, Emperor Nero was the first Roman political leader not to write his own declamations and oratories. The art of speechwriting, thus, is a very old one. I know of no major political figures of the last century or this one who wrote all their own speeches or even their books. (John F. Kennedy received the Pulitzer Prize for a book he purportedly made little contribution to actually penning.) Nobody is shocked and dismayed to find out that

Table 5.1.

United States Senators (Spring 2007) and New Media

Name	State	Party	Blog/Blog-like Diary or Report	Other
Jeff Sessions	Alabama	Republican		Podcast: http://sessions.senate.gov/rss/about.cfm
Richard Shelby	Alabama	Republican		Podcast: http://shelby.senate.gov/public/index.cfm?FuseAction=Rss.About
Lisa Murkowski	Alaska	Republican		
Ted Stevens	Alaska	Republican		
Jon Kyl	Arizona	Republican	Weekly Journal Entry: http://kyl.senate.gov/	
John McCain	Arizona	Republican	Has been a guest blogger at "Captain's Quarters": http://www.captainsquartersblog.com/mt/archives/008256.php Has been a guest blogger at "Porkbusters": http://porkbusters.org/2006/06/we_need_to_stop_this_now.php "Blogs" at Newsbull (actually a collection of press releases): http://www.newsbull.com/m.asp?id=591	Myspace profile (set up by supporters): http://profile.myspace.com/index.cfm?fuseaction=user.viewprofile&friendid=107589950
Blanche Lincoln	Arkansas	Democrat		Podcast of weekly conversation with reporters: http://demradio.senate.gov/actualities/lincoln/
Mark Pryor	Arkansas	Democrat		Audio clips of speeches: http://pryor.senate.gov/newsroom/
Barbara Boxer	California	Democrat		
Dianne Feinstein	California	Democrat		
Wayne Allard	Colorado	Republican		Podcast: http://allard.senate.gov/public/index.cfm?FuseAction=RSS.Podcast
Ken Salazar	Colorado	Democrat		Podcast: http://salazar.senate.gov/SenKenSalazarpod.xml
Chris Dodd	Connecticut	Democrat	Blog: http://dodd.senate.gov/index.php?q=blog/1	Podcast: http://dodd.senate.gov/podcasts/

Senator	State	Party		
Joe Lieberman	Connecticut	Independent / Democrat	Has been a guest blogger: http://www.myleftnutmeg.com/showDiary.do?diaryId=6070 Also has been a guest blogger at: http://ctlocalpolitics.net/2007/01/24/guest-post-senator-chris-dodd/	Voters encouraged to offer suggestions for his ipod, nicknamed the "DoddPod": http://www.chrisdodd.com/doddpod?page=1
Joe Biden	Delaware	Democrat	Online Campaign has a "blog" (collection of news stories): http://www.uniteourstates.com	Audio Files: http://lieberman.senate.gov/newsroom/actualities.cfm Video Files: http://biden.senate.gov/newsroom/media2006.cfm
Thomas Carper	Delaware	Democrat	Blog, "Carper's Corner": http://carper.senate.gov/acarpercorner.htm	
Mel Martinez	Florida	Republican		Podcast: http://martinez.senate.gov/public/index.cfm?FuseAction=RSS.Podcast
Bill Nelson	Florida	Democrat		
Saxby Chambliss	Georgia	Republican		Podcast: http://chambliss.senate.gov/public/index.cfm?FuseAction=RSS.About
Johnny Isakson	Georgia	Republican		
Daniel Akaka	Hawaii	Democrat	Blog, "Weekly Report": http://akaka.senate.gov/public/index.cfm	
Daniel Inouye	Hawaii	Democrat		
Larry Craig	Idaho	Republican		Interactive Podchat – Viewers submit questions in advance: http://craig.senate.gov/podchat.cfm Weekly Video, "Washington Report": http://craig.senate.gov/washreport.cfm
Mark Crapo	Idaho	Republican		Podcast: http://crapo.senate.gov/podcast.xml

(Continued)

Table 5.1. (*Continued*)

Name	State	Party	Blog/Blog-like Diary or Report	Other
Dick Durbin	Illinois	Democrat		
Barack Obama	Illinois	Democrat		Podcast: http://obama.senate.gov/podcast/ Myspace page (set up by supporters): http://profile.myspace.com/index.cfm?fuseaction=user.viewprofile&friend ID=5173909
Evan Bayh	Indiana	Democrat		
Dick Lugar	Indiana	Republican		Audio/Video Clips: http://lugar.senate.gov/press.html
Chuck Grassley	Iowa	Republican	Blog: http://grassley.senate.gov/index.cfm?FuseAction=Blogs.Detail&Blog_id=12	Weekly Webcast: http://grassley.senate.gov/index.cfm?FuseAction=Video.Webcasts Podcast: http://grassley.senate.gov/index.cfm?FuseAction=RSS.Podcast
Tom Harkin	Iowa	Democrat		Podcast: http://harkin.senate.gov/podcast/index.cfm
Pat Roberts	Kansas	Republican	Blog, "Roberts' Journal": http://roberts.senate.gov/public/index.cfm?FuseAction=PressRoom.Entries&ContentRecord_id=0f83cda2-802a-23ad-40d1-3be3b7541a8d&Region_id=&Issue_id=	Podcast: http://roberts.senate.gov/public/index.cfm?FuseAction=Rss.About
Sam Brownback	Kansas	Republican		
Jim Bunning	Kentucky	Republican		Audio/Video Clips: http://bunning.senate.gov/index.cfm?FuseAction=AudioVideo.Home
Mitch McConnell	Kentucky	Republican		Radio Clips: http://landrieu.senate.gov/news/radio.cfm Video of Senate Speeches: http://landrieu.senate.gov/news/video.cfm
Mary Landrieu	Louisiana	Democrat		

Name	State	Party	Notes	Media Links
David Vitter	Louisiana	Republican		Multimedia: http://vitter.senate.gov/?module=pressroom/media
Susan Collins	Maine	Republican		Podcast: http://collins.senate.gov/public/continue.cfm?FuseAction=Rss.Podcast
Olympia Snowe	Maine	Republican	Blog, "Weekly Updates": http://snowe.senate.gov/public/index.cfm?FuseAction=PressRoom.WeeklyUpdates	Audio Clips: http://snowe.senate.gov/public/index.cfm?FuseAction=PressRoom.AudioClips Video Clips: http://snowe.senate.gov/public/index.cfm?FuseAction=PressRoom.VideoClips
Ben Cardin	Maryland	Democrat	Blog/List of Articles: http://cardin.senate.gov/newsroom.cfm	
Barbara Mikulski	Maryland	Democrat		Audio/Video Clips: http://mikulski.senate.gov/Newsroom/audio.html
Ted Kennedy	Massachusetts	Democrat		
John Kerry	Massachusetts	Democrat	Blog, "John's Journal": http://kerry.senate.gov/v3/cfm/home.cfm Has been a guest blogger: http://www.savetheinternet.com/blog/2006/06/30/stopping-the-big-giveaway-by-john-kerry/ Additional Kerry blog, by "Violet Bliss Dietz"; http://blog.johnkerry.com/	Multimedia Downloads: http://kerry.senate.gov/v3/press/downloads.html Podcast: http://www.johnkerry.com/podcast/
Carl Levin	Michigan	Democrat		Audio Clips: http://levin.senate.gov/newsroom/radio/index.html
Debbie Stabenow	Michigan	Democrat	Blog, "Monthly Column": http://stabenow.senate.gov/press/columns/index.htm	
Norm Coleman	Minnesota	Republican		Podcast: Link to podcast: http://coleman.senate.gov/index.cfm?FuseAction=News.Podcasts

(Continued)

Table 5.1. (*Continued*)

Name	State	Party	Blog/Blog-like Diary or Report	Other
Amy Klobuchar	Minnesota	Democrat		Video Clips: http://klobuchar.senate.gov/multimedia.cfm
Thad Cochran	Mississippi	Republican		
Trent Lott	Mississippi	Republican	Blog, "Weekly Column": http://lott.senate.gov/index.cfm? FuseAction=Articles.Home	Weekly Radio Address: http://lott.senate.gov/index.cfm? FuseAction=AudioVideo.Home
Kit Bond	Missouri	Republican		
Claire McCaskill	Missouri	Democrat		
Max Baucus	Montana	Democrat		
Jon Tester	Montana	Democrat	(Website under construction at time of publication): http://tester.senate.gov/	
Chuck Hagel	Nebraska	Republican		Audio Clips: http://hagel.senate.gov/index.cfm?FuseAction=News.Multimedia
Benjamin Nelson	Nebraska	Democrat		
John Ensign	Nevada	Republican		
Harry Reid	Nevada	Democrat		
Judd Gregg	New Hampshire	Republican		Audio Clips: http://gregg.senate.gov/public/index.cfm? FuseAction=PressRoom.AudioClips Video Clips: http://gregg.senate.gov/public/index.cfm? FuseAction=PressRoom.VideoClips
John Sununu	New Hampshire	Republican		Audio Clips: http://www.sununu.senate.gov/radio.html Video Clips: http://sununu.senate.gov/video_clips.html
Frank Lautenberg	New Jersey	Democrat	Blog, "Frankly Speaking": http://lautenberg.senate.gov/newsroom/franklyspeaking.cfm	

Robert Menendez	New Jersey	Democrat	Video Archive: http://menendez.senate.gov/videos/archive.cfm Audio Archive: http://menendez.senate.gov/audio/archive.cfm
Jeff Bingaman	New Mexico	Democrat	TV / Radio Clips: http://bingaman.senate.gov/news/mediacenter.cfm
Pete Domenici	New Mexico	Republican	
Hillary Clinton	New York	Democrat	Video Clips: http://clinton.senate.gov/#Multimedia Myspace Page (by supporters, for supporters): http://www.myspace.com/hillaryclinton2008 Previously "blogged" on health care issues (not written by her, mostly press releases): http://health.yahoo.com/blog-for-hope/clinton/ Current "blog" not by Clinton but contains blog posts as well as YouTube clips, etc: http://www.votehillary.org/CMS/blog
Chuck Schumer	New York	Democrat	
Richard Burr	North Carolina	Republican	Audio Clips: http://burr.senate.gov/index.cfm?FuseAction=Audio.Home Video Clips: http://burr.senate.gov/index.cfm?FuseAction=Video.Home
Elizabeth Dole	North Carolina	Republican	Audio Clips: http://dole.senate.gov/index.cfm?FuseAction=Audio.Home Video Clips: http://dole.senate.gov/index.cfm?FuseAction=Video.Home
Kent Conrad	North Dakota	Democrat	Audio/Video Clips: http://conrad.senate.gov/press/press.html
Byron Dorgan	North Dakota	Democrat	Podcast: http://dorgan.senate.gov/newsroom/podcasts/podcast.xml

(Continued)

Table 5.1. (*Continued*)

Name	State	Party	Blog/Blog-like Diary or Report	Other
Sherrod Brown	Ohio	Democrat	Has been a guest blogger on Huffington Post: http://www.huffingtonpost.com/rep-sherrod-brown/end-the-standoff-on-stem-_b_21541.html	
George Voinovich	Ohio	Republican	Blog (Collection of Articles): http://voinovich.senate.gov/public/index.cfm? FuseAction=NewsCenter.SenVoinovichsColumns	Audio Clips: http://voinovich.senate.gov/public/index.cfm? FuseAction=NewsCenter.AudioClips Video Clips: http://voinovich.senate.gov/public/index.cfm? FuseAction=NewsCenter.VideoClips
James Inhofe	Oklahoma	Republican	Blog, "Jim's Journal": http://inhofe.senate.gov/public/index.cfm? FuseAction=PressRoom.JimsJournal	Podcast: http://inhofe.senate.gov/public/index.cfm? FuseAction=Rss.Podcast Video Clips: http://inhofe.senate.gov/public/index.cfm? FuseAction=PressRoom.VideoClips
Tom Coburn	Oklahoma	Republican	Blog: http://coburn.senate.gov/public/index.cfm? FuseAction=LatestNews.Columns	Podcast: http://coburn.senate.gov/public/index.cfm? FuseAction=RSS.Podcast TV Clips: http://coburn.senate.gov/public/index.cfm? FuseAction=LatestNews.TVClips
Gordon Smith	Oregon	Republican		Audio / Video Clips: http://gsmith.senate.gov/public/index.cfm? FuseAction=News.Multimedia
Ron Wyden	Oregon	Democrat		Audio / Video Clips: http://wyden.senate.gov/media/audio.html
Robert Casey, Jr.	Pennsylvania	Democrat		
Arlen Specter	Pennsylvania	Republican	Blog ("Articles"): http://specter.senate.gov/index.cfm? FuseAction=Articles.Home	Audio / Video Clips: http://specter.senate.gov/index.cfm? FuseAction=AudioVideo.Home
Jack Reed	Rhode Island	Democrat	Blog (of "selected Op-Eds"): http://reed.senate.gov/newsroom/Op-Ed.cfm	

Sheldon Whitehouse	Rhode Island	Democrat	
Jim DeMint	South Carolina	Republican	Blog, "Jim's Journal": http://demint.senate.gov/index.cfm?FuseAction=JimsJournal.Home Other Op-Eds: http://demint.senate.gov/index.cfm?FuseAction=PressReleases.Home&Type=Op-Ed	Audio Clips: http://demint.senate.gov/index.cfm?FuseAction=Audio.Home Video Clips: http://demint.senate.gov/index.cfm?FuseAction=Video.Home
Lindsey Graham	South Carolina	Republican		
Tim Johnson	South Dakota	Democrat	Blog ("Editorials/Columns"): http://johnson.senate.gov/editorials.html	Audio Clips: http://johnson.senate.gov/soundwaves.html
John Thune	South Dakota	Republican	Blog (Op-Eds): http://thune.senate.gov/public/index.cfm?FuseAction=Opeds.Home	Audio/Video Clips: http://thune.senate.gov/public/index.cfm?FuseAction=News.Multimedia
Lamar Alexander	Tennessee	Republican	Blog ("Weekly Column"): http://alexander.senate.gov/index.cfm?FuseAction=Columns.Home	Audio/Video Clips: http://alexander.senate.gov/index.cfm?FuseAction=News.Multimedia
Bob Corker	Tennessee	Republican		
John Cornyn	Texas	Republican		Podcast: http://cornyn.senate.gov/index.asp?f=page&pid=229&lid=1 Video Clips: http://cornyn.senate.gov/funct_media.cfm?funct=video Audio Clips: http://cornyn.senate.gov/funct_media.cfm?funct=audio
Kay Hutchison	Texas	Republican	Blog (Weekly Column of "Capitol Comments"): http://hutchison.senate.gov/capcoms.htm Other published articles: http://hutchison.senate.gov/articles.htm	Audio/Video Clips: http://hutchison.senate.gov/videoaud.htm
Robert Bennett	Utah	Republican		Audio/Video Clips: http://bennett.senate.gov/press/multimedia.cfm
Orrin Hatch	Utah	Republican		Podcast: http://leahy.senate.gov/POD/index.html
Patrick Leahy	Vermont	Democrat		Audio/Video Clips:
Bernie Sanders	Vermont	Independent		http://sanders.senate.gov/news/index.cfm?code=AV

(Continued)

Table 5.1. (*Continued*)

Name	State	Party	Blog/Blog-like Diary or Report	Other
Jim Webb	Virginia	Democrat		Audio/Video Clips: http://webb.senate.gov/newsroom/multimedia.cfm
Patty Murray	Washington	Democrat	Blog (From her trip to the Middle East): http://murray.senate.gov/middleeast/index.cfm Weekly "E-Newsletter": http://murray.senate.gov/news/#enews	Audio/Video Clips (Left side of page): http://murray.senate.gov/
Robert Byrd	West Virginia	Democrat		Audio Clips: http://byrd.senate.gov/newsroom/audio/audio.html
John Rockefeller	West Virginia	Democrat	Blog ("Editorials and Columns"): http://rockefeller.senate.gov/news/editorials_columns.htm	Audio/Video Clips: http://rockefeller.senate.gov/news/audio_video.htm
Russell Feingold	Wisconsin	Democrat	Blog (Op-Eds): http://feingold.senate.gov/news/opedpage.html Reposts selected material from other blogs: http://feingold.senate.gov/news/blog.html	Podcast: http://feingold.senate.gov/news/podcasts_index.xml Audio/Video Clips: http://feingold.senate.gov/news/podcasts.html
Herb Kohl	Wisconsin	Democrat	Blog, "Weekly Columns" (none since 2005): http://kohl.senate.gov/weekly_writings.html	
Michael Enzi	Wyoming	Republican		Podcast: http://enzi.senate.gov/public/index.cfm?FuseAction=Rss.Podcast Video Clips: http://enzi.senate.gov/public/index.cfm?FuseAction=NewsRoom.VideoClips Audio Clips: http://enzi.senate.gov/public/index.cfm?FuseAction=NewsRoom.AudioClips
Craig Thomas	Wyoming	Republican		Audio/Video Clips: http://thomas.senate.gov/index.cfm?FuseAction=News.Multimedia

Franklin Roosevelt, Ronald Reagan, or for that matter Hillary Clinton or George W. Bush spoke words written by others.

To what extent are words printed in political blogs owned by anyone? The topic can be both painful and funny. On the humorous side is an interchange between an MSNBC guest host on the *Hardball* program and former GOP House Speaker Tom Delay:

> Mike Barnicle, Guest Host: Do you get up first thing in the morning and start blogging away? Or how, what do you do?
>
> Former Majority Leader Tom Delay: Well, I'm not a very good writer. I have the ideas, and I have somebody else put the words together.

Blogwars may break out on the issue of who really blogs and who does not. In the spring of 2005, Representative Sherrod Brown of Ohio (D-Thirteenth District) wrote a letter to Senator Mike DeWine (R-Ohio) concerning the nomination to the Supreme Court of Samuel Alito and specifically enumerating what Brown represented as Alito's poor record on labor issues and workers' rights. Apparently, nearly the entire letter was what in traditional publishing would be called "plagiarized"—that is, originally either the ideas or the actual words of a political blogger, Nathan Newman, of the labor issues–oriented nathannewman.org. The *Cleveland Plain Dealer* revealed the lifting of the language after officials from DeWine's office alerted them. Mr. Newman, however, far from being angry about the incident, attacked Senator DeWine and the newspaper story itself, arguing,

> Who the hell cares if a Brown staffer copied a factual listing of legal cases into a letter? This was hardly a literary blog post using deathless prose for the ages. It was the facts that made this post interesting, not its literary value. . . . Guess what, Sherrod Brown's staffer was lazy and didn't do a rewrite of my blog post or put in an attribution line. But the report on this story was even lazier, doing an easy "call the campaigns for quotes" story instead of the harder work of dealing with the substance of Alito's anti-worker legal record. So the reporter saying that Brown's letter "was

plagiarized" is flatly inaccurate. The reality is that politicians used public domain sources in a host of ways and using my blog post was no different.[54]

We are on new ground here. A purist like me would love to say that the uncited and intentional portage of material, no matter what the source, the destination, or the outcome, is always unethical. But if almost all other forms of traditional political speech are falsely (but with a wink!) attributed to an author other than the original, then why not the content of political blogs? Perhaps we will see the emergence of another role for the political blogger: open-source or public domain speechwriter.

Polblogging from Ground Zero

The first-person quality of politicians' blogs is enhanced when they speak to us from interesting, even exotic, situations where we cannot or are unlikely to be ourselves, the blogger-as-reporter style mentioned in the last chapter. Patrick J. Leahy, the Vermont Democratic senator, for example, blogs in "real time" from the floor of the Senate. During Ronald Reagan's funeral, Representative Mike Pence (R-Indiana) stood inside the national cathedral and typed directly into his BlackBerry the following blog entry:

> My wife and I stand amidst the most powerful people in the world. . . . We have stood beside presidents and princes, prime ministers and leaders of every stripe but that is not what moved us these past two hours. There was the undeniable presence of the Spirit of the Lord in this place and it was a sweet presence. . . . [T]he casket swept by to our right, and tears filled my eyes.[55]

Similarly, a pol can emphasize the political importance of what he or she is doing. Former California governor and several-times presidential candidate Jerry Brown, while mayor of Oakland, blogged the following:

> This week I threw a switch that activated California's largest corporate solar power installation, a system that will provide 80 percent of the energy supply for the FedEx hub at Oakland International Airport. FedEx's system, designed by the

PowerLight Corporation, will reduce the load on our power grid and is an important step in the struggle for energy independence and greenhouse gas reduction.[56]

Then Brown proceeded to argue that this was no grip-and-grin photo op but a symbol of Washington's (i.e., the Bush administration's) failures on energy policy and thus, "We need more corporations to follow FedEx's lead and do their part to reduce pollution and stave off dramatic climate change." In short, tying in ordinary proceedings to bigger, more pressing, and more dramatic events boosts a polblog's merit.

In each case, we are not only invited to listen to the polblogger describing eyewitnessed events but to *feel* as if he or she were relating to us intimate asides about events to which we would normally have no access. More important to the politician, such utterances bypass big media; they can show and tell us at length, without being subject to outside editing or commentary by an interlocutor. As we have seen, however, such intimacy is no guarantee that the message won't be trumped by some else's personal use of new media.

Case Study: Blogging from Iraq with "The Troops"

Travels abroad, to zones of war or danger or diplomatic sensitivity, seem ready-made for "follow me" polblog narratives. When, in December 2004, then Senator Jim Talent (R-Missouri) made an official visit to the Middle East, including a stop in Iraq, his office posted "Sen. Jim Talent's special travel event blog"—which, after his lost reelection bid, has been taken down. Not surprisingly, the focus was on what the senator saw, what he thought about it, and his personal encounters with Missourians serving in the U.S. armed forces in the region. The first-person tense of the post is evident in the language ("I flew in"), its conversational quality ("I want to use most of this blog to talk about Iraq"), and the sense of straight author-to-reader connectivity ("I write this" and "I want to give the stream of my impressions"). The format is extremely effective from a political communications perspective. But was this Talent's own authentic voice? Was it streamed, or carefully written, rewritten, and then vetted by his advisers? Did he write this, as implied within the text, on an evening in Jerusalem? We might envision the senator hunched over his laptop, reading scratched notes from a pad, pausing, musing, and unleashing a flurry of typing. At-the-scene pictures add to the authenticity and the "I was there at Ground Zero" quality. Thus, even in an age of advanced communications, we expect our politicians to "be there" in person after natural disasters or terrorist attacks or in the war zone where "Sen. Talent has dinner with the Missouri soldiers of the First Cav."

The flood of such recollections and narrative works well to establish the intimacy as a twofold message. First, the politician *bodily* supports the troops and the mission and is both an accessible human being and also a political leader who, as noted, is someone with us and above us. Consider this photo caption: "A young Iraqi boy stands next to his drawing of the word 'good' above a First Cav division symbol." This is a left-handed, or perhaps right-handed, criticism of media reports emphasizing Iraqi resistance and opposition to the American presence in their country. Then Talent specifically unleashes an attack on the media. But it is not a Spiro Agnew direct-style assault:

> I also heard consistently, during my two days both in the South and in Baghdad, frustration at how the war is being reported. Everyone to whom I spoke, in the military, in the Iraqi cabinet, and in the State department, believes that the effort is going well—though everyone is very cautious—and that an unbalanced picture is being presented. The troops are particularly frustrated; I got an earful on this subject when I had dinner with the First Cav soldiers on Saturday night.

In all, Talent's postings seem to be a prime example of a successful form and function of a political blog, deftly establishing the senator as a user-friendly political leader exuding the powers of commilito and appealing to his conservative Republican base. Dealing with negative information is, of course, a political art: how to handle a touchy question at a press conference; what to say when the policy you advocated seems to go bad; how to deal with a combative opponent at a debate. And now how to blog.

But in the blogwars, personalization is a potent weapon for either side. Talent lost his seat in 2006, albeit by a narrow margin. He fell for several reasons, but one key issue that played a part was stem cell research. Television and film actor Michael J. Fox made an ad for Talent's Democratic opponent that exuded a much more personal level of appeal to voters. Shaking from his Parkinson's syndrome affliction, Fox spoke to the viewer: "As you might know, I care deeply about stem cell research. In Missouri, you can elect Claire McCaskill, who shares my hope for cures. . . . " The TV ad ran only a few times in one market in Missouri, but like all controversial political commercials, it was replicated through discussion and replay on news programs and then was posted by the McCaskill campaign on YouTube, where it found millions of viewers who had never seen the original television version. In addition, it was a major focus of blogs, left and right, during the weeks after its initial airing, and most left blogs and not a few right blogs included the link to the YouTube posting. Put in military terms, the episode demonstrates how all political media can serve as a force multiplier for all other media, whether television or blogs.

In parallel, Senator Patty Murray (D-Washington) blogged her own Middle East trip (http://murray.senate.gov/middleeast/). Murray has a very personable writing style that shows concern for both the soldiers and their families at home. She seems to be a politician who is not afraid to be informal at times yet knows when to be on target with issues (e.g., the war, leaders of foreign countries) in her discussions. She chronicles events in a comical yet very familiar way. "We did this amazing zigzag in—sort of spiral down very fast—and my ears felt horrendous," she said, describing the final approach to the Baghdad airport. "It was like a bad Disneyland ride as we veered left, right, up, and down to avoid an 'incoming' . . . and I have to admit my stomach was in my throat." Murray shows fellowship for the soldiers, even flying into the Green Zone of Baghdad with a soldier to get a better look. An example of her commilito is as follows:

> We then had dinner with the troops and ate in the mess hall—lots of calories there! Great conversation with troops who wanted to know latest details of everything from home! They also wanted us to know that they had done a lot of good here and that their work had been worthwhile. They fear the media is not showing the

good side of their work. I can understand that—they have given up an awful lot to be here and don't want it to be in vain.

Both the way she writes her blog and the significance of her actually taking the trip touch base with her readers. This is vital political communication: Those who oppose the war itself, or the way the war is being fought, obviously need to emphasize their support of the troops. Being there with them and making us feel that the connection is personal, not just a photo-op drop-in, finds authentic expression via the blog form.

Memo to Candidate Smith: Are Blogs the "New Iowa"?

I suspect that individual small blogs will have more of an effect and may tip the outcome in smaller "downballot" races, for alderman or even for Congress, than for higher profile senatorial or presidential contests. But 2006–2008 is the time of the invisible primary, so it is worth taking the perspective from political professionals thinking about the biggest ballot of all, the presidency. As Emily Metzgar, a Louisiana political columnist, and I found in the fall of 2005, there was considerable speculation about whether blogs were really a revolution, a wholly new form of political interaction between would-be presidential candidates and the people, or analogues of well-established campaign benchmarks.[57] A necessary starting point is to consider how similar blogs are, as a new medium or genre or venue, to traditional components of presidential politics. What follows is a sort of (unusually candid) "memo" that a staffer at a consulting firm might write, with the client being, let us say, a millionaire businessperson, not particularly conversant with blogs, considering running for the presidency in 2008. (Note: I will recapitulate here some points from the text, again from the point of view of a professional.)

> Dear Candidate Smith:
> At our last meeting you asked, "What can blogs do for me?" Let me try to answer that question by reviewing what blogs can do that is like or unlike forms of campaigns and elections with which we are already familiar.

Are blogs the new Iowa? Since the 1970s, it has been a rule that strong primary candidates do not arrive on the scene late (although the definition of "late" and "early" keeps shifting); rather, they surface early during the so-called invisible primary. The main geopolitical focus of their efforts is the first caucus state, Iowa, and the first primary state, New Hampshire, where they try to build party affiliations and ground organizations. But if the bloglands are a place, then they are the real "first in the nation" testing ground. Bloggers will decide whom to support for president (and whom to vociferously oppose) long before the first caucus-goers cast a ballot, whether in Iowa or the new "moved-up" states of South Carolina and Nevada. Candidates, however, must work blogs through old-fashioned retail politics one major (and many minor) blog at a time. Like residents of Ottumwa and Nashua, bloggers cannot be swayed with broadcast e-mails and one-size-fits-all pitches.

Are blogs fund-raising machines? In the primary runs, the more money you raise early, the more likely you are going to be the last candidate standing in a tough race. (Lack of funds is the reason Tom Vilsack, a well-résuméd, attractive candidate, is no longer in the race.) The Dean campaign theory of going to the blogs was that it was possible through the Internet to induce millions of people to raise small amounts of money to make up for their deficit in large donors. Moreover, blogging (and enabling technologies like MeetUp) allows viral marketing: people raising money from their physical and virtual friends. Look at sites like South Asians for Obama—started up by one American with no ties to the campaign. By cash-registered measures, the Web-as-fund-raiser plan worked in 2003–2004: Dean raised at least $20 million before a single vote was cast in Iowa. (Kerry would himself raise about $80 million online.) On the other hand, as Dean learned, using blogs does not make other campaign expenditures—staffs, transportation, GOTV (get out the vote) measures, and radio ad costs—disappear, and the Dean campaign's coffers were emptied within weeks. The Internet and blogs are gold mines, with many miners who will organize themselves, but they do not negate the high costs of a modern presidential bid.

Are blogposts new-tech campaign books or speeches? Modern presidential candidates create media content when they write books, make speeches, debate, and hold press conferences. But their books are little read, even by loyal followers; the other discourses are mainly delivery vehicles for the seven-second sound bites their media consultants hope will be picked up by television news. Furthermore, most of what modern presidential candidates say and "write" is concocted by professional speechwriters and campaign staff. Such in-house authoring is not considered a scandal; everybody does it. Blogs are a different animal of audience interaction. Bloggers read entire posts carefully, especially those of politicians, not just the talking points a campaign leadership might herald. Blog readers demand authenticity. Woe to the blog-cred of the candidate whose first-person blog is outed as prepackaged, committee-fashioned talking points.

Are blogs "smoke-filled rooms" of insider decision making? Politicians yesterday and today have "closed" briefings, talks, and discussions with staff, party leaders, donors, friends, family, and even sympathetic journalists. Blogposts can mimic for the public the intimacy of such encounters. But, if posting all your speeches, press releases, and voting records on the Web constituted a gold mine for your adversary's oppositional research in the late 1990s, then nowadays presenting the world with your stream-of-consciousness thoughts on issues of the day, your taste in restaurants, and meditations on parenthood offers your enemies a host of ammunition. The old political rule dictates that the more you say, the more there is to hang you with. On the other hand, excessive caution may result, as it already has, in dull blogging, with just as many filters of editing and focus group testing for a blog as for the average speech or debating points. The more controlled or canned a blog seems, the less it reads like a sincere blog. The great blog communicators of the future will find ways to straddle that divide.

Are blogs television ads? The era of the thirty-second candidate is alive and well; television and its massive budget outlays will always be part of any presidential campaign. But blogs offer advantages over the tube. Blog ads and video logs (vlogs) are not yet covered by campaign reform rules. Blogs and vlogs can test-market a TV video but also can be deployed as an instant response to opponents' attacks without the usual production-cycle and time-buying delays of regular media. Again, though, as in the case of Howard Dean's 2004 run, if bloggers don't like what you are broadcasting, they will inform you, and their criticism will become the fodder of negative big media coverage.

Are blogs virtual campaign rallies? A blog can be a candidate's megaphone, complete with an eager audience, but as Senator Durbin learned when he reversed himself on defense of his Guantánamo remarks, although bloggers can be a loyal constituency, they are not an unswerving one. Political bloggers tend to be passionate, idealistic about their politics, and less forgiving of the gamesmanship, issue flopping, expediency, and compromise on positions that are part of normal politicking for office.

Are blogs talk radio? So claim many political insiders. Bloggers can shout issues to prominence and echo them in a vast global chamber of repetition and reaction, a force multiplier of attack and defense. When Senator Barack Obama (D-Illinois) offered a long post defending Democrats who had voted for the John Roberts nomination to the Supreme Court, it was the talk of liberal cyberspace for weeks, the subject of tens of thousands of posts, comments, and debates. Remember how Newt Gingrich was able to build alliances with talk radio hosts to help set the public agenda and win Congress in 1994? Today, bloggers and talk radio can be allied just as synergistically. When Pennsylvania Senator Rick Santorum appeared on Hugh Hewitt's radio show asking for support for his reelection bid, and then Hewitt put a link to donate money on his blog, Santorum's fund-raising jumped 500 percent! New superblogs like TownHall tend to unify blogging and talk radio. But independent bloggers differ from DJs and radio hosts in one important way: No matter how intemperate they get, they can't be fired or influenced by political pressure, publishers, or advertisers. On the other hand, some can be bought or subsidized, and no current law requires disclosure of such ties during the election season itself.

In sum: Use blogs with other media and other traditional campaign vehicles and venues. They can't work alone.

A candidate reading this memo would conclude that blogs are both different from and similar to familiar methods of political campaigning and influence. What follows are some examples of that dynamic at work.

Polblogging Style

Of course, politicians have always needed to balance the base (partisans) and the middle. Blogs make this tension, if not more difficult, more public. In the bloglands, you can't pack the rooms with your supporters, shut out hecklers, and enforce message discipline. For example, candidate Obama pioneered the use of MySpace as a campaign tool, and most of the posters to the site offer positive and good-natured comments. But look at what happens when you open up the gates of interactivity to anyone, from kooks to your sworn enemies to supporters who embarrass you by their support. Among the July 2007 commenters on the Obama MySpace site, one hip-hopper "Namaste" signed on to say, "Fallin' thru ta show ya some luv and say wassup!! Have an Excellent, Blessed Day!! 'lid . . . never follow." Fair enough, but does the accompanying video graphic of a nude woman jiggling her buttocks help or hurt the Senator from Illinois in his march to the White House? Then there's the scary LostInQueens who signed on to assure the candidate, "you can count on my vote." His graphic is a masked man pointing a gun at the viewer. And MySpace sells advertising: In one ad on Obama's page, the conservative magazine *Human Events* offers readers a free report on "the real Barack Obama," detailing issues from "his radical stance on abortion to his prominence in the corruption scandals that has been virtually ignored by the mainstream media" and asserts that "Barack Obama is not fit to be Senator – not to mention the next President of the United States." Again, such voluntary associations Obama could do without.

Furthermore, any candidate (or other human being) who is not a dedicated blogger will find it difficult to respond to queries and comments at length and in depth without producing inaccuracies and gaffes that delight his or her opponents. So are the rewards and returns of blogging worth the risks and efforts?[58] Perhaps such intangibles explain why, as of summer 2007, only a few of the two dozen or so major and minor possibles and probables (and dropouts) to run for the presidency in 2008 had blogs or guest blogged. Politicians and their staffs and consultants continue to wrestle with many issues of interactivity. For example, on his ForwardTogether Political Action Committee's blog, Mark Warner's avatar appears in video to project commilito: "Thanks for taking the first step in joining our online community; I hope you enjoy reading our blog and will use it to share your own thoughts; be sure to create your own account so you can start participating today." But even as of summer 2006, when it was still assumed he would run for president in 2008, there were no posts by Warner himself, only by staff members, one of whom describes himself as a just-upgraded intern. Howard Dean Internet campaign vet and founder of MyDD Jerome Armstrong was a consultant for the blog, although he too rarely posted on it. In an interview, Armstrong, coiner of the term *netroots,* said, "What I'm really looking for is for the campaign to use the Internet as a field mechanism. That's where I really think it has power . . . making it a tool for neighbor-to-neighbor interaction and persuasion. Taking what the Bush campaign did and making it more personal."[59] Of course, as noted, when a blogger becomes a consultant some people are put off. One commenter stated in response to a MyDD post favorable to Warner and his fund-raising for other Democrats: "Is MyDD an official organ of the Warner campaign now??? Why does Warner get the headline for these activities when a lot of other candidates are doing the same thing?" MyDD responded in turn, not to the accusation about a pro-Warner bent, but registering John Edwards's party fund-raising.

In fact, Edwards, a prolific and prolix blogger and flesh-presser of bloggers, is almost alone in fully diving into the medium. His reasons for going to the blogs may be, as they were for Dean in 2003, partly practical; he has no place else to go. One of the main benefits of office-holding is being in the public eye. But Edwards's speaking tours and blog outreach may make up for that publicity deficit, at least among activists who are paying attention during the invisible primary. Indeed, Edwards's nascent campaign seems to be a good test case in what blogs can do for a candidate or what one can do with them. In addition, there is the time factor. Being a senator or governor means that every once in a while you have to spend time at your office acting as a senator or a governor. Edwards is unrestricted by anybody else's clock: He can devote his time to campaigning. Finally, the bloglands, for all its mine-fields of candor, may be a much safer place for a politician than elected office. If you are a senator or congressperson today, you are faced with voting on Iraq war appropriations, even on Iraq war pullout options; every alternative will anger somebody. Antiwar gold star mother Cindy Sheehan has demonstrated at the Bush ranch in Crawford, Texas, and also outside the New York offices of Senator Clinton; by July 2007 she planned to run against California Senator Nancy Pelosi if there was no Iraq pullout. The poll ratings of the Democratic Congress registered at the time as low as the president's. If there is a big anti-incumbent backlash in 2008, Edwards can avoid it. He can play "populist outsider," too, a role he plainly relishes.

Blogging by other 2008 hopefuls is sporadic and problematic. Senator Clinton's first lonely "blog" entries on breast cancer for the American Cancer Society's Blogs for Hope were press releases rather than real posts and were very safely worded at that. One can compre-hend her reticence. Should Hillary Clinton give a $1,000-a-plate speech that will be covered by the networks or post a blog entry that may or may not attract any big media attention? (Further, when she gives that speech, her staff can control the crowd to a great extent, organizing a friendly response, which is not possible in the bloglands.)

Wesley Clark is another example of someone who has embraced the new technologies of interactive media. He maintains sites on Facebook, MySpace, YouTube, and Frappr. But once again, the lesson is that sim-ply "blogging up" does not automatically save or resurrect presidential ambitions. Clark's lively community blog (http://securingamerica.com/) features posts by him and those who register for the site. But the Clark Community Network—as of winter 2007—would not immediately have sold any political professional on blogging. In December 2005, the site hosted "Live Blogging with General Clark" in which commenters asked general questions on many topics, from government wiretapping to relations with Serbia and other more exotic issues. Consider how the following exchange highlighted the problems, prospects, and hilarities of *real* interactivity between candidate and public.

> *meshuggah1324*[60] *on December 19, 2005—5:29pm, 5:31pm.* General Clark, as a former Supreme Allied Commander in Europe and [considering] your military background, have you ever been briefed on UFOs? Do you know what really crashed near Roswell New Mexico in 1947? Why does the U.S. Government feel the need to keep this information above top secret? What national security reasons would keep them from fully disclosing this information to us? What are your opinions on the UFO/ET subject. Thank you sir, I respect you very much. [Also] Do you think the alien technology we've recovered is the reason for the 50+ years of denial when it comes to UFOs? Do agree [sic] it's time for disclosure and some congressional UFO hearings so that the 400+ Disclosure Project witnesses can testify before congress like they wanted to do just before the 9/11 attacks? Thank you . . .
>
> *Wes Clark on December 19, 2005—5:48pm.* I've never been briefed on Roswell.

Clark gave direct, if careful, answers to some questions. But sometimes, he did not reply at all, presumably because the queries were coming too fast, were too complicated for him to just rattle off responses quickly, were too dangerous to take stances toward, or because he realized that some posters were pulling his leg. Still, Clark and his staff have worked hard, recasting the Clark Community Network in the summer of 2006 and holding more (and tighter) live blogs—for example, "I've been doing my best to speak out for Democrats while working to help as many great candidates as possible as we head towards the 2006 elections, and I would love to hear from you today and answer any questions you may have. So tell me what's on your mind!" Of interest is an attempt to create a visual symbol for the candidate—an analog of Dean's red bat—with the graphic of a very muscular donkey charging forward waving an American flag. Clark's blog is getting more refined, another sign of the battlefield trial-and-error part of deploying new weapons technology.

The former governor of Iowa, Tom Vilsack, also blogs, although not regularly. In September 2005, he guest blogged for a week at TalkingPointsMemoCafé (http://www.tpmcafe.com/user/tvilsack/diary). His language was oriented toward treating the blogs as I do here, as *lands*, a place to go to meet people. He wrote, "While I spend time with your community this week . . ." and then combined this sense of "other space" with his own over-the-shoulder description of his Walking Across Iowa tour. He explains,

> I've done so for the past six years and I find it exciting to be following the discussion here from my Blackberry the entire time. I want to take a moment now and respond to the great comments you had about the role of government, and the Democratic Party's message.

He then replied to comments on his previous posts, mostly on the role of government in people's lives. His tone was chummy, but the text was informative. It was a well-crafted anecdote. The hint that his experience as governor can be applied to higher offices is not lost: "Moving good state programs to the federal level starts with good state leadership." Vilsack obviously has no illusions that blogging will replace retail politics of the face-to-face kind but rather seems to understand that one can use blogging to complement local politicking. In the end, however, under the shadow of Barack Obama and the Clinton money machine, Vilsack withdrew from the presidential race; blogging alone could not make him a viable candidate. Presidential contenders, thus, should regard blogging as a tool, a special one that cannot be approached carelessly or appropriated willfully without regard to its possible blowbacks. Nor can it ever be seen as some sort of deus ex machina that will salvage a failing campaign or flawed message.

The premier example of the perils of polblogging came with the first blog blowup of campaign 2008. As mentioned, John Edwards, from almost the first days after the defeat of 2004, started working the blogs, talking to bloggers, blogging, and then hiring bloggers. Among the more prominent of the latter were Amanda (Pandagon) Marcotte and Melissa (Shakespeare's Sister) McEwan. The move was seen as a coup in the blog community. Marcotte posted the announcement:

> I feel that the best candidate for feminists to endorse is John Edwards. That Hillary Clinton is a woman is not enough for me, since she makes maneuvers that send up all sorts of red flags. In sum, I want Edwards to win and I want to help make that happen. The other reason I'm joining the campaign is because I think that they really understand the growing importance of the internet in politics. Seriously, look at how cool [John Edwards's] blog is already and this is all before I get my hooks into it. I want to make the internet a more important part of politics, and I see this campaign as a way to do that.

Marcotte's reasons for joining the campaign were revealing: ideology plus the feeling that Edwards understood the new medium like no other candidate.[61] As Jerome Armstrong put it: "Edwards [Is] Wrapping up the Left Blogosphere."[62] It was a reminder of the Carter–McGovern "people" strategy, but instead of street and organizational activists, Edwards was doing an end run around the Clinton money colossus by going after the feisty left partisans of the Web.

Then the unraveling began, with blog upon blog drive-bys. Michelle Malkin showcased some controversial quotes from Marcotte's writings, most drawn from those uncovered by other conservative bloggers:

> Today's "Jesus cries when women fuck" update by Amanda Marcotte. . . . Well, the Texas House of Representatives got Republican Jesus and he reminded them that out of all the things he hates, which are multitude, nothing incurs his wrath more than women's sexuality.
>> Don't relegate yourself to the used cunt lot
>> Of course, if you're a perverted religious nut, the blood and the pain of "cherry"-breaking is probably a de riguer [sic] part of a woman's life, both to give the man a cheap thrill of actual blood while enacting the sex-as-violent-possession construction that is

part of virginity fetishization and to remind the woman of her religious teaching that womanhood is suffering (see: Genesis).

Malkin commented,

> The question is: How long will the Edwards campaign want the "insightful" and "issues-oriented" Marcotte to be a part of them? Seems that everyone but the Edwards campaign has tracked Marcotte's foul-mouthed nutroots diatribes. Or perhaps the Edwards team is well aware of her lunatic blogging and can't wait for her to unleash her unbridled anger on their spiffy website to give him a gritty, "progressive" edge.[63]

Such thrusts and counterthrusts followed, but as with other blog impacts, the real heat began when the mainstream news took notice. A blogger on the ABC.com Web site asked: "Does John Edwards Condone Hate Speech?" The *New York Times* site weighed in on "Edwards's Blogger Blooper."[64] Most persistently, Bill Donohue, head of the 350,000-strong Catholic League for Religious and Civil Rights, charged Pandagon with anti-Catholicism and antireligious bigotry; he found platforms on shows like *The O'Reilly Factor* to repeat his indictments. One Pandagon quote he cited as being particularly offensive was as follows:

> Q: What if Mary had taken Plan B after the Lord filled her with his hot, white, sticky Holy Spirit? A: You'd have to justify your misogyny with another ancient mythology.

Queried Donohue: "Why [has Edwards] chosen to embrace foul-mouthed, anti-Catholic bigots on his payroll?" Marcotte was further accused of deleting posts from her blog archives to cover up her past rants. Left bloggers defended her, maintaining that it was a perfectly innocuous archiving problem.

The Edwards campaign took notice but seemed to experience difficulty in finding an appropriate counterstrategy. At first, Edwards hung tough, albeit with a left-handed uncertainty, stating,

> I talked personally to the two women who were involved. They gave me their word they, under no circumstances, intended to

denigrate any church or anybody's religion and offered their apologies for anything that indicated otherwise. I took them at their word. . . . It will not happen again. That you can be sure of.[65]

Edwards was praised by some left blogs for sticking by his allies. David Goldstein on a Huffington Post blog declared,

> By standing up to Malkin and Donohue when it would have been much easier to cave, Edwards has decided to take a blow on behalf of a nascent progressive netroots movement most establishment Democrats neither fully understand nor appreciate. Whether or not he is my candidate, this blogger is going to stand up for Edwards in return.[66]

But then came the collapse. Both bloggers resigned from the campaign and resumed their independent blogging. In context, they did so *after* receiving much hate mail (and even some personal drop-by threats) of the scariest kind. Marcotte printed on her blog e-mails that told her "you just need a good f˙king from a real man!" "It's just too bad your mother didn't abort you," and "YOU RACIST WHORE. FAT UGLY B˙˙˙H." (Even stronger language appeared that can't be reprinted in these pages.) Again, who would want a voluntary association that results in such attacks?

The painful experience for all involved highlighted some basic lessons about polblogging. First, the technology of blogger and blog vetting is tricky: Edwards notably admitted that before hiring the two left bloggers, he had never actually met them. Second, as noted, there is no code of ethics about deleting posts and rewriting them; every blogger is her or his own ombudsman and compliance officer. But on a larger level, the very qualities that make blogging refreshing in comparison to measured, bland campaign-speak also make them dangerous. A rant may initially read well—as I know from my own experience, especially if like-minded partisans share one's outrage du jour—but the same text may come off as embarrassing when highlighted in red on someone else's blog or dissected in the pages of a newspaper. The future will illuminate what lessons candidates learn in the tortuous process of incorporating blogs into campaigns for office. For now, we can understand why many politicians and political professionals are struggling over how, when, and if to become bloggers.

Finally, the political candidate who blogs—blogs seriously—will have to anticipate what happened in the Dean campaign: Bloggers will expect a passionate embrace or some validation of their zeal. One wonders, then, whether certain candidates, because of their low-key personalities, may not be the best fit—*blogfit* versus traditionally mediafit—for blogging. In fact, it is possible to make a prediction of a sort on this issue. If bloggers tend to be people who are more excited about their politics than the average person, then the profile of the candidate who will most attract them will be someone who is more sharply defined as either a conservative or a liberal. That does not mean, however, that bloggers (who, after all, are politically educating themselves as well as others) want to be the amen choir on the *Titanic*. Most political bloggers I have interviewed have no wish to support a lost cause; they would like their side to win, with as few compromises to truth and justice as possible. As Natasha Chart (Dean campaign, Pacific Views) said to me, "We work with who we have; we support them when they do right by us."

During the period of the primaries, this may be an attractive reciprocity: candidates vying for the Republican nomination appealing to the conservative base, and Democrats to their liberal base. Candidates who have strong positions will invite strong support from such an audience. It is unsurprising, for example, that Senator Russ Feingold (D-Wisconsin), who has consistently since 9/11 taken the most liberal and left positions on the war in Iraq, civil liberties, and a host of other issues, won the straw poll held on the DailyKos Web site, while a moderate centrist candidate, more beloved and thought of as "winnable" by party elders, insiders, and traditional players—Evan Bayh, governor of Indiana—received only 1 percent of support in the poll. Notably, neither chose to run for the 2008 presidency.

It is worth asking as a necessary correction whether some candidates should blog, can blog, or even more in the extreme, might consider being openly antiblog. No better subject presents itself for such a speculative enterprise than 2008 Democratic Party presidential hopeful Senator Hillary Rodham Clinton of New York.

Case Study: When Not to Blog—Hillary's Dilemma

I began *Blogwars* by asserting that my bias was "problog." Being pro-blog, however, is as nonspecific as being "profood." I am problogging as a concept, I am enamored of the technology, and I am supportive of useful (nutritious!) blogging. But I have also emphasized that political blogs are (a) hard work, (b) full of blowback perils, (c) difficult to maintain successfully, and (d) prone to eliciting excitement, passion, and verbal violence of a high degree. Perhaps it is fitting, then, to end this discussion of professional political blogging by making the case that sometimes politicians should not blog.

For many politicians, there can be good reasons not to blog. As shown with the Dean campaign, bloggers can take up time and effort; like any dating partner, they expect attention. Perhaps rather than disappointing bloggers, one should simply not blog at all. Alternatively, as was the case for Wesley Clark, interactivity can force one into a tight corner. From the point of view of the professional, the biggest red flag about blogging is its uncontrolled nature. The great dilemma becomes: Do we filter out anybody who might embarrass the candidate? On the other hand, if we "troll" too many people from a blog, it won't be credible as a blog. Finally, of course, the point made earlier about campaign Web sites being gold mines for oppositional research is even truer for blogs. Blogs seem primed for gaffes; their instant-everywhere, unerasable nature makes it likely that 2006–2008 will see some candidate somewhere blog some infernal blunder. It is equally unlikely that the Edwards blogger flap will be the only time a candidate is mortified by something a hired blogger has posted.

Such issues and others challenge Senator Clinton. As of spring 2007, the New York senator and former first lady has the largest war chest and the highest name recognition, and has topped ratings in national polls, of any Democrat in the pool for a possible presidential bid. Susan Estrich, in her book *The Case for Hillary Clinton*, argued that she was the perfect candidate because: "[W]hich of your safe white men are going to excite the base the way Hillary does, so they can spend all their time in the middle? I'll answer: None."[67]

In fact, part of the base, as reflected in left blogs, is hardly cheering on the junior senator from New York. She is faring poorly among the left-dem-liberal blogs and partisans precisely *because* of her consistent attempt to steer a "middle" policy course and win swing voters.[68] As one *Washington Post* headline put it: "Clinton Angers Left with Call for Unity: Senator Accused of Siding with Centrists."[69] Leading the left disparagement was Kos himself. In response, Bob Kunst, the long-time liberal Democratic activist who has led the grassroots Hillary Now group since 2003, argued that blogs represent only one section of the Democratic left. That assessment is correct, but the multimillion-visitor DK site gives Kos the largest independent soapbox on the Web. The press and the party take him seriously as a player, a sure sign that the blog has arrived in the circles of power. He is not alone among big left bloggers either. Arianna Huffington, editor and organizer of the major group blog named after her, posted a mock "red state" strategy memo for Clinton, making witty barbs against the New York senator's turn to the right. Items include "HRC sponsors bill authorizing president to use all available force against Satan—and the nations that harbor him—to spread freedom and democracy in Hell. . . ."

Moreover, blogs give voice (a megaphone) to people who used to be pretty much one-story human interest pieces in old-media formula journalism. Following is a diatribe from gold star mother and antiwar leader Cindy Sheehan on "Hillary as Warmonger":

> This was also the year that we also began to hold such Republicans in Democratic clothing like Hillary Clinton, Joe Lieberman, Joe Biden, and Diane Feinstein (list is by no means all inclusive) accountable for their support of what George is doing in Iraq. When we as Democrats elect our leaders we expect them to reject and loudly repudiate the murderous and corrupt policies of this administration, not support and defend them.[70]

Have such slings and arrows affected Clinton's poll numbers? Not yet, but in the long invisible primary, minor snags can signify major problems to come.

In fact, one major piece of evidence suggests that Hillary Clinton has been worried about her left flank.[71] In early 2006, the Democratic National Committee voted to insert one or two new first-tier caucuses and new primaries based on "criteria [of] racial and ethnic diversity;

geographic diversity; and economic diversity including [labor] union density." On the assumption that she were to run, this change could prove to benefit a 2008 Clinton presidential campaign by positioning "safe" Clinton states immediately after Iowa and New Hampshire. As history attests, Bill Clinton established himself as a front-runner even after losing both Iowa and New Hampshire in 1992 by winning southern states with huge African American Democratic bases. Similarly in 1984, Walter Mondale's campaign was saved by victories in Georgia and Alabama after Gary Hart's strong second place in Iowa and upset win in New Hampshire.

The proposed schedule change reflected the desire of a number of Democrats, such as members of the Congressional Black Caucus, to follow Iowa with "diversity" states such as South Carolina, which has a large black population, or perhaps another state that has a large Hispanic population. But the move was pro-Clinton and conducted by Clinton allies: Her greatest bulwark is her high level of support from black Americans and black Democratic officials. Bill Clinton was famously dubbed America's "first black president," and this two-way attachment was highlighted in 1992 when he won Georgia, South Carolina, and many Super Tuesday states where African Americans make up a huge percentage or even a majority of the voting Democratic base. As newsman Jim Lehrer put it, Clinton, after a string of early losses, came "back from the dead . . . with a lot of black votes." With such goodwill among a key Democratic constituency, the senator hopes for what sports fans know as a "three-peat" of the Clinton "southern" election strategies of '92 and '96. If Senator Clinton were to suffer an early reverse, it would be to her advantage that Democratic Party leaders build some friendly firewalls between and after the contests in the Hawkeye and Granite states. Such a strategy made perfect sense until Barack Obama declared his candidacy and then increasingly showed strong support among black voters.

In sum, it is clear that Hillary does have something to fear; hence, the need for her to ensure an early blowout. Yes, left-blog attacks and eruptions of irritation by her own grassroots supporters at Senator Clinton's strategies for a White House run are statistically on the fringe. But politicians and political professionals understand that wildfires on the edges of public opinion can spread to the center. Worse, activist bloggers, with their giant Web soapbox, can be heard by mainstream media who, hungry for new stories, might start fanning the "Clinton in trouble with left base" flames.

Until the late fall days of 2006, many were asking what Hillary's blog strategy should be; should she have one at all? Winning the presidency is still about money, and by some predictions, Hillary will be the first presidential candidate never to take public funding in primaries or afterward. Her war chest will be so large that, as one Republican fund-raiser, Rodney Smith, told me, "The only possible counterstrategy would be to run a billionaire against her." When sums as large as $200 to $300 million are being spent, do blogs matter at all, or will they be drowned out by television, direct mail (land mail and e-mail), and get-out-the-vote foot soldiering?

These were Clinton's choices in 2006 for 2007–2008:

1. *Ignore the left blogs.* Assume that victories in the primaries will eventually silence her internal critics; they will come on board as it is proven that she is the party's nominee and only hope for a Democratic presidency. Problems with this strategy are that (a) bloggers are not a herd to be led (by fiat or force) wherever a politician wants, (b) it is anathema for bloggers to shut up and get in line, and (c) while in 2004 Kerry could count on anti-Bush loathing on the left, it is not as clear that the 2008 Republican nominee (say, Mitt Romney or John McCain) will generate as much antipathy.

2. *Co-opt the left blogs.* Clinton could, as does John Edwards, meet with left bloggers, brief them, show (or feign) respect for them, make the case that she must attract a majority of the electorate, and ask for left-blog help in the crusade to retake the White House. And in some instances, she can buy cooperation: hire any major left blogger who will sign on as a consultant. Of course, as I have said, political bloggers, if one can generalize about them, tend to be honest and passionate about their ideologies. I believe they are less likely to be bought off, spun, or sweet-talked than the average local party boss.

3. *Attack the left blogs.* An intriguing option for Hillary Clinton is to use (or rather abuse) left blogs to push forward her appeal to middle voters. Thus far, with many positions like supporting an anti-flag-burning amendment, she has been engaging in *countertyping.*[72] This is when a politician offers up imagery, symbolism, and words that counter an established negative prejudice that an audience might have. So a female Democratic candidate would send campaign messages that portray her as "strong on defense" and "tough on crime," featuring scenes of her slamming jail cell doors or shaking hands with Marines. A male Republican candidate might try to appear "compassionate" and "caring" by showing himself touring a day care center, and so on.

If Clinton's main concern was the general election contest—that is, winning the middle and swing voters—then she (and her lead live-in political strategist) may have considered a Sister Souljah moment, with the symbolic target this time being antiwar left bloggers. An SS moment refers to the time in 1992 when Bill Clinton criticized the black, female rap artist for sounding like David Duke for a comment she made on the lines of "why not have a week and kill white people?" (Souljah said the remark was taken out of context.) The political implication was that Clinton came off as a moderate Democrat not beholden to an "extremist" of the left and thus was more acceptable to sociocultural moderates and conservatives.

Do left bloggers present such a target of opportunity today? In politics and war, people judge you by your friends and your enemies. The idea behind the SS moment strategy is to pick an enemy who can win you more friends. John Cole of Balloonjuice blog put it best: "Most politicians would pay to have this kind of opposition."[73] Surely, one option would have been to attack the left, via blogs, to gain even more of a reputation as a moderate. The downside here is obvious—a huge cyberspace blowback—but if all Clinton cares about is poll numbers, then she and her advisers might decide that a sharp elbow jab to the left might be symbolic proof to middle voters that her moderate views are not just electoral cant.

It might have been tempting, then, if the Clinton team is confident their "base" numbers are solid, to challenge a left blog, preferably one that has made some heated statement about the Iraq war that is beyond the pale of mainstream American public opinion. The danger is that, in mass communication terms, this is not 1992. Sister Souljah could only complain to the big media and her friends (by phone). Or write a song. Blogs have their own instant platforms, outreach, and weaponry. There is more danger (and here is a warning to all political candidates) that in attacking *some* blogs, bloggers may take offense that you are attacking blogging itself. There is a difference, but Bill Clinton, after all, deftly attacked some lyrics of one rap singer; he did not attack rap itself. Such are the intricacies, for politicians, of whether to blog or not blog.

By the first days of 2007, however, Hillary would embrace blogs—sort of—and then YouTube. Three events swiftly demonstrated that blogs really were part of presidential elections and that the leading Democratic candidate and her team felt they could not be ignored, dismissed, or "dissed." First, to great fanfare on the bloglands, former President Bill Clinton invited to lunch left bloggers such as Atrios, MyDD's Matt Stoller, and DailyKos's mcjoan. The picture of the bloggers posing with a former president seemed to herald a new era indeed: the iconoclasts invited into the temple—although, for many left bloggers, affection for Bill does not transfer to Hillary, her perceived opportunism, or her policies. Second, Hillary hired Peter Daou, of Salon.com's Daou Report and director of blog operations for John Kerry in 2004, to be her blogger in chief. Then came the defining moment. Clinton announced that she was formally running for president in true (or attempted true) blog style: Her online announcement appeared before she made her spoken declaration. Furthermore, the signature line of her announcement speech was that as part of a goal of "listening to the American people" she desired a dialogue; she put forth the invitation: "Let's talk." (Her later *Sopranos*-inspired video on YouTube reemphasized that she would not concede the new media battleground to anyone else.)

That such an obvious stylistic paean to blogs arrived about ten years after the term *weblog* was first coined reflects a certain symmetry.

However, a crucial coda that has not escaped politicians, even potential presidents, is that interactive media are a sword that many can wield, not just the powerful, and can swing in all directions. As I have noted, a number of my students and not a few bloggers I have interviewed for this book have found the personal price of interactivity too high. Will candidates pull back from interactive technologies because they work too well rather than because they don't work at all?

Barack Obama seems aware of such paradoxes, but like the rest he is not sure what can be done about them. In his autobiography, *The Audacity of Hope*, he relates that in the summer of 2005, he was asked to give a short speech during the dedication of the Abraham Lincoln Presidential Library and Museum in Springfield, Illinois. Obama praised Lincoln's eloquence and also the martyred president's initiative in rising from poverty to the highest office in the land. Subsequently, *Time* magazine asked Obama to contribute a mini-essay on Lincoln but requested something "more personal" (i.e., bloglike) than the speech. Obama thus wrote for the world's leading newsmagazine: "He never won Illinois' Senate seat. But in many ways, he paved the way for me. . . . In Lincoln's rise from poverty, his ultimate mastery of language and law, his capacity to overcome personal loss and remain determined in the face of repeated defeat—in all this, he reminded me not just of my own struggles . . . "[74] It was an innocuous comment. Obama was clearly not claiming "I am Lincoln." But columnist Peggy Noonan could not resist saying that Obama was "explaining he's a lot like Abraham Lincoln, only sort of better." In response, Obama noted,

> As soon as Ms. Noonan's column hit, it went racing across the Internet, appearing on every right-wing website as proof of what an arrogant, shallow boob I was (just the quote Ms. Noonan selected, and not the essay itself, generally made an appearance on these sites). In that sense, the episode hinted at a more subtle and corrosive aspect of modern media—how a particular narrative, repeated over and over again and hurled through cyberspace at the speed of light, eventually becomes a hard particle of reality; how political caricatures and nuggets of conventional wisdom lodge themselves in our brain without us ever taking the time to examine them.

No insight and incident better sum up the situation that modern politicians face when confronted by blogging and the many interactive, instant, always-on viral media technologies to come.

Finally, it all boils down to control. There will always be among human beings differentiations of power; societies numbering more than a few hundred people that have tried to level us typically only succeed in creating another class of elites. I do not agree with those who say that the new media world will be egalitarian, but (and here is the key) the novel technologies, styles, and attitudes *allow* for upsets, reversals, and overturns of authority. Is it a surprise that the first, and still the most famous and most viewed, "commercial" of the 2008 presidential race was the "Vote Different" ad created by an individual, posted on YouTube, and virally transmitted to, well, everybody? Yes, ParkRidge 47 (Phil de Vellis), the author of the Apple 1984 parody attack on Hillary as Big Brother, is a political media professional, although he was unemployed at the time. But he demonstrated that the basement interactor can—with luck, wit, and skill—get the political attention of the nation. The little guy scored big, and the big institutions took note. There is something very hopeful, and very American, about the possibility of such bootstrap success in the global marketplace of ideas.

Afterpost: Continue the Conversation

I started this book about blogging by saying that its medium, venue, and style heralded a wave of interactive technologies that will change our society, culture, and politics. In this regard, the headliner of 2007 is certainly YouTube. In the spring, building on its new status as the network of record for our culture, the user-generated video online service started up a Choice08 section featuring political clips of the presidential race ranging from those provided by campaigns (e.g., "Romney on Iraq") to the indy-viewer parody (e.g., several minutes of John Edwards primping to the soundtrack of *Westside Story*'s "I Feel Pretty"). To someone like me, who grew up in the pre-remote-control, three-network evening news era, Choice08 is yet another example of something amazing happening in the world of mediated politics. To echo Thomas Paine, "our style and manner of thinking" is indeed undergoing a revolution. Yet the new needs the old as much as the old is transforming itself to work with the new. CNN partnered with YouTube to host debates of the candidates, complete with videoed questions and comments submitted by viewers. Mash-up debates followed.

Such linkages are crucial. Neither blogs nor any other interactive media will elect presidents unaided. We know this from the many cases of blog-originated stories that became consequential news items only when caught up by the bigger media. We also understand the importance of a multimedia approach to blogs through polling data. A study by the Pew Research Center found most people "viewing" four YouTube videos (the Clintons' parody of *The Sopranos* finale; Obama Girl's "I Got a Crush on Obama"; John McCain's joking about bombing Iran; and John Edwards' "I Feel Pretty") were more likely to see them on television than on the Internet.[1] On the other hand, another study by Pew found that Americans' public affairs knowledge has actually declined since the creation of the commercial Internet in 1989.

We can, therefore, with caveats in mind, state certain probabilities about the present and future of political blogging.

1. *Political blogging is the province of people who are passionate about politics, policies, and public affairs and will work to change the world.* In spring 2007, I, my colleague Dhavan Shah of the University of Wisconsin, and his doctoral students conducted a survey of some 150 prominent political bloggers.[2] Among our findings: They were least enthused to start and maintain their blogs by the lure of money; they were most motivated by the following:

- to provide an alternative perspective to mainstream media
- to help society
- to influence public opinion
- to help a political party or cause

In short, they wanted to make a difference. As we know, one of the primary criticisms of blogs is that they tend to be partisan champions of the left or the right. Bloggers will respond by saying that enthusiasm and taking a strong stance is a virtue.[3] Often, bloggers will poke fun at their open partisanship by using the term *rant* in reference to their own postings. Temperament also plays a role: News and political professionals are sometimes taken aback by bloggers' zeal. Traditional journalists, for example, are supposed to be calm, cool, and collected on air and in print. The personality conflict is reminiscent of the brusque reaction of '70s fictional news director Lou Grant to reporter Mary Richards on her first day of work in broadcast news: "You've got spunk. I hate spunk." That enthusiasm, however, leads the young to take up blogging; from that same cohort will emerge the next generation of political leaders in America. Blogging will be a portal and training ground for the campaign and election workers, political media consultants, and even candidates of the future.

2. *Unless you buy them off, bloggers cannot be controlled from above or from real or virtual headquarters.* Political bloggers, because of their commitment and even irascibility, are much less susceptible to being duped or led willy-nilly by political masters. Although bloggers are not quite a herd of veritable cats, the blog form demands independent decision making while at the same time encouraging group association. It follows that, while blogs will swarm issues, only a rare concern will elicit agreement among all bloggers. Furthermore, if one seeks to understand a microcosm of oppositional opinions on any one issue, blogs are a good place to look first. Voluntary alliances are much more likely to be fruitful ones.

3. The essence of understanding blog interactivity is its personal relationship building: Roman fellow soldiership, or commilito. If it is true that successful mass communication is that which best approximates successful personal communication, then the blog is an ideal form of political expression and participation. A blog allows interactivity of such a high degree that it is not clear whether there is a separate sender and receiver or communicator and audience but rather an interactor alternating between both. Someone who comments frequently on Little Green Footballs feels like an LGF blogger in a way that no viewer of the *CBS Evening News* in the 1970s felt that they were on the broadcast team. The camaraderie of blogging through voluntary association is its social mainstay; the challenge for anyone seeking to penetrate that assembly is to be seen as sincerely interested in interaction and sustain it.

4. *Blogs have achieved greatness, not had it thrust upon them, nor are they a fad or accident; that is why they will become part of almost every political campaign.* Political bloggers have attained their power, prominence, and popularity because they offer speedy deployment, group accretion of knowledge, freedom from the structural rigidity of managerial bureaucracies and megaprofit-driven industries, and rapid revision to incorporate new information. They expose and overcome perennial problems in the existing political-media system. Bloggers do

not represent "the people" per se, but they can speak for an influential and powerful segment of the body politic.

5. *The mission of those who appreciate blogs and see their potential is to educate the public about the most efficacious ways to use blogs to enrich knowledge of politics and public affairs and stimulate healthy political activism and participation.* Salon.com managing editor Scott Rosenberg once commented, "The rise of blogs does not equal the death of professional journalism. The media world is not a zero-sum game. Increasingly, in fact, the Internet is turning it into a symbiotic ecosystem—in which the different parts feed off one another and the whole thing grows."[4] Indeed, like a marketplace within the greater marketplace of *all* media, the various oppositional voices in the bloglands constitute many rich possibilities of replicating the kind of ideal debate about issues that the founders of this country had in mind when they envisioned a free and open press. Conversely, if people seek out and listen to only what communication scholars call "feedback that fits"—that is, political expression that repeats and confirms our existing political beliefs—no one gains.

6. *Although blogging notoriety is often related to high-profile, "sexy," big stories, there are many journeymen bloggers who are pioneering the bloglands and focusing on issues on the local level.* Bloggers are performing many admirable political education functions. Instead of worrying about their excesses, we should be teaching ourselves and our children to emulate their successes, such as creating dialogues where previously there were only top-down monologues and infusing new energy into the watchdogging of government—local, national, and international.

7. *Blogs can teach us to stop and think about the nature of information in a hyperkinetic, mediated data world.* Because we encounter political blogs on the Internet, a medium that we associate with quickness of transport and instantaneous updating, does not mean that blogs cannot serve for everyone a function analogous to slow (and nutritious) food versus fast (but junk) food. The best blogging, I have argued, is deep analysis; it freezes a moment, pondering, researching, considering, and offering observations that arrest the accelerated and shallow sensationalism of most regular media. I know of no better way to teach

my students how to be scrutinizing consumers of political information, and even creators of it, than for them to construct blogposts that inform as well as entertain their peers.

8. *My students—the I-D-S (Internet-digital-satellite-selfcasting) generation—want to create and build (as well as remix/mash up), not just consume and witness.* Media that do not adapt to their wants and preferences will simply be ignored by them, as the music industry and the movie business are learning to their cost. Only something bloglike in its interactivity will engage them in news and public affairs. All of us, from the traditional print journalist to the entrepreneur podcaster, should work toward developing venues that help our eighteen-year-olds become engaged and informed political citizens. In particular, the young political class, the engaged campaign correspondents and workers of today and tomorrow, is extremely blog sympathetic.

9. *Those who recoil at the vitriol of blogs, who see in them the face of the undeservedly self-important cartoon Calvin, the populist villain Lonesome Rhodes, or the scribbling poison-pen mercuries, miss the point that argumentation can be enlightening.* As noted, John Milton supported "liberty of unlicenc'd printing" and the clash of opposing ideas despite the fact that he was a very partisan political advocate. You would be as ill served using a single blog as a sole source of political information as would a behavioral theorist whose only data source for a generalized psychological insight was one mouse. To get the most out of blogs, you need to peruse them, develop relationships based on trust, and appreciate those blogs that you believe faithfully inform you, accurately, eloquently, and insightfully. Above all, read blogs that infuriate you and with which you disagree and use their contrarian logic and positions to question your own system of political beliefs.

10. *Blogs, or whatever blogging becomes, instead of spurring political cynicism, will rejuvenate political participation by making us all more responsible citizens.* A recent research study found that viewers of the *Daily Show* tended to become more cynical about politicians but also felt "increased confidence in their ability to understand the complicated world of politics."[5] Blog information gathering and argumentation will help as well in making more of us—especially our youth—feel more empowered to participate in democracy, more as stakeholders than

as an audience for politics. As Kathleen Hall Jamieson wrote shortly before the arrival of blogs in the political marketplace,

> The likelihood that the public will be misled is minimized if the competing views are available and tested by advocates, audiences, and the press, if all sides engage in warranted argument, and if they accept responsibility for defending their own claims and the claims others offer on their behalf. This concept sounds idealistic, but unless a certain critical degree of substantive interchange is preserved among candidates, the people, and the media that control their encounters, the possibility of a critical information deficit will exist.[6]

An updated notation is that we can no longer trust politics to the politicians, journalism to the journalists, or for that matter, education to the educators. To borrow again from our ancient protoblogger Isocrates, somebody needs to be "waging war against the false pretenders to wisdom."[7] Through blogs, we can stimulate a "substantive interchange" of facts, ideas, and arguments among voters as well as candidates. Blogs offer many competing views and allow us to try to identify and remedy our self-evident "critical information deficit" about so many issues that involve our lives, our nation, and our world. And, as noted, perhaps most important, the political workers, players, and powers of the future will grow up tutored in politics by interactive media such as blogs.

I see such a phenomenon at work in my students: yes, some are turned off from blogging due to the rough-and-tumble nature of the beast. But even in disappointment, even in failed interactivity, some people find more reason to get involved, to do something positive. To wit, one major event that confirmed that the old and new media were building upon each other was the July 2007 debate among Democratic presidential hopefuls. Broadcast on CNN, the interchange featured questions selected from about 3,000 videos submitted via the megavideovlog YouTube. One of the younger respondents was a student at my university who described himself as "floored" when he saw his twenty-seven-second video on television. His query was directed at Senators Clinton and Obama and dealt with the race and gender issues of the election . . . but that's not the whole story. Jordan Williams, age twenty, told our local paper that he was "a little bit dismayed when Sen. Obama made a joke. . . . But they didn't answer the question, so I was immediately a little annoyed." Indeed, but Williams, a member of the Campus Young Democrats organization, expressed his continuing interest in following political news and being a good "citizen." He added: "I just think it's very important. Some people care about what Lindsay Lohan's doing on the weekend, and I like to care about what speech [John] Edwards recently gave."[8]

But blogging no longer speaks truth to power just virtually. Political candidates, as we have seen, now regularly meet with bloggers in person, at group lunches, or by speaking to their conventions. In fact, as I was reviewing the proof pages of this book, a coda to the first great chapter of blogging's ascent into politics and policymaking arrived in my e-mail box. John Donovan, the Kansas milblogger of Argghhh!, announced cryptically that big news was coming soon. Forty-eight hours later, he reported on his blog that he and other milbloggers such as Matt Burden (BlackFive), Mrs. Greyhawk (Mudville Gazette), NZ Bear (TTLB and the Victory Caucus), and Mohammed (Iraq the Model) had met with President Bush in the White House, with a number of high officials and aides in attendance. The commander in chief of the United States said, "I looked at my schedule today, and I found it interesting that I would be sitting down with bloggers." On his blogpost about the event, Donovan added, "No more interesting than we found it, Sir. Trust me on that." Bloggers had literally entered the corridors of power. I believe they will never be shut out again.

That does not mean that we are at the end of the history of blogs, and that they will ride off into the sunset hand in hand with voters and politicians. As I hope I have documented here, political blogging *can* enrich us, but we should never forget its frequent employment and great potential as a weapon. For example, one innovative use of political blogs, shown early in the 2008 campaigns, was to cite them in negative radio and television political advertising as an authoritative source. Whereas once an electronic political ad would refer to something negative said about an opponent in a newspaper, now one can quote an antagonistic blog about them. The ethics of this practice are questionable, especially when the blogger is anonymous (or is a paid operative of the attacker) and the information is erroneous.

Blogging, thus, is a means, not an end, to a new political culture, but its possibilities, perils, and promises are so great that all of us—scholars, professionals, amateurs, and anyone who cares about the state of American politics and the health of the republic—should become part of the conversation. If you consider this book to be a long blogpost, realize that it is incomplete without the thread of reader insights that the best blogging incites. I hope that process can begin now because 2008 is the beta test for blogging public policy, campaigns, and elections. In politics and media technology, although the future is uncertain, it will not go unblogged.

Notes

Preface

1. David D. Perlmutter, "The Internet: Big Pictures and Interactors," in *Image Ethics in the Digital Age*, 2nd ed., eds. Larry Gross, John Stuart Katz, and Jay Ruby (Minneapolis: University of Minnesota Press, 2004), 1–26.

2. "Tech Helps and Hurts Politicians," emarketer, April 13, 2007, http://www.emarketer.com/Article.aspx?id=1004797.

3. Edelman Group, *A Corporate Guide to the Global Blogosphere* (New York: Edelman Group, 2007), 4, 9.

4. Daniel W. Drezner, "Which Blogs Are Read by the Media?" (May 31, 2004), http://www.danieldrezner.com/archives/001321.html.

5. Brad DeLong, "We're Certainly Getting Our Money's Worth from Senator Boxer" (February 12, 2005), http://www.j-bradford-delong.net/movable_type/2005-3_archives/000344.html.

6. M. Manuel, "Election 2004," *Atlanta Journal-Constitution*, July 25, 2004, 1E; M. Manuel, "Election Affirms Net's Influence," *Atlanta Journal-Constitution*, November 14, 2004, 4A.

7. Tom Price, "Do Computers and the Internet Enhance Democracy?" *CQ Researcher* 14, no. 32 (September 17, 2004): 757–780.

8. D. G. Bystrom, M. C. Banwart, T. Robertson, and L. L. Kaid, *Gender and Political Candidate Communication: VideoStyle, WebStyle, and NewsStyle* (New York: Routledge, 2004); Kaye Trammell, "Blogging and Hyperlinking," Paper presentation, Political Communication Division, International Communication Association (May 2004).

9. Lee Rainie, "The State of Blogging" (January 2, 2005), http://www.pewinternet.org/pdfs/PIPbloggingdata.pdf.

10. Lee Rainie and John Horrigan, "Election 2006 Online," *Pew/Internet* (January 17, 2007), http://www.pewinternet.org/PPF/r/199/report_display.asp.

11. Interview by Shearon Roberts (May 2006), State Representative Aaron Pena (D-Texas) for District Forty in south Texas.

12. Richard Benedetto, *Politicians Are People, Too* (Lanham, Md.: University Press of America, 2006), 108.

13. Deborah Wallace, "2005 Session" (March 14, 2005), http://hdc.leg.wa.gov/members/wallace/blog_archive_2005session.asp.

14. Kate Kaye, "Survey Shows the Blogosphere Is Breaking Out," *ClickZNews* (April 26, 2006), www.clickz.com.

15. Hugh Hewitt, in his book *Blog*, compares the blogswarm (bloggers joining to fight over any given issue) to military formations of air and submarine warfare. Hugh Hewitt, *Blog: Understanding the Information Reformation That's Changing Your World* (New York: Nelson, 2005).

16. Michael S. Malone, "Moore's Law Hits Blogosphere" (August 4, 2005), http://abcnews.go.com/Business/SiliconInsider/story?id=1026500&page=1.

Chapter 1

1. Matthew M. Reavy and David D. Perlmutter, "Presidential Web Sites as Sources of Information," *Electronic Journal of Communication* 7, no. 3 (1997). [online]

2. George Norlin, ed. and trans., *Isocrates* (New York: Putnam, 1927), xviii, 49.

3. Norlin, *Isocrates,* 49.

4. Isocrates, *Speeches and Letters*, ed. George Norlin, "Panathenaicus," http://www.perseus.tufts.edu/cgi-bin/ptext?doc=Perseus%3Atext%3A1999.01.0144&query=head%3D%2312.

5. This point was made to me by Charles Marsh.

6. Isocrates, "Panathenaicus."

7. Jay Cost, "Nine Tips for Bush on [Filling] the Supreme Court Vacancy" (August 1, 2005), http://www.redstate.org/story/2005/7/1/17522/11385.

8. J. A. Wilson, *The Culture of Ancient Egypt* (Chicago: University of Chicago Press, 1956), 246.

9. H. Goedicke, ed., *Perspectives on the Battle of Kadesh* (Baltimore: Halgo, 1985), 93.

10. Kenneth Jost and Melissa Hipolit, "Blog Explosion: Passing Fad or a Lasting Revolution?" *CQ Researcher*, June 9, 2006, 505–528.

11. Quoted in John Keane, *Tom Paine, A Political Life* (New York: Grove Press, 1995), 231.

12. According to the Nexis/Lexis database.

13. Quoted in David D. Perlmutter and Misti McDaniel, "The Ascent of Blogging," *Nieman Reports,* 59, no. 3 (Fall 2005): 60–64.

14. Perri Peltz, James Hattori, and Rick Lockridge, "Internet Delivers Love at First Sight," *CNNdotCOM* (July 8, 2000), http://transcripts.cnn.com/TRANSCRIPTS/0007/08/cnncom.00.html.

15. Kate Kaye, "Survey Shows the Blogosphere Is Breaking Out," *ClickZNews* (April 26, 2006), www.clickz.com.

16. SusanG, "Yearly Kos: The Magic of People Power Made Manifest" (June 9, 2006), www.dailykos.com/storyonly/2006/6/9/115348/0341.

17. Tom Curry, "At Vegas Blog-fest, It's Not Politics as Usual" (June 12, 2006), http://www.msnbc.msn.com/id/13190686/.

18. Julian Brookes, "Yearly Kos," *Mother Jones* (June 12, 2006), http://www.motherjones.com/mojoblog/archives/2006/06/yearly_kos_when.html.

19. Rebecca Blood, *Weblog Handbook* (Cambridge, Mass: Perseus, 2002); F. Y. Peng, N. I. Tham, and H. Xiaoming, "Trends in Online Newspapers," *Newspaper Research Journal* 20, no. 2 (1999): 52–64; J. Stromer-Galley and K. A. Foot, "Citizen Perceptions of Online Interactivity and Implications for Political Campaign Communication," *Journal of Computer-Mediated Communication* 8, no. 1 (2002), http://jcmc.indiana.edu/vol8/issue1/stromerandfoot.html.

20. "Blog Reading Is a Free-Floating Affair," *EMarketer* (March 7, 2007), www.emarketer.com/article.aspx?1004656.

21. See compilation at http://ezraklein.typepad.com/blog/2005/10/the_politics_of.html#comments.

22. Christian Crumlish, *The Power of Many: How the Living Web Is Transforming Politics, Business, and Everyday Life* (San Francisco: Sybex, 2005); Albert-Laszlo Barabasi, *Linked: How Everything Is Connected to Everything Else and What It Means* (New York: Perseus, 2002); Malcolm Gladwell, *Tipping Point: How Little Things Can Make a Big Difference* (New York: Little, Brown, 2000); Howard Rheingold, *Smart Mobs: The Next Social Revolution* (Cambridge, Mass: Perseus, 2002); James Surowiecki, *The Wisdom of Crowds* (New York: Doubleday, 2003); David Weinberger, *Small Pieces Loosely Joined: A Unified Theory of the Web* (Cambridge, Mass.: Perseus, 2002).

23. Harvey Mitchell, *America After Tocqueville: Democracy Against Difference* (Cambridge: Cambridge University Press, 2002), 52.

24. Jennifer Stromer-Galley, "New Voices in the Public Sphere: Political Conversation in the Internet Age" (PhD dissertation, University of Pennsylvania, 2002); S. Sundar, S. Kalyanaraman, and J. Brown, "Explicating Web Site Interactivity: Impression Formation Effects in Political Campaign Sites," *Communication Research* 30, no. 1 (2002): 30–59.

25. Andrew Paul Williams, Kaye D. Trammell, Monica Postelnicu, Kristen D. Landreville, and Justin D. Martin, "Blogging and Hyperlinking," *Journalism Studies* 6, no. 2 (2005): 177–186.

26. Jay Rosen, "Readers and Viewers," *Columbia Journalism Review* (May 2003), http://www.cjr.org/issues/2003/5/alt-rosen.asp.

27. Blood, *Weblog Handbook,* 114–115.

28. Jon Fine, "All the News That's Fit to Dis," *BusinessWeek* (October 10, 2005), http://www.businessweek.com/bwdaily/dnflash/oct2005/nf20051010_7117_db042.htm.

29. Lada Adamic and Natalie Glance, "The Political Blogosphere and the 2004 U.S. Election: Divided They Blog" (March 4, 2005), http://www.blogpulse.com/papers/2005/AdamicGlanceBlogWWW.pdf.

30. Steve Livingston, "The 'Nokia Effect,'" in *From Pigeons to News Portals: Foreign Reporting and the Challenge of New Technology,* eds. David D. Perlmutter and John M. Hamilton (Baton Rouge: Louisiana State University Press, 2007), 46–69.

31. James Boswell, *Life of Johnson,* chap. 35, http://www.worldwideschool.org/library/books/hst/biography/LifeofJohnson/chap36.html.

32. Cited in Chester F. Chapin, *The Religious Thought of Samuel Johnson* (Ann Arbor: University of Michigan Press, 1968), pp. 129–30.

33. Cyril Connolly, *Enemies of Promise* (Boston: Little, Brown, 1939): 14.

34. Bill Watterson, *The Complete Calvin & Hobbes, Book Three* (Kansas City: McMeel, 2005), 59.

35. Lee Rainie, "The State of Blogging," *Pew Internet & American Life Project* (January 2, 2005), http://www.pewinternet.org; Lee Rainie, "New Data on Blogs and Blogging" (May 2, 2005), http://www.pewinternet.org; Michael Cornfield et al., "Buzz, Blogs, and Beyond" (May 16, 2005), http://www.pewinternet.org/ppt/BUZZ_BLOGS __BEYOND_Final05-16-05.pdf.

36. *The Wall Street Journal,* "Two-Fifths of Americans Online Have Read Political Blogs" (April 13, 2005), http://online.wsj.com/article/0,,SB111332546086804781,00.html.

37. "What Blogs Cost American Business," *AdAge.com* (October 24, 2005), http://adage.com/news.cms?newsId=46494.

38. Kaye D. Trammell and Ana Keshelashvili, "Examining the New Influencers: A Self-Presentation Study of A-List Blogs," *Journalism and Mass Communication Quarterly* 82, no. 4 (Winter 2005): 968.

39. Trammell and Keshelashvili, "Examining the New Influencers."

40. Blood, *Weblog Handbook.*

41. Clay Shirky, "Power Laws, Weblogs, and Inequality" (February 8, 2003), http://www.shirky.com/writings/powerlaw_weblog.html.

42. D. W. Drezner and H. Farrell, "Web of Influence," *Foreign Policy* (December 2004), 32–41.

43. Research conducted by Moore Information group for Tom Edmonds Consulting. *USA Voters: Political News Sources* (February 2007).

44. Edelman Group, *A Corporate Guide to the Global Blogosphere* (New York: Edelman Group, 2007), 8.

45. Ted Schadler and Charles S. Golvin, "The State of Consumers and Technology: Benchmark," *Forrester's Consumer Technographics* (July 29, 2005).

46. 5. Nema Milaninia, "A Tehran Bias: Why We Iranian Bloggers Were Wrong About the Election Commentary," Pacific News Service, June 22, 2005. http://news.pacificnews.org/news/view_article.html?article_id= 32bb498ec49e9d314476713cdf9ab35a.

47. Steven Levy, "Blogging Beyond the Men's Club," *Newsweek* (March 21, 2005), http://www.msnbc.msn.com/id/7160264/site/newsweek/.

48. Svetlana V. Kulikova and David D. Perlmutter, "Blogging Down the Dictator? The Kyrgyz Revolution and 'Samizdat' Websites." *International Communication Gazette* 69, no. 1 (2007): 29–50.

49. Ed Keller and John Berry, *The Influentials* (New York: Free Press, 2003), 147–148; Daniel Terdiman, "Dems Hold the High Ground Online," *Wired* (April 23, 2004), http://www.wired.com/news/politics/0,1283,63183,00. html; "Political Influentials Online in the 2004 Presidential Campaign," Institute for Politics, Democracy and the Internet, http://216.87.14.57/UploadedFiles/ political%20influentials.pdf; Convio, Inc, "Using the Internet to Raise Funds and Mobilize Supporters" (December, 2003), http://www.convio.com/downloads/ Dean_WhitePaper_121703.pdf.

50. Keller and Berry, *The Influentials*.

51. "Political Influentials Online," as reported in E. Schwartz, "Don't Write Off Blogs Yet," *InfoWorld.com* (April 11, 2005): 10.

52. "Political Influentials Online"; Brian Michael King, "The Net Matures as a Democratizing Medium," *Interlink* (2002), http://www.interaction.org/ict/ dem_medium.html.

53. G. O'Malley, "Study: Blog Readers an Elite Minority," *Media Daily News* (March 14, 2005), http://publications.mediapost.com/index .cfm?fuseaction=Articles.showArticleHomePage.

54. Barbara K. Kaye, "It's a Blog, Blog, Blog World: Users and Uses of Weblogs," *Atlantic Journal of Communication* 13, no. 2 (2005): 73–95.

55. Kaye, "Survey Shows."

56. Edelman Group, *A Corporate Guide*, 5.

57. Rhodes Cook, *The Presidential Nominating Process: A Place for Us?* (Lanham, Md.: Rowman & Littlefield, 2004), 109.

58. Quoted in Kevin Anderson, "American Media vs. the Blogs," *BBC News* (February 22, 2005), http://news.bbc.co.uk/1/hi/world/americas/ 4279229.stm.

59. Quoted in David Meerman Scott, "The Web Isn't a Newspaper, It's a City," *Econtentmag* (February 21, 2005), http://www.ecmag.net/Articles/ArticleReader.aspx?ArticleID=7628&AuthorID=44.

60. Eric Engberg, "Blogging as Typing, Not Journalism," *CBS News* (November 8, 2004), http://www.cbsnews.com/stories/2004/11/08/opinion/main654285.shtml.

61. Victoria Brownworth, "The Long Arm of the Blog," *Baltimore Sun,* May 15, 2005, 10F.

62. Thinkprogress, "O'Reilly Tonight: How Blogs Are Destroying America" (October 4, 2005), http://thinkprogress.org/2005/10/04/oreilly-blogs/.

63. Steve Lovelady, "Towards a Journalism of Reality," *Columbia Journalism Review Daily online* (November 22, 2004), http://www.cjrdaily.org/politics/towards_a_journalism_of_realit.php.

64. G. L. Jackaway, *Media at War: Radio's Challenge to the Newspapers, 1924–1939* (Westport, Conn.: Praeger, 1995), 128.

65. Jackaway, *Media at War,* 128; indeed, the parallels to blogs and bigger media in 2003–2006 are striking.

66. Isocrates, *Speeches and Letters,* "Panathenaicus," ed. George Norlin, http://www.perseus.tufts.edu/cgi-bin/ptext?doc=Perseus%3Atext%3A1999.0 1.0144&query=head%3D%2312.

67. Robert Putnam, *Bowling Alone* (New York: Simon & Schuster, 2000), 173.

68. Cass Sunstein, *Republic.com* (Princeton, N.J.: Princeton University Press, 2001), 49.

69. Manual Castells, *The Rise of the Network Society* (Cambridge: Blackwell Books, 1996); Marshall Van Alstyne and Erik Brynjolfsson, "Electronic Communities: Global Village or Cyberbalkanization?" Working paper (Cambridge: Massachusetts Institute for Technology, March 1997); Bruce Bimber, "The Internet and Political Transformation: Populism, Community, and Accelerated Pluralism," *Polity* 31 (1998): 133–160; Andrew Shapiro and Richard Leone, *The Control Revolution* (New York: Public Affairs, 1999).

70. T. Neil Sroka, *Understanding the Political Influence of the Blogosphere* (Washington, D.C.: George Washington University & the Institute for Politics, Democracy, & the Internet: April 2006), 26.

71. Adamic and Glance, "The Political Blogosphere."

72. Robert Ackland, "Mapping the U.S. Political Blogosphere: Are Conservative Bloggers More Prominent?" (April 25, 2005), http://incsub.org/blogtalk/images/robertackland.pdf.

73. Adamic and Glance, "The Political Blogosphere."

74. Brad Stone, "A Call for Manners in the World of Nasty Blogs," NYTimes.com, April 9, 2007, http://www.nytimes.com/2007/04/09/technology/09blog.html?ex=1184644800&en=0c56e21c13bdaef5&ei=5070; see also

David D. Perlmutter & Mary Schoen, "If I Break a Rule, What Do I Do, Fire Myself? Ethics Codes of Independent Blogs," *Journal of Mass Media Ethics* 22, no. 1 (2007): 37–48.

75. Jill, "A Follow-up," *Feministe* (January 4, 2006), http://www.feministe.us/blog/archives/2006/01/04/a-follow-up/.

76. Minnesota Lefty Liberal, "Forced to Go Dark" (June 24, 2005), http://www.mnleftyliberal.blogspot.com. Also via personal e-mail contact, June 26, 2005.

77. Blackfive, "Sign of Success?" (November 2005), http://www.blackfive.net/main/2005/11/sign_of_success.html.

78. M. Sutcliffe, "Employers' 'Dooce' Powers Trump Speech Rights," *Canada.com* (January 20, 2007), http://www.canada.com/ottawacitizen/news/business/story.html?id=73a58e35-5dcf-4d47-be30-a75181229f4d.

79. Michael Calderon, "Is New Orleans a Prelude to Al-Qaeda's American Hiroshima?" (September 2, 2005), http://moonbatcentral.com/wordpress/?p=1069.

80. Justin Raimondo, "A Death Threat: The Perils of Punditry" (September 5, 2005), http://www.antiwar.com/justin/?articleid=7154.

81. William Powers, "The Massless Media," *Atlantic Monthly* 295 (January–February 2005): 122–126.

82. Richard M. Perloff, *Political Communication: Politics, Press, and Public in America* (New York: Erlbaum Associates, 1998), 149.

83. John Horrigan, Kelly Garrett, and Paul Resnik, "The Internet and Democratic Debate" (October 2004), http://www.pewinternet.org/pdfs/PIP_Political_Info_Report.pdf.

84. Eszter Hargittai, "Cross-Ideological Discussions Among Bloggers" (May 26, 2005), http://www.webuse.org/news/2005/05/26/crossideological-conversations-among-bloggers/.

85. Suzanne Stefanac, *Dispatches from Blogistan: A Travel Guide for the Modern Blogger* (San Francisco: Peachpit/New Riders, 2007).

86. Rowan Scarborough, "Gitmo Called Death Camp," *Washington Times* (June 16, 2005), http://www.washingtontimes.com/national/20050616-121815-1827r.htm.

87. Paul Mirengoff, "Senator Durbin's Trifecta" (June 16, 2005), http://powerlineblog.com/archives/010758.php.

88. Hugh Hewitt (June 16, 2007), http://www.hughhewitt.com/old_site/cgi-bin/calendar.pl?month=6&view=Event&event_id=785.

89. David Neiwert, "Eliminate Them" (June 17, 2005), http://dneiwert.blogspot.com/.

90. Steve Gilliard, "Torture? No Big Deal. They Deserved It" (June 16, 2005), http://stevegilliard.blogspot.com/2005/06/torture-no-big-deal-they-deserved-it.html.

91. Kos, "The Latest Moronic Right-Wing Smear Attack" (June 15, 2005), http://www.dailykos.com/storyonly/2005/6/16/25826/4241.

92. Dean Barnett, "Why the Rise of the Left-Wing Blogosphere Has Been Bad for the Democratic Party," *Weeklystandard.com* (July 15, 2005), http://www.weeklystandard.com/Content/Public/Articles/000/000/005/823tdfin.asp?pg=1.

93. Captain Ed [Morrissy], "Durbin Apologizes Weakly a Week Later" (June 21, 2005), www.captainsquartersblog.com/mt/archives/004776.php.

94. See Zack Pelta-Heller, "Building Blogs," *AlterNet* (February 22, 2005), http://www.alternet.org/mediaculture/21316/.

95. Rick Ellis, "Dan Rather for a Day" (October 19, 2004), http://allyourtv.com/rickonmedia/comments.php?id=107_0_1_0_C.

96. Interview by Shearon Roberts (May 2006); Patrick Ruffini, e-campaign director at the RNC (runs the Web site Gop.com).

Chapter 2

1. Barbara K. Kaye, "It's a Blog, Blog, Blog World: Users and Uses of Weblogs," *Atlantic Journal of Communication* 13, no. 2 (2005): 73–95.

2. P. Nixon and H. Johansson, "Transparency Through Technology: The Internet and Political Parties," in *Digital Democracy*, eds. B. Hague and B. D. Loader (London: Routledge, 1999), 135–153; Bruce Bimber and Richard Davis, *Campaigning Online: The Internet in U.S. Elections* (Oxford: Oxford University Press, 2003); M. Margolis and D. Resnick, *Politics as Usual: The Cyberspace "Revolution"* (Thousand Oaks, CA: Sage, 2000).

3. R. Klotz, "Virtual Criticism: Negative Advertising on the Internet in the 1996 Senate Races," *Political Communication* 15 (1998): 347–365.

4. R. K. Whillock, "Cyber-politics," *American Behavioral Scientist* 40, no. 8 (1997): 1208–1225.

5. D. Wring and I. Horrocks, "The Transformation of Political Parties?" in *New Media and Politics*, eds. B. Axford and R. Huggins (London: Sage, 2000), 191–209.

6. Edwin Diamond, Martha McKay, and Robert Silverman, "Pop Goes Politics: New Media, Interactive Formats, and the 1992 Campaign," *American Behavioral Scientist* 37, no. 2 (1993): 257–261; Kenneth L. Hacker, L. Lowl, M. Scott, and R. Steiner, "Uses of Computer-Mediated Political Communication in the 1992 Presidential Campaign," *Communication Research Reports* 13, no. 2 (1996): 138–146; D. D. Myers, "New Technology and the 1992 Clinton Presidential Campaign," *American Behavioral Scientist* 37, no. 2 (1993): 181–187.

7. Wendell Cochran, "The Boys on the 'Net," *American Journalism Review* 18 (April 1996), 40–42.

8. Matthew M. Reavy and David D. Perlmutter, "Presidential Web Sites as Sources of Information," *Electronic Journal of Communication* 7, no. 3 (1997);

David A. Dulio, Donald L. Goff, and James A. Thurber, "Untangled Web: Internet Use During the 1998 Election," *PS: Political Science and Politics* 32, no. 1 (1999): 53–58; Lynda L. Kaid and Diane G. Bystrom, *The Electronic Election: Perspectives on the 1996 Campaign Communication* (Mahwah, N.J.: Erlbaum Associates, 1997).

9. James Katz, Philip Aspden, and Warren Reich, "Elections and Electrons," in *Citizens and the Internet: Diversifying Information Sources in Cyberspace*, eds. Marion Just, Ann Crigler, and Montague Kern (Chicago: National Speech Communication Association, November 1997), 2.

10. Cochran, "The Boys on the 'Net."

11. John Tedesco, "Changing the Channel: Use of the Internet for Communicating About Politics," in *Handbook of Political Communication Research*, ed. Lynda Lee Kaid (New York: Erlbaum Associates, 2004), 507–510.

12. Bruce Bimber, "The Internet and Political Transformation: Populism, Community, and Accelerated Pluralism," *Polity* 31 (1998): 133–160.

13. Robert Benedict, Matthew J. Burbank, and Ronald J. Hrebenar, *Political Parties, Interest Groups and Political Campaigns* (Boulder, Colo.: Westview Press, 1999); Pew Research Center for the People and the Press, *One in Ten Voters Online for Campaign '96: News Attracts Most Internet Users* (Washington, D.C.: Pew Research Center for the People and the Press, 1996).

14. Robert Klotz, "Positive Spin: Senate Campaigning on the Web," *PS: Political Science and Politics* 30, no. 3 (1997): 482–486.

15. Reavy and Perlmutter, "Presidential Web Sites as Sources of Information."

16. Richard Davis, *The Web of Politics: The Internet's Impact on the American Political System* (Oxford: Oxford University Press, 1999), 87.

17. Davis, *The Web of Politics*, 103.

18. Dulio, Goff, and Thurber, "Untangled Web."

19. Davis, *The Web of Politics*, xi.

20. Bimber and Davis, *Campaigning Online*, 26.

21. Richard T. Griffiths, "History of the Internet," http://www.let.leidenuniv.nl/history/ivh/frame_theorie.html.

22. P. Krasilovsky, *Community Resources on the Web* (Bethesda, Md.: Markle, 1998).

23. Mitchell Kapor, quoted in John V. Pavlik, *New Media Technology: Cultural and Commercial Perspectives* (Boston: Allyn & Bacon, 1996), 317; see also Graeme Browning, *Electronic Democracy: Using the Internet to Influence Politics* (Wilton, Conn.: Online Inc., 1996); Robert A. Dahl, *Democracy and Its Critics* (New Haven, Conn.: Yale University Press, 1989), 339; Amitai Etzioni, *The Spirit of Community: Rights, Responsibilities, and the Communitarian Agenda* (New York: Crown Publishers, 1993); Lawrence K. Grossman, *The Electronic Republic: Reshaping Democracy in America*

(New York: Viking, 1995); Nicholas Negroponte, *Being Digital* (New York: Vintage, 1995), 165.

24. J. C. Tedesco and L. L. Kaid, "Candidate Web Sites and Voter Effects: Investigating Uses and Gratifications," paper presented at the National Communication Association Convention, Seattle, November 2000.

25. L. L. Kaid, "Political Advertising and Information Seeking: Comparing Exposure via Traditional and Internet Channels," *Journal of Advertising* 31 (2002): 27–35.

26. Nicholas Jones, *The Associations of Classical Athens: The Response to Democracy* (Oxford: Oxford University Press, 1999).

27. John Kloppenborg and Stephen Wilson, *Voluntary Associations in the Graeco-Roman World* (London: Routledge, 1996).

28. Steven Epstein, *Wage & Labor Guilds in Medieval Europe* (Chapel Hill: University of North Carolina Press, 1991).

29. Douglas Verney, *The Analysis of Political Systems* (London: Routledge, 1965), 129.

30. Howard Rheingold, *The Virtual Community* (Reading, Mass.: Addison-Wesley, 1993).

31. Denise Bostdorff, "The Internet Rhetoric of the Ku Klux Klan," *Communication Studies* 55, no. 2 (2004): 340–361.

32. David Weinberger, *Small Pieces Loosely Joined: A Unified Theory of the Web* (Cambridge, Mass.: Perseus, 2002).

33. E. Cone, "Web Politics 2.0," *CIO Insight* (November 5, 2004), http://www.cioinsight.com/article2/0,1540,1714560,00.asp.

34. Kaye Trammell, "Celebrity Blogs" (PhD dissertation, University of Florida, 2004).

35. David D. Perlmutter, *Visions of War: Picturing Warfare from the Stone Age to the Cyberage* (New York: St. Martin's, 1999).

Chapter 3

1. Rebecca Blood, "Weblogs: A History and Perspective" (September 7, 2000), http://www.rebeccablood.net/essays/weblog_history.html.

2. Paul Boutin, "Robot Wisdom on the Street," *Wired News* (July 2005): 99.

3. Peter Merholz, http://www.peterme.com/archives/00000205.html.

4. Joshua Marshall, "Talking Points Memo" (December 10, 2002), http://www.talkingpointsmemo.com/archives/week_2002_12_08.php#000480.

5. Dan Goodgame and Karen Tumulty, "Tripped Up by History," *Time* (December 23, 2002), http://www.time.com.

6. Mark Glaser, "Trent Lott Gets Bloggered . . . Weblogs Credited for Lott Brouhaha," *Online Journalism Review* (December 17, 2002), http://www.ojr.org/ojr/glaser/1040145065.php.

7. See time line in Jeffrey A. Dvorkin, "Lott Controversy Makes Some Reporters Pause—Except One," *NPR Online: Media Matters* (December 20, 2002), http://www.npr.org/yourturn/ombudsman/021220.html.

8. Washingtonienne, "I Got a Raise Today! Now I Make $25K" (May 14, 2004). Was posted at: http://washingtoniennearchive.blogspot.com/2004/05/i-got-raise-today-now-i-make25k.html. Now offline.

9. Richard Lieby, "The Hill's Sex Diarist Reveals All (Well, Some)," *Washington Post,* May 23, 2004, D3.

10. Cf. Howard Kurtz, "Why So Late on Lott?" *Media Notes/Washington Post* (December 10, 2002), http://www.washingtonpost.com/ac2/wp-dyn/A34186-2002Dec10?language=printer.

11. Quoted in David D. Perlmutter and Misti McDaniel, "The Ascent of Blogging," *Nieman Reports,* 59, no. 3 (Fall 2005): 60–64.

12. Pamela O'Connell, "Internet Matchmaking," *New York Times,* November 14, 2005, F26.

13. Matthew Klam, "Fear and Laptops on the Campaign Trail," *New York Times Magazine* (September 26, 2004), http://www.matthewklam.com/nonfiction/trail.html.

14. "What They Were Thinking," *Wired* (August 2005): 109.

15. Evan Thomas (and *Newsweek* Staff), *Election 2004* (New York: Public Affairs, 2004), 118.

16. Teachout's post that revealed this information (http://zonkette.blogspot.com/2005/01/financially-interested-blogging.html) has been taken down. Quoted in Chris Suellentrop, "Blogging for Dollars," *Slate.com* (January 14, 2005), http://www.slate.com/id/2112314/fr/rss/.

17. Rachel Smolkin, "The Expanding Blogosphere: Political Blogs," *American Journalism Review* (June 2004): 38.

18. Talkleft, "Hewitt and O'Reilly Should Read the News" (January 15, 2005), http://talkleft.com/new_archives/009336.html.

19. Bill Gates, Nathan Myhrvold, and Peter Rinearson, *The Road Ahead* (New York: Penguin, 1996), 4. Actually, the evidence is that later writers conceived that a market could be perfect, but Smith did not. See Heinz Lubasz, "Adam Smith and the Invisible Hand—of the Market?" in *Contesting Markets: Analyses of Ideology, Discourse and Practice,* ed. Roy Dilley (Edinburgh: Edinburgh University Press, 1992), 37–56; Jacob Viner, "Adam Smith and Laissez Faire," *Journal of Political Economy* 35 (1927): 198–232.

20. *Kudlow & Company,* CNBC (2005).

21. J. Dube, "A Blogger's Code of Ethics," *Cyberjournalist* (April 15, 2003), http://www.cyberjournalist.net/news/000215.php; Martin Kuhn, "Blog Ethics Analysis 2004," http://blogethics2004.blogspot.com/.

22. Jerome Armstrong, January 6, 2007, a personal narrative of the Dean campaign. Provided to author.

23. Armstrong, personal narrative.

24. "What They Were Thinking," 107.

25. Jennifer Stromer-Galley and Andrea B. Baker, "Joy and Sorrow of Interactivity on the Campaign Trail: Blogs in the Primary Campaign of Howard Dean," in *The Internet Election: Perspectives on the Web in Campaign 2004,* eds. A. Williams and J. Tedesco (Lanham, Md.: Rowman & Littlefield, 2006), 111-131.

26. Joe Trippi, "Foreword," in *Extreme Democracy,* eds. Jon Lebkowsky and Mitch Ratcliffe (San Francisco: Creative Commons, 2005), 6–14.

27. Brian King, "The Net Matures as a Democratizing Medium," *Interlink,* http://www.interaction.org/ict/dem_medium.html.

28. Joe Trippi, "Down from the Mountain," O'Reilly Digital Democracy Teach-In, San Diego, February 9, 2004. IT Conversations Audio, http://www.itconversations.com/transcripts/80/transcript-print80-1.html; Joe Trippi, "New Media, Old Politics?" (October 14, 2004), MIT Forum, http://web.mit.edu/comm-forum/forums/new_media_old_politics.html.

29. Stromer-Galley and Baker, "Joy and Sorrow of Interactivity."

30. M. D. Lord, "Constituency Building as the Foundation for Corporate Political Strategy," *Academy of Management Executive* 17 (2003): 1–16.

31. Trippi, "Foreword."

32. Clifford Brown, Lynda Powell, and Clyde Wilcox, *Serious Money: Fundraising and Contributing in Presidential Nomination Campaigns* (Cambridge: Cambridge University Press, 1995).

33. Thomas B. Edsall, "Gay Community Gave Dean Early Boost," *Washington Post,* January 1, 2004, A08.

34. The Pew Research Center for the People and the Press, "The Dean Activists: Their Profile and Prospects" (April 6, 2005), http://people-press.org/reports/pdf/240.pdf.

35. Alexis Rice, *Campaigns Online: The Profound Impact of the Internet, Blogs, and E-Technologies in Presidential Political Campaigning,* Center for the Study of American Government at Johns Hopkins University, *Campaigns Online.org* (January 2004), http://www.campaignsonline.org/reports/online.pdf.

36. Thomas, *Election 2004,* 20–22; Paul Maslin, "The Front-Runner's Fall," *Atlantic Monthly,* May 2004, 96–104.

37. This figure was widely cited but is probably an exaggeration.

38. Pew Research Center, "The Dean Activists."

39. Maslin, "The Front-Runner's Fall."

40. R. Smolkin, "Blogosphere," *American Journalism Review* (June–July)04): 39–43.

41. Chris Matthews, "Weekend: Bedford, New Hampshire," *Chris atthews Show* (January 24–25, 2004). Was http://www.thechrismatthewsshow m/012404.html but now offline.

42. Howard Kurtz, "After Blogs Got Hits, CBS Got a Black Eye," *Washington Post*, September 20, 2004, C1.

43. Quotes are from message board at *Freerepublic.com* (September 8, 2004), http://www.freerepublic.com/focus/f-news/1210516/posts?page=107#107.

44. Mickey Kaus, "The Case Against Editors," *Slate.com* (October 28, 2003), http://www.slate.com/id/2090405/.

45. Charles Johnson, "Bush Guard Documents: Forged," *Littlegreen-footballs* (September 9, 2004), http://littlegreenfootballs.com/weblog/? entry=12526_ Bush_Guard_Documents-_Forged.

46. Corey Pein, "Blog-gate," *Columbia Journalism Review* 43, no. 5 (January–February 2005): 30.

47. 10ksnooker, "Deep Throat" (June 2, 2005), polipundit.com/wp-comments-popup.php?p=8002&c=1.

48. Hunter, "TANG Typewriter Follies; Wingnuts Wrong" (September 10, 2004), http://www.dailykos.com/story/2004/9/10/34914/1603.

49. Corey Pein, "Yes, CBS Screwed Up Badly in 'Memogate'—but So Did Those Who Covered the Affair," *Columbia Journalism Review*, http://www.cjr.org/issues/2005/1/pein-blog.asp.

50. A. Bay, "Shakespeare Blogged," *The Masthead*, Spring 2005, 14–15.

51. Dick Thornburgh and Louis D. Biccardi, "Report of the Independent Review Panel" (January 5, 2005), 172, http://wwwimage.cbsnews.com/htdocs/pdf/complete_report/CBS_Report.pdf.

52. Stephen D. Cooper, *Watching the Watchdog: Bloggers as the Fifth Estate* (Seattle: Marquette Books, 2006).

53. T. Neil Sroka, *Understanding the Political Influence of the Blogosphere* (Washington, D.C.: George Washington University & the Institute for Politics, Democracy, & the Internet: April 2006), 21.

54. Jimmy Orr, "Ask the White House" (July 29, 2004), http://www.whitehouse.gov/ask/20040729.html.

55. Jerome Armstrong, "Early VNS Exit Polling" (November 2, 2004), http://www.mydd.com/story/2004/11/2/135756/299.

56. From the right came conspiracy theories that "faulty" exit polls were intended to discourage would-be Bush voters. See Dick Morris, "Those Faulty Exit Polls Were Sabotage," *The Hill* (November 4, 2004), http://thehill.com/dick-morris/those-faulty-exit-polls-were-sabotage-2004-11-04.html; John Wambough, "Election 2004: Exit-Poll Disinformation Hoax Backfires?" *Renew America* (January 7, 2005), http://www.renewamerica.us/columns/wambough/050107.

57. SoCalDemocrat, "Kerry Winning Exit Polls—FRAUD LOOKS PROBABLE," *Democraticunderground* (November 2, 2004), http://www.democraticunderground.com/discuss/duboard.php?az=show_topic& forum=132&topic_id=1290765.

58. S. Rosenbush, "Too Much Buzz on the Blogs," *BusinessWeek Online,* November 4, 2004; Frank Barnako, "Bloggers Blew It: Much Posting, Little Impact," *CBS.MarketWatch.com* (November 3, 2004), http://www.market watch.com/News/Story/Story.aspx?guid=%7BC2B2EB99-2DB8-49ED-99FD-F94D01701BAA%7D&siteid=mktw.

59. J. Horn, "Election 2004: The Internet, Exit Polls Bog Down the Blogs," *Los Angeles Times,* November 3, 2004, 33.

60. Staff Reporters of the *Sun,* "Bloggers Botch Election Call: Networks Cautious, Steady," *New York Sun* (November 3, 2004), http://www.nysun.com/article/4183.

61. Eric Engberg, "Blogging as Typing, Not Journalism," *CBSNews.com* (November 8, 2004), http://www.cbsnews.com/stories/2004/11/08/opinion/main654285.shtml.

62. Antonia Zerbisias, "A Hard Day's Slogging in Cyberspace," *Toronto Star,* November 3, 2004, B04.

63. Evaluation of Edison/Mitofsky Election System 2004 prepared by Edison Media Research and Mitofsky International for the National Election Pool (NEP) (January 19, 2005), http://www.exit-poll.net/election-night/EvaluationJan192005.pdf.

64. Armstrong, "Early VNS Exit Polling."

65. Buzzflash, "Early Exit Polling Shows Kerry Ahead . . . " (November 2, 2004), http://www.buzzflash.com/alerts/04/11/ale04086.html.

66. Ana Marie Cox, "A Little Birdie Told Us" (November 2, 2004), http://www.wonkette.com/archives/a-little-birdie-told-us-024776.php.

67. Quoted by Rex Sorgatz, "ONA, Day 2: Wonkette Wonks" (November 13, 2004), http://www.fimoculous.com/archive/post-727.cfm.

68. Horn, "Election 2004," 33.

69. Ana Marie Cox, "Ask Wonkette: Polling All Our Exits" (November 2, 2004), http://wonkette.com/politics/campaigning/polling-for-victory-is-this-election-thing-still-on-24823.php.

70. Mark M. Blumenthal, "The Methods and Accuracy of Polling: Toward an Open-Source Methodology; What We Can Learn from the Blogosphere," *Public Opinion Quarterly* 69, no. 5 (2005): 655–669.

71. Ana Marie Cox. "Pollster-Pundits Lead Media Astray on Wisconsin Primary," STATS, George Mason University (February 23, 2004), http://www.stats.org/stories/2004/Pollster_pundits_wisconsin.htm.

72. Edelman Group, *A Corporate Guide to the Global Blogosphere* (New York: Edelman Group, 2007), 4, 9.

73. Tom Brokaw, "Decision 2004: Election Night," *NBC Evening News,* November 3, 2004.

74. Lee Rainie, "The State of Blogging" (January 2, 2005), http://www.pewinternet.org/pdfs/PIPbloggingdata.pdf.

75. N. Z. Bear, "A Post-Election Blog Funk?" *Tech Central Station* (January 11, 2005), http://www.tcsdaily.com/article.aspx?id=011105B.

76. Heather Hopkins, "YouTube, the US Midterm Elections and UK Politics," *hitwise.com* (November 6, 2006), http://weblogs.hitwise.com/heather-hopkins/2006/11/youtube_the_us_midterm_electio.html.

77. Rick Perlstein, "Who Deserves Credit for the Democratic Comeback? Plan of Attack," *New Republic: Tnr.com* (November 8, 2006), http://www.tnr.com/doc.mhtml?i=w061106&s=perlstein110806; Daniel McQuade, "'Net Gains: Local Bloggers Helped Steer Last Week's Elections Leftward," *Philadelphia Weekly.com* (November 15, 2006), http://www.philadelphiaweekly.com/view.php?id=13394.

78. "Did Blogs Have an Impact on the Midterm Election?" *Blogcampaigning. wordpress.com* (November 12, 2006),http://blogcampaigning.wordpress.com/2006/11/12/did-blogs-have-an-impact-on-midterm-election/.

79. Matthew Mosk, "Donations Pooled Online Are Getting Candidates' Attention," *Washington Post*, March 11, 2007, A07.

Chapter 4

1. John Hiler, "How Weblogs Influence a Billion Google Searches a Week," *Microcontent News* (February 26, 2003), http://www.microcontentnews.com/articles/googleblogs.htm.

2. Interview by Shearon Roberts (May 2006), Ari Rabin-Havt, director of Online Communications for Senator Harry Reid and the Democratic Caucus, http://www.giveemhellharry.com/blog.

3. Pamela, "FALLACI!" (November 29, 2005), http://atlasshrugs2000.typepad.com/atlas_shrugs/2005/11/i_leave_shreds_.html.

4. David Loewenstein, *Representing Revolution in Milton and His Contemporaries: Religion, Politics, and Polemics in Radical Puritanism* (Cambridge: Cambridge University Press, 2001).

5. Paul A. Rahe, "An Inky Wretch: The Outrageous Genius of Marchamont Nedham," *National Interest* (Winter 2002), http://www.highbeam.com/library/docFree.asp?DOCID=1G1:95841629.

6. John Morrill, "Cromwell and His Contemporaries," in *Oliver Cromwell and the English Revolution,* ed. John Morrill (New York: Longman, 2004), 259–281.

7. See discussion in Stephen D. Cooper, *Watching the Watchdog: Bloggers as the Fifth Estate* (Seattle: Marquette Books, 2006), 288–301.

8. Mark Baard, "Reporter Takes His Weblog to War," *Wired* (March 14, 2003), http://www.wired.com/news/conflict/0,2100,58043,00.html.

9. Christopher Albritton, "Resume," http://web.mac.com/callbritton/iWeb/Clips%20from%20Allbritton/E0965612-3785-40B7-AD2D-2A5359FA4288.html.

10. D. W. Drezner and H. Farrell, "Web of Influence," *Foreign Policy* (December 2004), 32–41.

11. Peter Maass, "Salam Pax Is Real," *Slate.com* (June 2, 2003), http://slate.msn.com/id/2083847/.

12. Neil A Lewis, "In Rising Numbers, Lawyers Head for Guantanamo Bay," *New York Times,* May 30, 2005, A10.

13. Arthur Hadley, *The Invisible Primary* (Englewood Cliffs, N.J.: Prentice Hall, 1976).

14. Robert E. Denton Jr., *The 2000 Presidential Campaign: A Communication Perspective* (Westport, Conn.: Praeger, 2002), 19.

15. David Damore, "A Dynamic Model of Candidate Fundraising: The Case of Presidential Nomination Campaigns," *Political Research Quarterly* 50 (1997): 343–364; Randall E. Adkins and Andrew J. Dowdle, "The Money Primary: What Influences the Outcome of Pre-Primary Presidential Nomination Fundraising?" *Presidential Studies Quarterly* 32, no. 2 (2002): 256–275.

16. Katharine Hinckley and John Green, "Fund-raising in Presidential Nomination Campaigns: The Primary Lessons of 1988," *Political Research Quarterly* 49 (1996): 693–718; Diana Mutz, "Effects of Horse-Race Coverage on Campaign Coffers," *Journal of Politics* 57, no. 4 (1995): 1015–1042; Damore, "A Dynamic Model of Candidate Fundraising."

17. Matt Vella, "John Edwards, the E-Candidate," *BusinessWeek Online* (January 22, 2007), http://www.businessweek.com/technology/content/jan2007/tc20070122_842933.htm; Chris Cillizza and Dan Balz, "On the Electronic Campaign Trail," *Washington Post,* January 22, 2007, A01.

18. Inara Verzemnieks, quoted in Sam Hieb and Edward Cone, "For Some Bloggers, All Politics Is Local" (February, 2, 2005), http://www.personaldemocracy.com/node/323.

19. Eriposte, "How the Liberal Media Myth Is Created—Part 2," *theleftcoaster.com* (March 24, 2005), http://www.theleftcoaster.com/archives/003980.php.

20. C. Lankshear and M. Knobel, "Do-It-Yourself Broadcasting: Writing Weblogs, in a Knowledge Society." Presented at the American Education Research Association annual meeting, Chicago, 2003; M. Manuel, "Election 2004: Covering the Conventions," *Atlanta Journal-Constitution,* July 25, 2004, 1E; M. Manuel, "Election Affirms Net's Influence," *Atlanta Journal-Constitution,* November 14, 2004, 4A.

21. Lawrence Soley, *The News Shapers* (New York: Praeger, 1992).

22. David D. Perlmutter, *Picturing China in the American Press: The Visual Portrayal of Sino-American Relations in* Time *Magazine, 1949–1973* (Lanham, Md.: Rowman & Littlefield, 2007).

23. R. H. Bernstein and R. Munro, *The Coming Conflict with China* (New York: Knopf, 1997), 77; K. Silverstein, "China's Hired Guns," *Multinational Monitor* 17, no. 4 (1996): 26; K. Silverstein, "The New China Hands: How

the Fortune 500 Is China's Strongest Lobby," *The Nation,* February 17, 1997, 11+; Ian Urbina, "The Corporate PNTR Lobby: How Big Business Is Paying Millions to Gain Billions in China," *Multinational Monitor* 21, no. 5 (2000): http://multinationalmonitor.org/mm2000/00may/urbina.html.

24. Victor Navasky and Christopher Cerf, *The Experts Speak: The Definitive Compendium of Authoritative Misinformation* (New York: Random House, 1994).

25. Robert F. Kennedy Jr., "Deadly Immunity," *commondreams.org* (June 16, 2005), http://www.commondreams.org/views05/0616-31.htm.

26. Lindsay Beyerstein, "Simpsonwood, Thimerosal, and Vaccines (II)" (July 2006), http://majikthise.typepad.com/majikthise_/2005/06/simpsonwood_thi_1.html.

27. Jon Friedman, "Brian Williams May Surprise America," *CBS. MarketWatch.com* (November 30, 2004), http://www.marketwatch.com/news.

28. Lada Adamic and Natalie Glance, "The Political Blogosphere and the 2004 U.S. Election: Divided They Blog," Intelliseek Corporation (2005), 15, http://www.blogpulse.com/papers/2005/AdamicGlanceBlogWWW.pdf.

29. David D. Perlmutter, *Photojournalism and Foreign Policy: Framing Icons of Outrage in International Crises* (Westport, Conn.: Greenwood, 1998).

30. David D. Perlmutter, "Witness to something sleazy." *MSNBC.com* Opinions, August 24, 2001. [no longer online].

31. Stephen D. Cooper, *Watching the Watchdog: Bloggers as the Fifth Estate* (Seattle: Marquette Books, 2006).

32. House Bill No. 1677 (January 12, 2005), prefiled December 17, 2004, http://leg1.state.va.us/cgi-bin/legp504.exe?051+ful+HB1677.

33. Janette Rodrigues, "Del. Cosgrove Appears on 'Nightline' About Blogs," *The Virginian-Pilot,* March 10, 2005, B4.

34. "Eternal Vigilance Is the Price of Liberty: HR1677—A Reply from Delegate Cosgrove" (January, 2005), http://democracyforvirginia.typepad.com/democracy_for_virginia/2005/01/eternal_vigilan.html.

35. "A Blog Fog for Del. Cosgrove," *The Virginian-Pilot,* January 13, 2005, B10.

36. Dave Addis, "Good for Us, Pregnancy Bill Is Nipped in the Bud," *The Virginian-Pilot,* January 12, 2005, B1.

37. See reviews of this research in David D. Perlmutter, *Photojournalism and Foreign Policy: Framing Icons of Outrage in International Crises* (Westport, Conn.: Greenwood, 1998); David D. Perlmutter and Gretchen L. Wagner, "The Anatomy of a Photojournalistic Icon: Marginalization of Dissent in the Selection and Framing of 'A Death in Genoa,'" *Visual Communication* 3, no. 1 (2004): 91–108; David Domke, David Perlmutter, and Meg Spratt, "The Primes of Our Times? An Examination of the 'Power' of Visual Images," *Journalism* 3, no. 2 (2002): 131–159.

38. Perlmutter, *Photojournalism and Foreign Policy.*

39. Perlmutter, *Photojournalism and Foreign Policy.*

40. Zombie, "The Zombie Hall of Shame," http://www.zombietime .com/hall_of_shame/.

41. James Gleick, *Faster: The Acceleration of Just About Everything* (New York: Random House, 1999).

42. David Shenk, *Data Smog: Surviving the Information Glut* (San Francisco: Harper, 1997).

Chapter 5

1. Quoted from *National Review Online,* "Kos Mania!" (July 6, 2006), http://media.nationalreview.com/post/?q=YmRiMjNiMDI3N2FjNGFm Mzk1OGVlMzliNGZmN2Y2NzM=.

2. Kos, "Really Quick" (June 24, 2006), http://www.dailykos .com/story/2006/6/24/194520/430.

3. Chris Suellentrop, "Disclosures That Bloggers Have Been Paid by Political Campaigns to Post Positive Stories or Spread Rumor," *National Public Radio,* January 17, 2005; Charles Babington and Brian Faler, "A Committee Post and a Pledge Drive," *Washington Post,* December 18, 2004, A16.

4. Kathryn Jean Lopez, "A Kerry-League Play," *National Review Online* (October 22, 2004), http://www.nationalreview.com/lopez/lopez200410221133.asp.

5. Hugh Hewitt, "Trouble in South Dakota for Tom Daschle," *Weekly Standard* (July 8, 2004), http://www.weeklystandard.com/Content/Public/ Articles/000/000/004/290luazp.asp.

6. J. Stanton, "Bloggers Targeted Daschle and the Press," *National Journal* 36, no. 46–47 (2004): 3540–3542; B. Faler, "On Bloggers and Money: Some Seek Disclosure Rules for Web Sites Paid by Candidates," *Washington Post,* May 3, 2005, A19; Frank Rich, "Gonzo Gone, Rather Going, Watergate Still Here," *New York Times,* March 6, 2005, 2-1; Nick Coleman, "'Pay-to-Play' Writers Need to Be Stopped," *Star Tribune,* January 12, 2005, 2B.

7. Jennifer Sanderson, "Blogging: A Venue to Rant, Rave and Review," *Argus Leader,* August 9, 2004, 1A; see also David D. Perlmutter, "Political Blogs: The New Iowa?" *Chronicle of Higher Education* (May 26, 2006): B6–8.

8. David D. Perlmutter and Mary Schoen. "If I Break a Rule, What Do I Do, Fire Myself? Ethics Codes of Independent Blogs," 22(1): 37–48, *Journal of Mass Media Ethics,* 2007.

9. Georg Simmel, *Conflict and the Web of Group-Affiliations,* trans. K. H. Wolff and R. Bendix (New York: Free Press, 1955); L. Coser, *The Functions of Social Conflict* (New York: Free Press, 1956); L. Coser, *Continuities in the Study of Social Conflict* (New York: Free Press, 1967).

10. R. E. Clark, *Reference Group Theory and Delinquency* (New York: Behavioral Publications, 1972), 87–88.

11. Edward Shils, "Primary Groups in the American Army," in *Continuities in Social Research: The Studies in the Scope and Method of the American Soldier,* eds. R. K. Merton & P. Lazersfeld (New York: Free Press, 1950), 16–39. See also review in David D. Perlmutter, *Visions of War: Picturing Warfare from the Stone Age to the Cyberage* (New York: St. Martin's, 1999).

12. A. M. Bartholdy, *The War and German Society: The Testament of a Liberal* (New Haven, Conn.: Yale University Press, 1937), 286.

13. R. K. White, "Images in the Context of International Conflict: Soviet Perceptions of the U.S. and U.S.S.R.," in *International Behavior: A Socio-Psychological Analysis,* ed. H. C. Kelman (New York: Holt, Rinehart & Winston), 238–276.

14. Sam Keen, *Faces of the Enemy: Reflections of the Hostile Imagination* (San Francisco: Harper & Row, 1986).

15. Pliny (the Younger), *Letters and Panegyricus,* trans. Betty Radice (Cambridge, Mass.: Harvard University Press, Loeb Classical Library, 1969), 13, 15.

16. J. B. Campbell, *The Emperor and the Roman Army, 31 B.C–A.D. 235* (Oxford: Clarendon, 1984), 47.

17. Paige P. Edley and Montague Kern, "Women Candidates Going Public: The 30-Second Format," *Argumentation and Advocacy* 31 (1994): 80–95; B. E. Gronbeck, "Negative Narrative in the 1988 Presidential Campaign Ads," *Quarterly Journal of Speech* 78 (1992): 333–346; K. H. Jamieson, *Eloquence in an Electronic Age: The Transformation of Political Speechmaking* (New York: Oxford University Press, 1988).

18. David Ryfe, "Franklin Roosevelt and the Fireside Chats," *Journal of Communication* 49 (1999): 80–103; Lenart Silvo, *Shaping Political Attitudes* (Thousand Oaks, Cal.: Sage, 1994).

19. Gary Dean Best, *The Critical Press and the New Deal: The Press Versus Presidential Power, 1933–1938* (Westport, Conn.: Praeger, 1993); Gwenyth L. Jackaway, *Media at War: Radio's Challenge to the Newspapers, 1924–1939* (Westport, Conn.: Praeger, 1995), 136–138.

20. Ryfe, "Franklin Roosevelt and the Fireside Chats"; Michael Emery and Edwin Emery, *The Press and America* (Englewood Cliffs, N.J.: Prentice Hall, 1988), 355; Arthur Molella and Elsa Bruton, *FDR, The Intimate Presidency: Franklin D. Roosevelt, Communication and the Mass Media in the 1930's* (Washington, D.C.: Smithsonian Institution, 1981), 4. For a particularly in-depth and comprehensive discussion of Roosevelt's use of radio and his relationship with the press, see Betty Houchin Winfield, *FDR and the News Media* (New York: Columbia University Press, 1994).

21. Franklin D. Roosevelt and B. D. Zevin, *Nothing to Fear: The Selected Addresses of Franklin Delano Roosevelt, 1932–1945* (Boston: Houghton Mifflin, 1946), 18.

22. Gary Dean Best, *Pride, Prejudice, and Politics: Roosevelt Versus Recovery, 1933–1938* (Westport, Conn.: Praeger, 1991), 2.

23. Best, *Pride, Prejudice, and Politics*, 2.

24. Edward Chester, *Radio, Television and American Politics* (New York: Sheed & Ward, 1969), 31.

25. Halford Ryan, *Franklin D. Roosevelt's Rhetorical Presidency* (Westport, Conn.: Greenwood Press, 1988), 23.

26. Ryan, *Franklin D. Roosevelt's Rhetorical Presidency*, 24.

27. Ryfe, "Franklin Roosevelt and the Fireside Chats," 81.

28. Victor Kamber, *Poison Politics: Are Negative Campaigns Destroying Democracy?* (New York: Plenum Press, 1997), 28–29.

29. Jules Witcover, *No Way to Pick a President* (New York: Farrar, Straus and Giroux, 1999), 53.

30. Martha Kumar, "Does This Constitute a Press Conference?" *Presidential Studies Quarterly* 33 (2003): 221.

31. Craig Allen, *Eisenhower and the Mass Media: Peace, Prosperity and Prime-Time TV* (Chapel Hill: University of North Carolina Press, 1993).

32. Martin Medhurst, *Dwight D. Eisenhower: Strategic Communicator* (Westport, Conn.: Greenwood Press, 1993), 4.

33. Louis Liebovich, *The Press and the Modern Presidency: Myths and Mindsets from Kennedy to Election 2000* (Westport, Conn.: Praeger, 2001), 3.

34. John Bartlow Martin, Newton N. Minow, and Lee M. Mitchell, *Presidential Television* (New York: Basic Books, 1973), 38–39.

35. Joseph P. Berry Jr., *John F. Kennedy and the Media: The First Television President* (Lanham, Md.: University Press of America, 1987), 66, 142.

36. Martin, Minow, and Mitchell, *Presidential Television*, 41–43.

37. *Public Papers of the President of the United States: Richard Nixon, 1971* (Washington, D.C.: U.S. Government Printing Office, 1971), 819–820.

38. Yawei Liu, "The United States According to Mao Zedong: Chinese-American Relations, 1893–1976" (PhD dissertation, Emory University, 1996), 65.

39. William Safire, *Before the Fall: An Inside View of the Pre-Watergate White House* (New York: Doubleday, 1975), 414.

40. Richard Madsen, *China and the American Dream: A Moral Inquiry* (Berkeley: University of California Press, 1995), 69.

41. Madsen, *China and the American Dream*, 73.

42. Richard Nixon, *RN: The Memoirs of Richard Nixon* (New York: Grosset & Dunlap, 1978), 557–558, 560; H. R. Haldeman, *The Haldeman Diaries* (New York: G. P. Putman's, 1994), 411–413.

43. Madsen, *China and the American Dream*, 73.

44. *Public Papers of the President of the United States: Richard Nixon, 1972* (Washington, D.C.: U.S. Government Printing Office, 1972), 379.

45. Matthew A. Baum and Samuel Kernell, "Has Cable Ended the Golden Age of Television?" *American Political Science Review* 93 (1999): 99–114.

46. George Hackett and Eleanor Clift, "For Members Only," *Newsweek*, November 14, 1988, 22.

47. Kathleen E. Kendall, *Communication in the Presidential Primaries: Candidates and the Media, 1912–2000* (Westport, Conn.: Praeger, 2000), 182.

48. Timothy E. Cook, *Making Laws and Making News: Media Strategies in the U.S. House of Representatives* (New York: Brookings Institution, 1989), 100.

49. Robert V Friedenberg and Judith S. Trent, *Political Campaign Communication: Principles and Practices* (Westport, Conn.: Praeger, 2000), 226.

50. Dan Nimmo, "The Electronic Town Hall in Campaign '92: Interactive Forum or Carnival of Buncombe?" in *The 1992 Presidential Campaign: A Communication Perspective*, ed. Robert E. Denton Jr. (Westport, Conn.: Praeger, 1994), 207–226.

51. Dan Balz and Ron Brownstein, *Storming the Gates: Protest Politics and the Republican Revival* (Boston: Little, Brown, 1996), 184.

52. H. Wilensky, "The Professionalization of Everybody," *American Journal of Sociology* 70 (1964): 137–158.

53. K. Waldman and Kathleen Hall Jamieson, *The Press Effect: Politicians, Journalists, and the Stories That Shape the Political World* (New York: Oxford University Press, 2003).

54. Nathan Newman, "Becoming Part of Sherrod Brown Campaign Story" (November 8, 2005), http://www.nathannewman.org/laborblog/archive/003529.shtml.

55. Brian Wingfield, "The Latest Initiative in Congress: Blogging," *New York Times*, February 24, 2005, A4.

56. Jerry Brown, "Let the Sun Shine on Politics of Global Warming" (August 11, 2005), http://jerrybrown.typepad.com/jerry/2005/08/let_the_sun_shi.html.

57. David D. Perlmutter and Emily Metzgar, "Could Blogs Trump Stumping in Iowa?" *Christian Science Monitor*, November 3, 2005, 9.

58. The "instant publish" form of the blog may lead to imprudent posting and subsequent retribution. A high-ranking official within the Liberal Party of Canada resigned after it was reported that he posted on his blog pictures of an opposition politician (a woman whose last name was Chow) that contrasted her with the Chinese breed of Chow dog. Tara Brautigam, "Liberal Exec Quits over Slurs on Web," *CNews* (December 26, 2005), http://cnews.canoe.ca/CNEWS/Politics/CanadaVotes/2005/12/26/1369003-cp.html. [now taken down]

59. Quoted in Tom Curry, "Blog Pioneer Maps Political Strategy for 2008," *MSNBC.com* (March 2, 2006), http://www.msnbc.msn.com/id/11624919/.

60. Meshuggah means "wildly unreasonable" in Hebrew. Was the fellow a crackpot or a joker?

61. Amanda Marcotte, "Pandagon Changes" (January 30, 2007), http://pandagon.net/2007/01/30/pandagon-changes.

62. Jerome Armstrong, "Edwards Wrapping Up the Left Blogosphere & Obama's Got the Millennials," *MyDD* (February 1, 2007), http://www.mydd.com/story/2007/2/1/112654/0387.

63. Michelle Malkin, "How to Become a Leading Democrat's Blogmaster Updated/Correction—and More Wit and Wisdom of Amanda Marcotte" (February 3, 2007), http://michellemalkin.com/archives/006818.htm.

64. Kate Phillips, "Edwards's Blogger Blooper" (February 2, 2007), *New York Times online*.http://thecaucus.blogs.nytimes.com/2007/02/07/ edwardss-blogger-blooper/.

65. Nedra Pickler, "Edwards to Retain Embattled Bloggers," *Associated Press* (February 8, 2007), http://www.washingtonpost.com/wp-dyn/content/article/2007/02/08/AR2007020800878.html.

66. David Goldstein, "John Edwards Takes One for the Netroots," *Huffington Post* (February 8, 2007), http://www.huffingtonpost.com/david-goldstein/john-edwards-takes-one-fo_b_40764.html.

67. Susan Estrich, *The Case for Hillary Clinton* (New York: HarperCollins, 2005).

68. A Cook Political Report/RT Strategies Poll of December 2005 showed a third of Democrats supporting, respectively, a "classical liberal," a liberal with "moderate appeal," or a centrist as their ideal 2008 candidate. Charlie Cook, "Looking for the Right One," *National Journal* (December 13, 2005), http://nationaljournal.com/about/cookcolumn.htm.

69. Dan Balz, "Clinton Angers Left with Call for Unity: Senator Accused of Siding with Centrists," *Washington Post,* July 27, 2005, A03.

70. Cindy Sheehan, "Cindy Sheehan's Message for the New Year," *Indybay* (December 29, 2005), http://www.indybay.org/newsitems/2005/12/29/17929511.php.

71. David D. Perlmutter, "Under the Radar, Clinton for President?" *Christian Science Monitor,* January 30, 2006, 9.

72. David D. Perlmutter and Guy Golan, "Counter-Imaging: Myth-Making and Americanization in Israeli Labor Party Campaign Ads, 2003," *Visual Communication* 4, no. 3 (2005): 304–332.

73. John Cole, "It Is Tough Being Hillary" (December 28, 2005), http://www.balloon-juice.com/?p=6402.

74. Barack Obama, *The Audacity of Hope* (New York: Random House, 2006), 123, 124.

Afterpost

1. Pew Research Center, "Campaign Internet Videos: 'Sopranos' Spoof vs. 'Obama Girl' Made for the Web but Viewed More on TV than Online," July 12, 2007, http://pewresearch.org/pubs/539/campaign-web-video.

2. Dhavan Shah, David D. Perlmutter, et al., "Bloggers and the Blogosphere: Motivation, Perception, and Mobilization." Presented at the Association for Education in Journalism and Mass Communication Conference, Washington, D.C., August 8–13, 2007.

3. Tom Johnson and Barbara K. Kaye, "Wag the Blog," *Journalism and Mass Communication Quarterly* 81, no. 3 (2004): 622–642.

4. Quoted by Jay Rosen, "Print Bloggers vs. Journalists Is Over," *Pressthink* (January 21, 2005), http://journalism.nyu.edu/pubzone/weblogs/ pressthink/2005/01/21/berk_essy.html.

5. Jody Baumgartner and Jonathan S. Morris, "The Daily Show Effect: Candidate Evaluations, Efficacy, and American Youth," *American Politics Research* 34, no. 3 (2006): 341–367.

6. Kathleen Hall Jamieson, *Everything You Think You Know About Politics—and Why You're Wrong* (New York: Basic Books, 2000), 56.

7. Isocrates, *Speeches and Letters*, ed. George Norlin, "Panathenaicus," http://www.perseus.tufts.edu/cgi-bin/ptext?doc=Perseus%3Atext%3A1999.0 1.0144&query=head%3D%2312.

8. George Diepenbrock, "KU Student's YouTube Question Featured in Presidential Debate," *Lawrence Journal World,* July 25, 2007, http://www2 .ljworld.com/news/2007/jul/25/ku_students_youtube_question_featured_ presidential/.

Index